The J

By
Catherine Birch

This book is dedicated to my dearest friends Lady Marian and Colin who is sadly no longer with us. Together we walked hundreds of miles through the Atacama Desert, we camped under the stars and made memories that will stay with us forever.

In 2011 and 2012 Marian, Colin and I travelled to the Chile to take part in the Atacama Crossing race. The race is an ultra-marathon multistage event over six days. Each competitor must carry everything they need for the six days and are supplied with water and share a tent with up to seven other competitors at night. 2012 was the year we completed the event and during that time we had some incredible experiences. The landscape in the Atacama is truly inspirational, it is a stunning place. I have drawn on some of those experiences as inspiration for this book. All the characters and events in the book are fictional.

Prelude

The late afternoon sun caught the paintwork on the red Harley Davidson, and it glinted as she took the corner. The machine snarled like an untamed beast as its mechanical heart pounded between Dakota's slim leather clad legs. She twisted the accelerator feeling the power surge beneath her and the bike moved up a gear. Flying along the road Dakota could feel the bite of the cold Scottish air against her bare neck below her helmet. The snarling machine surged on, effortlessly eating up the miles of road beneath its tyres.

The journey was taking her northwards from her home in London to Scotland. Her trip had started that morning. The trouble she was in with her family had made her realise she needed time away to sort things out in her head. As dawn was creeping over the horizon, she slipped away leaving it all behind her.

For the hundreds of miles she had travelled, her mind was full of the pain she had caused her family. She had left Miles, the man her parents wanted her to marry, to have a family with. Her mother had been furious, how could Dakota do that to them she had wanted to know, she was to be ashamed of herself. Her father had sat at the dining table, lit his pipe then scratched his head wondering aloud if he would ever find suitable husbands for his daughters. Then came another argument with her younger sister Nina who'd complained bitterly about their father's comments. Things had worsened when she told her family that she had handed her notice in at work and was going away. She needed to sort herself out and she hoped that by the time she returned Miles would have moved out of her house and she wouldn't have to endure this any longer.

Dakota knew her family would never understand her, they would never see she just couldn't be tied down, she was a free spirit. Trying to push the thoughts from her mind, she rode the bike harder and faster along the last few miles of the road that would lead her to Fort William. So engrossed in her thoughts she failed to see the logging truck pull out of a forest road until it was too late. Gasping she pulled on the brakes with all her force, but it was too late, she was riding too fast. The bike skidded sideways leaving thick black marks on the road, it twisted and bucked underneath her before crashing to the ground. She heard the shrieking of tortured metal against the road surface as her bike continued its onward journey taking her with it before finally coming to rest under the wheels of the logging lorry.

Chapter One

It was April, the sun was beating down and it was incredibly hot. The red motorcycle stood in the early afternoon sun outside the truck stop cafeteria, the metal creaking in the intense heat, the chrome reflecting the glare of the sun. Dakota sat in the cool of the air conditioning inside the café sipping at hot coffee, her elbows on the table, her hands cradling the coffee beaker. She was staring out of the window far into the distance past the shining paintwork of the Harley. Her dark mane of hair was hanging down loose around her shoulders and her sunglasses were perched on the top of her head. Her boots were covered in a film of dust.

Her gaze shifted to the beautiful machine in front of the window. She knocked back the dregs of coffee, pushed back her chair and pulled out of her jeans pocket a crumpled note to leave a tip on the coffee-stained table. As she opened the door of the cafeteria the hot air hit her cool face as if someone had opened a hot oven. She straddled the bike pulling the helmet over her head she fumbled with the strap before fixing it and adjusted her shades. She was ready!

Dakota fired the machine into life, pushed back the stand and slowly pulled out of the truck stop onto the tarmac road. A smile touched the corner of her lips, today would be the day she would make it to San Pedro. Her plan on arrival was to check in and get a shower. The dust from riding the Chilean roads got everywhere. The two nights before she had slept under the star-studded sky, the vast expanse that spanned the whole of the Atacama Desert. Tired from riding all day she'd made camp just off the road and behind rocks making sure she was invisible to passers-by. She had used up the food provisions she'd bought with her, at some stage during her stay she would need to stock up again for the ride back to Santiago.

Dakota needed this holiday; she had to get away from life at home and all the problems that came with it and this time in Chile was for her. If she wanted to sleep under the stars she could and if she didn't shower for days, there was nobody here to judge her.

1

She would please only herself arriving at that decision whilst half asleep on the long flight from London to Santiago. At Madrid she'd sat and consumed several cups of coffee, booked the hotel, the bike and planned her trip. Although that was very clear in her mind, the memory of making the decision to leave London for Chile eluded her but she was here, and she knew in her heart it was the best thing she'd done. The ride from Santiago had been incredible, she had seen so much of Chile, met people at truck stops, chatted to tourists and just fell in love with the place. She had an overpowering sense of belonging here.

After riding for a while, the small town of San Pedro came into view sprawled out down below her. She slowed and rode into the sandy desert town. The eyes of the local townsfolk followed her, not accustomed to seeing a slight woman riding a large motorcycle.

The road soon deteriorated, and she found herself riding along not much more than a dirt track. The Harley growled as she changed gear and slowed again to accommodate the road conditions. She had ridden past a small bar she thought would be ideal for her dinner and a few beers later.

The hotel was basic but clean and nicely decorated. Dakota walked slowly around her room taking note of the signs in the bathroom asking guests not to put towels to be washed unless necessary, not to drink the local water and to not waste any water due to the Atacama being the driest desert, having hardly any rainfall each year. She would make a note to hang her towels up once she had finished with them. For now, she wanted to unpack her bike, shower and grab some food and a beer.

Outside it was even hotter. She hurriedly unpacked the panniers and took her bags back to her room. She shook out and hung her small collection of clothes. Hot weather clothes. Dakota had made the right decision to discover the Atacama Desert now, it was halfway through the Chilean autumn. It was thirty degrees outside and part of her plans included getting a tan and returning to London looking a healthier colour than she did now.

The jet of hot water pounded on her head and skin washing away the shampoo and soap she had lathered generously over herself. She watched the brown water leave her body and made its way down the plughole. She hurriedly dried herself relishing the feel of the rough hotel towel then hung it up so it could dry taking heed of the notice on the bathroom wall. Selecting shorts and a t-shirt from her small wardrobe Dakota dressed, ran a comb quickly through her damp hair and left the hotel. It was a very short walk into town, she briefly looked into the windows of the small knitwear and craft shops she had passed earlier casually casting her eyes over the array of goods on display.

The beer was ice cold, just what she needed. She ordered a pizza and clutching her beer she wandered outside to find a seat and soak up the last rays of the setting sun. She closed her eyes and instantly her head started to fill with the memories of the trip to Italy her and Miles had taken. He had surprised her, she remembered, with a spur of the moment trip to Rome. He'd left the airline tickets on the coffee table in her lovely house – there for Dakota to find. Why had he decided to take her to Rome she would never know, she was certainly not the type of woman who'd enjoy walking around the Vatican or the Sistine chapel not even the Colosseum would interest her. She'd tried hard to look interested more for his sake but deep inside she questioned if he knew her at all.

The trip had bored her to tears and had been largely instrumental in her realisation she couldn't spend the rest of her life with this man. The only thing she'd enjoyed was the food. Dakota had spent the entire trip increasingly worried Miles might have brought her to Rome to propose. She had felt great relief to land back on home soil and not have to tell her parents she'd declined him. As she sat in the late sun, she relived all the feelings of guilt she'd harboured and still to a greater or lesser degree felt. The hurt she'd caused him and her family too, but she had to be true to herself, life was too short for mistakes and marriage to the wrong man was one of them.

With another beer ordered the memories of her past life with Miles continued to invade her mind. They'd met via a mutual friend who'd set them up on a blind date. He'd taken her out to a very expensive restaurant and wined and dined her. At first Dakota thought he was the best thing that'd ever happened to her, he was good looking, generous and kind. She'd been very young, and very much under the influence of her parents who constantly reminding her what a good husband he would make, what great

3

prospects he had and what a nice person he was. Yes, he'd been all of those things but after five years with him he'd driven her crazy with all of his daily, weekly and monthly routines and she had to break free.

Miles had taken the end of their relationship badly; he'd wasted no time calling Dakotas parents to tell them what she'd done before she'd even had a chance to speak to them herself. It'd been difficult for her to live with them again, but she'd felt so terrible for hurting Miles, and she wanted to afford him the time to get his life together and move out. Initially they'd tried living together as friends, but it'd proven too much of a strain. He was always trying to win her back; he was desperate, and she'd began to detest him. One evening she'd sat him down and explained she had to move out and so did he. Six months came and went, and he was still in her house. She hoped he'd be gone by the time she returned to England; she was so fed up with living with her controlling parents. All these thoughts tumbling through her head had started to darken her mood. She dropped her head and stared at her beer desperately wondering if her life would ever become what she'd hoped for.

"Excuse me lady, is this seat taken?" a man's voice with a very heavy Spanish accent made Dakota jump and spill her beer. Standing, wiping spilt beer from her top with a paper napkin she glanced up and into the deepest brown eyes she had ever seen. He was dressed in a t-shirt, dirty ripped jeans and biker boots. His shades were resting on the top of his thick black hair, he was unshaven, and he had the most arresting smile she had ever seen. His lips were dry and slightly cracked from the sun but that didn't detract from his smile. Dakota stared at the man standing in front of her, still wiping the beer from her top "No, it's free."

"Mind if I sit here then?" he asked still smiling, the smile she was aware of but the eyes she couldn't take hers away from. "No if you want to." She replied hurriedly finishing her wiping and screwing the tissue into a ball. The man pulled out the metal chair, Dakota couldn't help but notice his strong, tanned hand with grubby nails, she could tell that hand had seen hard work.

Her pizza arrived at the table at the same time as her guests. The waitress handed out well-worn knives and forks wrapped in paper napkins. Dakota thanked the waitress and placed the

4

cutlery on the table. Before starting his pizza the man clumsily stood up, wiped his hands on his jeans then held his hand out to her. "I'm Javier," he said. Slowly she took his hand. His grasp was strong, his hands rough and calloused but warm against her soft skin. "I'm Dakota." She said slowly shaking his hand, unable to drag her gaze away from his brown eyes, he unable to let go of the small soft hand that was encompassed in his.

"Dakota, that's a name I've not heard before". He let go of her hand and sat in the chair taking in her slim athletic figure whilst unwrapping his cutlery.

"It is native American" she mumbled through a mouthful of pizza.

"Oh!" He took a large mouthful of his beer. They sat and ate pizza in silence for a while giving her a chance to take in the man before her. He was a bit rough around the edges but wow, he was hot! Just the sort of man her parents would have a heart attack over if she'd taken him home. A small smile touched her lips at the thought. "D'you live here?" she asked breaking the silence, "You look like you might be local?" She smiled, a lock of dark hair catching the corner of her eye which she quickly wiped away. "Yeah, I live here for my sins." He replied taking another gulp of his beer and the final mouthful of his pizza.

She swallowed hard, "What d'you do, for a job I mean?" she asked taking a pull on her beer, feeling the icy cold liquid soothe her dry throat. She coughed covering her mouth with the back of her hand and hurriedly apologised.

"I support sporting events with my bike, extreme sports events and the like. Work is seasonal but I get by. You want another beer?" he asked waving the waitress over to their table. "Yeah thanks" she handed the empty bottle to the waitress. "So, are you on holiday here in San Pedro?" Javier asked interested to see what a beautiful woman like her would be doing out here on her own.

"Um, well yes sort of. I'm doing a bit of touring around Chile. I started in Santiago and thought I'd make my way to San Pedro, have a look around and ride back perhaps go down south for a bit I'll see what I fancy doing."

"Oh! so you want to see the big old desert, is that why you came to San Pedro?"

"Yes, we don't have such things in not-so-sunny England where I'm from," she laughed, "so I thought I'd enjoy a bit of sun, sand and riding around seeing the sights." Javier was studying her. She was beautiful, had the most stunning smile he'd ever seen, her eyes were framed by the longest lashes and her jet-black mane hung around her shoulders still slightly damp framing her petite but beautiful features.

"What do you ride?" he asked trying to prise his eyes from her, very aware he was staring.

"A Harley Road King Classic" she said casually.

"Whoa, that isn't a woman's bike!" he slammed his beer down on the table, "that's one mean machine!" He leaned back on his chair crossing his arms over his chest and cocked his head to one side, what was going on with this woman sitting opposite to him he wondered. He'd never met anyone like her before. A tiny dot of a woman out here all alone on a bike a man would struggle to ride. She certainly was one in a million. "You like riding bikes then?" he asked, his dark eyes flashing, waiting for her reaction. Dakota felt her stomach do a somersault, she swallowed hard, completely aware the somersault wasn't from the pizza or the beer but rather the effect the man sitting opposite to her was having.

"Yeah, I have one back home so thought what better way to see somewhere than on a bike?"

The rest of the evening things were easy between them, they drank beer, they laughed a lot and talked about bikes. He rode a trials bike, something that could handle desert conditions easily and could ride up and down dunes all day. He advised her she'd need to stick to roads on her Harley if she wanted to see more of the Atacama or she'd risk getting the heavy machine stuck in the sand. Time ticked by, they drank more beer, and the evening faded into darkness. The vast carpet of stars that fills the Atacama at night was out. It was past eleven when Dakota finally stood up to leave feeling slightly wobbly having consumed rather too many beers. "Well, I'm off back to my hotel now for a good sleep and to recoup from two nights out under the stars. Thanks for tonight it was nice to meet you, Javier!" She held her hand out, he took it but didn't shake it, just held onto it for a few seconds their eyes met then he let go, she turned to leave.

"Which hotel are staying at?" he asked quickly before she could leave and walk out of his life. She liked how his hand had felt holding hers, it was warm and strong. "That's information for another time!" she whispered looking up into those dark and mysterious eyes; his mop of jet-black hair, his shades still on his head. She turned away from him and strode off into the small town. He watched her until she disappeared into the crowds that were still milling around despite the time, then she was gone.

Javier sighed, he'd liked Dakota, she was a unique type of girl. There were no airs and graces about her, she was relaxed, she liked bikes and was very down to earth. She seemed honest and not phased at all by him asking to sit with her after he'd spotted her sitting alone in the evening sunshine looking stunning and drinking beer. He knew from what she'd said when they had been talking, she was an independent woman who could handle herself and in addition to all that she was just gorgeous. Sitting in her t-shirt and shorts with beer spilt down her front, her glossy hair falling around her shoulders – still wet from her shower then that drop dead smile! In those very short hours, he'd become quite fond of her, they'd got along really well, she made him laugh, something he hadn't done in a very long time…. But now she'd walked away from him, he didn't know if he'd even see her again.

Javier stood, brushed off the last crumbs of his pizza and made his way back to his flat. He let himself in to the kitchen and flicked the kettle to make a sobering coffee. Outside the town was alive with the happy noise of tourists bustling around. He closed the window and sat on the sofa sipping the hot strong liquid. His thoughts returned to the woman he'd just met.

Dakota walked back to her hotel her head was full of Javier. What on earth had just happened? Some stranger had approached her, asked to sit and dine with her and they'd shared the evening together. Something she'd never have done in her past life. He seemed very nice, and he was certainly good looking if a bit scruffy around the edges but that was what she'd liked about him; what she was attracted to. He'd been easy to talk to and laugh with, something she hadn't done in a long time. But she didn't know if she'd ever see him again. Perhaps he wasn't even single.

7

Taking control of her thoughts, she gave herself a mental shakedown. She'd come to Chile to get over a relationship, to recover from the damage it'd caused and the inevitable heartache. She wasn't here to run head-first into another one, what was she even thinking? But he had been nice. She shoved her hands into her pockets and strolled the short distance across town back to the hotel.

Chapter Two

The sun streaming into her room woke Dakota the following morning. For the first time in what seemed an eternity she felt happy. She stretched, yawned loudly and walked over to the window to take a look at what the day outside held. There was a small bird pecking at crumbs someone had left. She watched as it hopped around pecking at the dry, dusty earth. After showering she walked over to the hotel restaurant for a bite of breakfast before heading out into the town again.

The restaurant was very basic but it did the job. Who needed frills when something like this would do just fine, she thought as she heaped her plate with toast, cheese, butter and jam and helped herself to a large cup of coffee. She chose a table and placed everything she'd precariously balanced on her arm down on the well-scrubbed wood before pulling out the old wooden chair. Sitting alone by the window she looked out over the small garden and onto a slabbed area where the pool was located. The pool was tiny, but it had sun loungers scattered around and looked inviting in the morning sunshine. People were already out there putting towels and books out to reserve the best spot. First breakfast, then walk around town and finally sun lounger with her book! Her plans decided, she revisited the breakfast bar to add a bowl of cereal to her tally and refreshed her coffee.

The small town of San Pedro was a great place to visit as a tourist. It was bustling with life and had a happy atmosphere. In the street where everything from donkeys to alpacas, babies to motorcyclists were about all sharing the same piece of road and being courteous to each other. Dakota walked along the rutted and worn dusty road covering her boots in a light film as she wandered further into town. She visited the small knitwear shops she'd passed the night before and carefully inspected the handmade crafts that were on sale just about everywhere. She bought only a few things wishing she had more room on the bike so she could buy the hand knitted mittens and jackets that hung from every beam. The shopkeepers were friendly, and she made conversation with them.

Stopping at a small bar Dakota ordered coffee and sat outside people watching. She closed her eyes and leant back against the chair feeling the hot sun bake down on her face. She felt happy and settled, this place had a good feel about it, a good vibe. She was glad she'd settled on San Pedro for her last stop before heading home. She'd stay here a while; she liked the town.

Placing her empty coffee mug back in the saucer Dakota left the bar and walked to the church in the main square. A beautiful, very old building that smelled of age and well weathered timber. The outside of the building was painted white and it looked well cared for. Inside the ancient wide timber floorboards were uneven only adding to the beauty of the place. There were small annexes dotted around with religious statues Dakota was only too aware she should've known who the statues were. If her mother had been with her, she'd have been annoyed by her lack of knowledge.

Dakota walked slowly around the church taking in everything - the smell, the sights and sounds of this amazing place. She sat on one of the pews and watched a couple of small children walking around with their mother each holding her hand and asking so many questions. The mother patiently answered their questions and kept hushing them as their voices got louder and louder. She watched the townsfolk come in and out, change flowers and clean. When she was completely alone Dakota whispered a silent prayer, asked God to guide her and help her. Please could he send someone she'd love and be happy with and not lead a lonely life now she and Miles had parted. She asked for a life that'd be good and honest with a man who'd want to share the same values with her. She wondered if she was asking too much.

The sun was high in the sky and beating down hard as she made her way back to the hotel. Her thoughts turned again to her family back home in London. Her younger sister Nina had been so angry with her when she'd left Miles. Nina hoped once Dakota was married her family would turn their attentions to her and boyfriend Karl who she was desperate to marry. Nina was the girl Dakota's parents had wanted her to be. She was obedient, loyal and trustworthy. She did exactly what her parents wanted without question unlike Dakota. The times Dakota had sat in her room

10

and had wished she could be like Nina, and God alone knew she'd tried but now aged twenty-four she'd finally realised it was her life and Miles was not part of her future, nor was the job she had been working so hard at. She knew she'd hurt her family deeply when she'd rebelled against them, getting away was the best thing she could do until they calmed down and forgave her. She'd caught the first available flight to Chile hoping it was far enough away from all the heartache at home.

At the hotel bar Dakota ordered a cheese and tomato sandwich on brown bread and took it to her room. She unpacked the things she'd bought and packed them neatly into her paniers. Changing into her bikini she stole bites from the sandwich whilst applying factor twenty-five sun cream to her body. She was of American Indian descent, so she'd not burn easily. She grabbed her book and walked out to the pool area to choose her sun lounger. As she walked out of the reception she looked up at the huge volcano in the distance. There was snow on the top of Licancabur. Dakota thought it looked strange considering it was thirty degrees down in the town at one o'clock in the afternoon. She'd take a ride up to the volcano before she went home, see what it was like that far up above sea level. She'd wondered on the flight over if she'd suffer altitude sickness but so far, she hadn't had any sign. She knew the summit of Licancabur stood at 5916 metres, but she wouldn't be venturing to the summit.

There was nobody around the pool area, it was so very quiet. She adjusted her towel; the lounger was put into the reclining position. Half an hour later Dakota was asleep sprawled over the sun lounger on her beach towel. As she slept the pool area started to fill up with afternoon residents, they all looked over at the girl who was sleeping, her dark hair cascading around her like a halo. When she woke, she looked at her watch. She'd slept for hours. Glancing around the pool she could see so many people had arrived since she had taken her place that afternoon.

Children splashed in the pool and mothers ran around after them with tubes of cream rubbing it into their pale skin. Elderly people were sitting in the shade reading books with sun hats on and pool staff were collecting glasses and empty bottles from the tables. Dakota yawned and walked to the bar to get a drink. She ordered herself a pint of orange juice. She wanted a beer, but she'd probably be dehydrated from sleeping in the sun for hours. The beer would have to be later back in the town with her dinner, sipping the orange through a straw she wondered if she would meet Javier again. She hoped he'd be around, but the reality was he wouldn't be out looking for her, he'd be busy, probably working. Dakota regretted not telling him where she was stopping when he'd asked the night before. She took the suncream bottle and slapped a handful of it onto her arms and legs. Her skin had already tanned being out in the sun just a few hours.

Hiding behind her shades Dakota studied the people who had joined her that afternoon. She wondered what their lives back home were like. The elderly couple sitting at the table under the tree reading. She thought they looked like they'd been married for at least fifty years, they looked so comfortable together. Dakota wondered if she'd find someone, she'd feel that safe and secure with, who she would always love through the good times and bad. Over by the pool where the parents with the children who didn't want sun cream applying. The mother was trying to hold the child down with one hand and rub cream in with the other. She was getting angry with the child and her voice was loud and fast trying to explain to the child why he had to have the cream applied. The father lay on his lounger ignoring his wife's plight. Dakota thought if she'd been the wife she'd give the man a damn good slap and get him to help her with the disobedient child. Her eyes turned to the young couple that looked as though they were on honeymoon. They were drinking beer on their loungers, holding hands and gazing into each other's eyes. What it must be like to be in love like that she thought.

Retrieving her well-worn paperback Dakota lay back on the beach towel. The sun baked down, and the laughter of the children filled the air. Away somewhere in the distance she could hear a motorbike and wondered if it was Javier. She'd liked him a lot. He'd been friendly and obviously recognised a fellow biker and had treated her well. He had given her food for thought on how she was going to manage her massive bike through the desert. He'd explained she'd need to stick to the main roads but that wasn't what she'd planned. Dakota wanted to go off the beaten track and explore. Perhaps she'd be able to borrow or hire a trials bike instead that'd be much more desert worthy.

It was late afternoon; the lure of the sun lounger had passed. Dakota stood in her room with her hands on her hips perusing her small wardrobe trying to decide what to wear that evening. Finally, she decided on a vest top, jean shorts and pumps. She showered and dressed and took herself off into the town for the second time that day. She chose a different bar but found the clientele were not really her type. The bar was filled with families, she'd had enough of children running around that afternoon. She wanted to be in the company of adults and people she could talk to if she chose but would leave her alone if she didn't want to socialise. She picked up her small bag and walked back to the bar she'd eaten at the night previously by the old church and square.

Sitting at the only outside table, the same as the night before in the warm evening air and perusing the menu a familiar voice behind her asked, "Do you always frequent these places alone?" It was Javier! He placed a hand lightly on her shoulder, "D'you mind?" he nodded to the chair next to her.

"Of course not, sit down," she replied trying to hide her delight at seeing him again, "I've just ordered a beer, but I'm sure the waitress can bring two if I go in and ask?" She stood and strode inside the dimly lit but cosy bar and ordered another beer for her visitor. She was glad he'd returned to the same bar; she could spend a second evening with him.

"What've you been doing today?" Javier asked after she returned with the beers. "This and that. Walked around town this morning and sat around the pool with my book this afternoon," she recalled the events of the day, "I fell asleep for a few hours and when I woke up, I'd been joined by half of the tourists in San Pedro," she complained wrinkling her nose. "But I suppose it is the season, isn't it?"

"Always here we have tourists," he replied running his hands through his thick hair, "San Pedro used to be used in western films so lots of people come, that is what keeps the small businesses going."

"Are you eating?" he asked studying her as she perused the menu. Tonight, she looked even more stunning he noted, she wore a vest top and jean shorts showing her tanned slender legs. Her hair was loose and wet as it had been the night before. Her eyes were framed with long dark lashes with the smallest amount of mascara and her lips showed just the faintest slick of lipstick.

"Yeah, but not sure what yet." She re-read the menu options, frowning slightly as she did so. "Maybe I have a veggie burger and chips or something like that?"

"You don't eat meat?" Javier looked horrified.

"No not for a very long time. Are you eating or have you already eaten?" she asked laughing at the look of shock on his face.

"Eating but eating *meat!*" he replied with mock defiance. Over the top of her menu, she studied him further. He was around five feet ten inches tall and medium build but very dark skinned. He wore the same ripped jeans and a black t-shirt. She noticed his lips still looked dry but that wouldn't have stopped her locking her lips onto them if the chance were to arise she thought then blushed, embarrassed by her own thoughts, and those dark brown eyes she could stare into forever. He had stubble on his cheeks, but it wasn't the designer type Miles had tried to grow, it was unkempt, natural stubble. She thought it was sexy and suited him.

After they finished their burgers, they sat in almost darkness outside the bar. A natural lull formed in their chatter and they were silent for a while. The wind had got up and tumbleweed was blowing around the small square where they were seated. "It's weird seeing that stuff blowing around," Dakota commented watching the fluffy balls bounce around, "we don't have that in England we only see it on telly."

"Tons of the stuff finds its way into town," Javier spoke softly never taking his eyes from her as the weed blew around gathering speed with each warm gust of wind. "What are you up to tomorrow, have you got any plans?" he asked still watching her as she looked on at the tumbleweed, "Have you been out to the desert yet?" he asked knowing full well that she hadn't. He waited for her response.

"Not sure about tomorrow. I was thinking about taking my bike out into the desert just to see how it'd manage. Obviously, I'd stick to the roads, I don't fancy hauling that beast out of a sand dune!" She drained the last of her beer and placed the bottle down on the table wondering how she would manage to pull the Harley out should it get stuck in the sand.

"D'you want another beer?" Javier waved the waitress over and ordered two more beers. "I'm not working tomorrow, I can take you out there, show you the best tracks if you'd like?" he casually suggested folding his hands on the table in front of him. Her gaze met his. For a few seconds they stared into each other's eyes both wondering where this was going.

"That'd be cool if you don't mind or have anything else on?" she replied resisting the urge to put her hand on top of his as it rested on the table.

"I've not got any plans to do anything really so we can ride out. Where and what time shall I meet you?" he asked trying to stay cool.

"I'll meet you here and we can take the road up and out of San Pedro and into the Atacama?" Dakota suggested. She really wanted to see more of the great Atacama Desert and to ride through it. She'd been a little apprehensive of going alone, not everyone in Chile spoke English and her Spanish left a lot to be desired and if she was to get stuck, she knew she'd be in trouble.

Chapter Three

Javier pulled up alongside Dakota on his very tired, dusty and battered bike. It was a lot smaller than Dakota's Harley and looked very worn and used against her gleaming red machine. "That is one huge bike you ride lady!" he commented looking enviously at the bike Dakota was mounted upon and thinking how sexy she looked astride such a machine, "I'd love to buy something like that and tour round one day if I'm ever able to afford it and take time off work."

"Well, I really wouldn't recommend my choice of bike for desert locations," Dakota chuckled. "Come on let's go and see the great wilderness!" She revved the accelerator, and the Harley pounced into life. Javier led the way out of San Pedro. They passed small shrines on the side of the road as they climbed up and out of the town. The road was good, they rode for an hour before they pulled over to look across desert and admire the sheer size as the plains rolled out on either side of them. It was quiet, not a single sound could be heard. "We can take this small track off down here or we can carry on, depends on how much you want to see, and d'you only want to see from the road or are you up for a bit of an adventure?" Javier turned to her, only his dark shades visible through the helmet and his voice was muffled.

"Let's take this track down here." Dakota turned the handlebars on the Harley and let out the clutch carefully turning onto the track. They rode slowly, the Harley wasn't handling the sandy road conditions very well, but they managed to ride about four miles down the track. "Off up there is a river crossing, you can ride for miles, but the track isn't suitable for your bike, its more for things like this or walking." Javier brought his bike to a halt and pointed to the river. "Looks like I need to get myself a different bike for the short term then" Dakota felt disappointed and annoyed with herself for not thinking about the terrain she'd need to ride across. She'd been enjoying the off-road ride but knew the Harley wouldn't be able to take her further. "D'you know anyone who has a spare trials bike I could borrow or hire maybe?" She asked. Javier thought for a moment before replying.

"Um, no, I don't. Mine is the only one around here that's why I get the work." He stopped for a minute looking thoughtful then turned to her, "Just an idea though, can you ride a horse?" He raised a questioning eyebrow. Dakota frowned and looked puzzled, "Yes I used to ride a lot when I was younger," she replied. "Why are you asking me?"

"I have a friend who has horses, they'd be able to take us much further into the desert, to places I'd struggle with even on my bike," he turned his bike around before she could say anything further and rode off calling over his shoulder. "Come on, we may as well carry along the main road for a bit longer."

They rode further and further out, late in the afternoon as the sun was reaching its hottest, they decided to turn back to San Pedro. Dakota wanted to discover more of the Atacama and had mulled over the offer of horses whilst they'd been out on the bikes. It was very late in the afternoon when they arrived back at Dakota's hotel. They and their bikes were covered in a thick film of dust, a reminder of their adventure. "Can I buy you dinner tonight as a thank you for today?" she asked Javier as she dismounted her bike and removed her helmet. She shook her head and ran her fingers through her ruffled hair and smiled at a rather stunned Javier. "That'd be cool. Where were you thinking?"

"You tell me, you know San Pedro better than I do. Where would be a suitable venue do you think and please no children running around?"

"I'll have a think. Can I pick you up around eight, is that okay?" he asked now he knew where she was staying.

"That sounds like a plan. I'll see you later then and thanks again for today I really had fun" she smiled, he realised for more than the first time that day what a stunning woman she was. He turned and rode away feeling completely out of his depth with a woman like Dakota. Why was he even kidding himself, she would never look twice at him romantically.

The restaurant Javier had chosen was lovely. Wooden floors and plain painted plaster walls were adorned with prints of the desert. The tables were plain scrubbed wood, but the place was cosy. They took a table inside and ordered beers and poured over the menu. "Not sure what to have tonight. I'm starving!" she exclaimed.

"I'm having a steak with all the trimmings," Javier put down the menu and looked over at her, his eyes searching for hers. "Have you thought any more about hiring the horses?" he asked patiently waiting for her reply.

"Yeah. The thing is I'd like to stop out in the desert for a few nights under the stars. I really want to experience the whole thing 24/7 and not spend all my time in a hotel. That isn't quite what I came for" she replied, "I suppose that's out of the question isn't it?" she looked disappointed.

"It can be arranged if you want to camp out. My friend Al who has the horses arranges treks with overnight camping. I can ask him if he'd give me the map, we could follow the route. If we did that, we'd have water and supplies for the horses each night. But only if you are up for it, I don't want you to feel uncomfortable. I could ask him to book you in for a trek with a group if you'd prefer that?" he suggested hoping that she'd say she wouldn't and wondering if he had pushed his luck a bit too far.

"Really? You would do that for me Javier? That would be brilliant!" Dakota's face lit up. She had not expected to end up seeing the desert from horse back at the kindness of a stranger, she'd owned ponies when she was a child and had ridden friends' horses and was a very accomplished rider. "When are you wanting to head out? I'll need to go and see Al tomorrow sometime. I can let you know more detailed plans after I've spoken to him?" Javier asked already planning in his head where he'd take her, so she'd have the best trip for her time in Chile.

"Any time after tomorrow would be good with me. Thanks so much Javier, I really appreciate you going out of your way to help me out." She reached over the table and took his hand. It felt so big and warm in hers and right somehow too.

"Thing is, we don't know when you'll come back to San Pedro, so we need to make sure you see all you want to this time." He took a gulp of the cold beer and smiled, knowing that her time in San Pedro was limited and one day very soon she would be gone. He was determined to make her time in Chile memorable, for her to be able to see and do everything she wanted, and he would be the one to make it happen for her.

They walked back to Dakota's hotel through the diminishing crowds, stopping at the hotel bar for a late-night drink. Dakota pulled out a bar stool and ordered a Pisco sour and Javier a whisky. "Ugh no, I don't know how you can drink those things, they're vile." He pulled a face at the glass Dakota was holding containing the opaque liquid.

"You don't get these things easily in England, so I'm making the most of it now," she explained as she sipped the sour contents, "and I really like it!" Javier pulled another face and finished the whisky. Putting down the glass he slid from the stool. "Right, I'd better get back, busy day tomorrow sorting out horses and things."

"Thanks again I do really appreciate it and please let me know what I owe you when you have spoken to your friend." Dakota stood from her stool preparing to go to her room. It had been a long but exciting day and tomorrow looked even better. "We can sort something out, I'm sure. I'll catch up with you tomorrow then?" his hand brushed the top of hers briefly and she felt her stomach make another somersault.

"Sure. Let's meet up at the bar in the square at seven?"

"Great!" He turned away wishing he had the nerve to kiss her even if only on the cheek, but he didn't want to spoil things, she might not have liked it. She watched as he left the bar and walked back to his flat.

Dakota was so excited about their trip on horseback. It'd been a few years since she'd ridden but she'd loved it and knew this would be an experience she would never forget. She'd need to make a speedy trip around town tomorrow and pick up some freeze-dried food, but she had everything else she and Javier had put on the list written on the back of a paper napkin as they'd sat in the bar that night excitedly planning. She gulped back the last of her drink and went back to her room.

That night she slept heavily and didn't wake until mid-morning. She'd missed her breakfast slot so grabbed herself a coffee and made her way into the town to collect her shopping. There were a few shops that stocked freeze-dried food, but she was limited on her vegetarian choice. She managed to pick up a selection for Javier, she had her chilli, vegetarian stew and a couple of vegetarian sausage casseroles. What they would taste like was anyone's guess she thought as she read the back of the pack in Spanish. Well, she was limited, and beggars couldn't be choosers! She purchased some fruit and a large container of orange juice for the trip.

Later she was laying on the sun lounger by the pool making a very poor job of trying to read her book. She couldn't really be bothered with it, the trek into the Atacama was far more exciting to think about than reading. It was another baking hot day and Dakota was making the most of it. She'd packed all the food bought earlier into her backpack along with the things she'd need for the trip. She lay in her bikini stretched out mulling over the trip when gentle hand touched her shoulder, "Hi, I just came by to check if you're available around ten tomorrow morning?" She sat up with a start, her book falling to the floor. It was Javier, he was trying to hide a smirk, his hand to his mouth covering his amusement. She saw this and smiled, "You damn made me jump Javier, don't you go sneaking up on people when they're not expecting it" she scalded poking a finger into his ribs and making him laugh.

"Tomorrow?" he continued, "Al has the horses already out in the desert and to save him bringing them back here we can ride out on the bikes and go on from where the horses are stabled. We can leave the bikes out there, is that okay with you?" he asked raising his eyebrows. Her face lit up as she realised what Javier was talking about. "Yes, tomorrow's great," she swung her legs over the side of the lounger and faced him, he was now sat on the lounger next to her. "Sorry, you startled me earlier" she added. Again, he found himself drawn in by her smile and how she looked smothered in sun cream in that very small bikini. He couldn't help but wonder if this trip was going to be a mistake, but he would never know if they didn't go. He smiled, watching her from beneath his dark shades. She looked so good in that bikini, her hair tied back, and her dark skin glistened with sun cream. He wanted to lean over and kiss her as she sat there completely oblivious to what he was thinking chatting away about their trip. "So, ten is okay for tomorrow have you got all you need?" his accent sounded heavier causing Dakota to pause for a second before her response.

"I've managed to get some freeze-dried food today, some orange juice and fruit for us. Have you got what you need?" she asked.

"I've freeze-dried. Live on the stuff when I'm supporting the ultra-races, so I always have piles of it around."

"Oh, I bought you some in case you didn't have, sorry I didn't think you'd already have a stash." She blushed a little feeling foolish, of course he'd have loads of the stuff, he'd have to live on it when he was out supporting races.

"That's kind of you though, thanks." He leant over and squeezed her arm with a tenderness, he'd done it before he realised but made no effort to remove his hand. She didn't move from his touch; her stomach was doing somersaults, but she felt powerless to move away from his hand as if he was holding her to the spot, to the sunbed. "D'you want a drink whilst you're here?" she asked finally breaking the spell he'd cast over her. He removed his hand from her arm, "No thanks I must get back and pack some things. I didn't ask you how long you wanted to go trekking for, I sort of loosely agreed five days but if that is too long, we can change it?" He cast his eyes down and made a job of straightened out his shirt, avoiding her gaze, unsure if he'd overstepped the mark with five days.

"*AMAZING*" she shrieked; her hand flew to her mouth realising people were looking over at them. "Five days is cool. See you later then?"

"Sure" he pushed his hands into his pockets and sauntered off. She watched him go. He was a lovely man who'd done all he could to ensure she had a great holiday doing what she had come to Chile to do. She was glad they'd met.

"What do you mean you don't want to sleep in a tent?" Javier's eyes were wide. He put his knife and fork down, put his elbows on the table and stared at Dakota. "Where d'you want to sleep then?" He asked puzzled.

"Outside, under the stars. My sleeping bag is rated to minus twenty, so I'll be warm enough and we'll have a campfire, so I don't see the problem with not taking a tent, Javier?" How could he say no, she was flashing those lashes at him, he was all but helpless.

21

"No problem. No problem at all but I have to say you're the first woman I've met who doesn't want a tent and privacy," he chuckled drinking the remains of the beer, "I'll get us another." He pushed back his chair and sidled off to the bar. After he'd gone Dakota wondered if she should request a tent after all, but she'd wanted to sleep under the Atacama stars. Every night she'd looked up in awe at the star-studded sky. She'd never seen so many stars in the sky and she didn't want that hidden by canvas. She'd be warm enough and when it came to getting dressed, she'd put her underwear on inside the sleeping bag. She was sure Javier was no stranger to women in underwear he had seen her in her bikini that afternoon and surely that was only the same as underwear. She thought back to that moment when he'd arrived and she'd felt very self-conscious, he was looking down at her stretched out in a very un-lady like fashion on her beach towel. He hadn't seemed bothered; she felt sure he wouldn't mind.

He returned with more beers, and they drank and spoke more of the trip. They watched the tourists pass by and enjoyed the balmy evening air. After dinner was finished, they walked back to Dakota's hotel, Javier didn't stay for a late-night drink, he was going back to finish his packing. She lay in bed that night thinking of him. She was about to go into the desert for five days with a man she barely knew but she felt she'd known him forever. Their time together was so right, so comfortable and nice, she felt so at ease with him, he was kind to her, but she felt something else was growing inside, feelings she shouldn't be having if she was listening to her head. One day soon she was going to have to get on a plane and fly back to London, to her family, her home and Miles. She turned over and drifted off into a long and peaceful sleep.

Chapter Four

Dakota sat astride her Harley in the hotel car park drumming her fingers on the petrol tank, waiting for Javier. He was late but she wasn't worried. He had stuff to do, people to see before he could go off radar and out into the great Atacama for five days with a stranger. She heard him before she saw him pull into the car park followed by a cloud of dust.

"Hey sorry I'm late I had bike problems this morning." Beneath his helmet his eyes looked stressed and had a smear of oil across his cheek which Dakota thought added to his appeal. "Are you okay, ready to go?" he asked.

"Yes I sure am." She started the bike feeling a great sense of excitement at what the days ahead would hold. She followed him up and out of San Pedro back onto the road they'd ridden along two days before. The sun shone down and it felt as though they were riding through an oven it was so hot.

After an hour of riding along the beautifully tarmacked road they pulled onto a small track. They rode cautiously along for a short while then came across a cluster of small single-story buildings. Javier pulled over and parked his bike inside one of the buildings. Dakota followed his lead. On the other side from the building that housed the bikes stood a few horses. An elderly man and woman were holding and stroking the creatures as they waited for their riders. "Hola Javier," the old man smiled and reached for his friend's hand clasping it tightly in his own withered one. "Hola Al, Catalina, this is Dakota, the lady who wants to go on this ride" Dakota stepped forward and shook both Al and his wife Catalinas hands. "You can choose the horses you want to take, and I'll take the other two back to San Pedro in the lorry later." Al said holding out the reins to his friend. "Which one would you like to ride?" he asked Dakota.

"I really don't mind, how about the one that's done the least amount of work recently and will be ready for a five-day trip?" Catalina stepped forward and handed her the reins of one of the horses she was holding. The horse was strawberry roan in colour and had a long black mane and tail. She was called Cherry.

Cherry was kitted out with a very different saddle to the one Dakota was used to riding on. The old woman explained in broken English how she would need to neck rein on the horse so instead of using reins as you would riding the English way you steered the horse by taking the reins on the horse's neck to the left or right. Dakota had ten minutes practice around the buildings then they were ready to go. Repacking their provisions from their packs into the saddlebags on their horse's backs they were all ready for their trip. Mounting up they turned their horses into the Atacama and their adventure began.

Javier and Dakota rode for two hours carefully picking their way across rough terrain before stopping for a short lunch break. Sitting on a rocky outcrop they could see for miles and miles ahead of them nothing but the Atacama Desert and all its raw beauty. The horses stood quietly behind them tethered to a tree in the shade. Tumbleweed gently blew past them bouncing on the sandy floor.

"Just look at it all," Dakota was awe struck, "the huge desert as far as you can see spread out in front of us, it is just so beautiful and quiet, I can't believe you can't hear a thing out here." She waved her arm across the endless expanse before them. "It certainly is big that I can guarantee," Javier agreed, "I hope we don't get lost out here!" he joked.

"We have a map though, don't we?" She turned to him and saw he was teasing her.

"It's actually a really good map and covers most areas I'm quite familiar with, we'll be fine I'm sure Dakota, don't you worry your pretty head about that" his big cheeky smile assured her.

"How long d'you come out here for with your work, when you cover the ultra-marathons and things?" Dakota asked through mouthfuls of apple.

"It varies, usually around five days or so. Sometimes I get a chance to go back to San Pedro and refuel in the day and grab a change of clothes, sometimes I don't."

After lunch they returned to their horses and tightened the girths on the saddles. Javier helped her mount and then swung up into his saddle with ease. Dakota watched him from behind her shades, he looked a very accomplished horse man, just something else to add to the list of what she found attractive about him she thought as she pulled alongside his horse Diego.

They rode over sand dunes for some of the afternoon and it was hard work for the horses, so they dismounted and walked leading their horses. They chatted for a while, Dakota found Javier an easy listener, she told him why she was in Chile; the troubles and strife she had suffered from her family back home. He listened and didn't say a lot, things must've been really difficult for her to have to run away so far from home. He told her he was glad she'd decided on Chile to run to and that had made her smile.

Camp that night was by a small wooden shack. It was late in the afternoon when they arrived. Javier bedded the horses down inside and lit a small fire where they were camping a short distance away. He boiled water in a small tin and added it to their dried dinners juggling the hot bag whilst trying to mix the contents. He handed Dakota her pack, she took it from him, thanked him and retreated to sit inside her sleeping bag propped up against a rock. She felt an overwhelming sense of happiness she didn't remember ever feeling before, a great sense of calm had come over her as she sat and consumed her dinner. Javier hunkered over the fire and poured them a coffee each then shuffled over to sit next to her. "Are you okay?" he asked pushing his shoulder against hers for a response. He wasn't looking at her, he was staring into his pack of food. "Yeah, I am thanks, I'm happier today than I've been in a very long time." She cradled the metal coffee mug in both hands and sipped the hot brown liquid watching him over the rim of her mug.

"Really?" he turned to her; she looked so small huddled over her coffee with her legs pulled up in the sleeping bag. Her hair loose around her shoulders. He wanted to hold her, to protect her from everything that had hurt her before here and now. He knew that was never going to happen, he looked away and back into his dinner pack. She couldn't see his feelings in his brown eyes. "Really. I'd come here to escape my life back home as you know. Things were difficult, I thought I'd probably be here and just be thinking about it all the time despite seeing the sights and riding around on the bike and that was the case really until I arrived in

San Pedro" and what she wanted to add was when she had met him, but she stopped herself, careless words could spoil things.

Javier was silent for a while he couldn't imagine a life like that, where she'd felt she had to leave her homeland to escape what she was going through, nor could he imagine her family not supporting her. Life was so different in England he'd heard that said several times when he'd been covering the ultra-marathons.

"How long are you planning on staying in Chile?" he asked.

"I don't know really, a few weeks maybe then I'll need to go back and face the music I suppose, you can't run forever, can you? Miles will have moved out by then I hope so at least I can go back to my house and not have to move back in with my family," she took another sip of the coffee and looked over at him. "D'you think I'm awful?" She spoke quietly unsure of what his reaction would be.

"No, I don't think that at all. Life is short, you only get one go at it. If Miles wasn't the right man, you did the right thing and the same with your job." She felt relief, unsure of why this man's opinion mattered to her so much when they hardly knew each other. "So, what goes with you then? We've talked about me all afternoon now it's your turn" Dakota asked changing the subject. "Not a lot really, not compared to your life anyway." He stared down into the empty coffee mug "I support these sporting events on my bike as and when they happen. Don't have a more regular job than that. I don't have a girlfriend although I did have one for seven years and then she got a job in Santiago and that was the end of it. We didn't survive a long-distance relationship, so she ended it. I've been on my own for two years now, I think, it might be more, I lose track sometimes, I live in a tiny one-bedroom flat." He poked the fire with a stick and put fresh wood on top of the embers. "Your life sounds good now though?" she quizzed, "I wish mine was so uncomplicated."

"It's tough though, making ends meet in the winter when there's no work. I must live very carefully with my money" he explained. They talked on into the night getting to know each other just a little bit better as every hour passed. Eventually sleep took them, the only sound to be heard was the horses softly munching alfalfa in the stables.

The following day the cool early morning breeze tickled Dakotas face. She woke, it was still dark, she lay quietly in her sleeping bag gazing up at the stars. She watched as they started their departure, to allow the sun to rise on another day. It was cold outside her bag, she snuggled down into it pulling the cord to keep the draught out. She could hear the horses in the building behind them moving around. Javier was asleep next to her and the fire had gone out. She lay for another hour quietly watching the night sky and then the sun broke through, and it was starting to get warmer. Dakota hurriedly dressed inside her sleeping bag; it was too cold to brave dressing outside. She quietly unzipped and crawled out.

Gathering the left-over wood, she managed to start the fire and went to feed and water the horses. They whinnied to her as they watched her arrive with their feed. She refilled the water buckets and by that time the fire had taken hold. She filled the small pot with water as she had watched Javier do the night before and spooned coffee into their mugs. Javier stirred in his bag but didn't wake so she rolled her bag up and packed it in the saddlebag. She made herself a coffee and filled the water back up in the pot on the fire. Javier woke and stretched. He yawned, sat up and looked bleary eyed over at their camp. His hair was messy, and Dakota smiled to herself thinking he was long overdue a haircut. "You've got up already and you've got the fire started?" He asked yawning again and stretching.

"I'm not totally useless you know?" she laughed, "I've fed and watered the horses too and this is my second coffee." She held up the mug she had been drinking from, "I'll make you one now you're awake." She poured the hot water into the metal mug and handed it to him, "Here. What are you wanting for breakfast, the choice on the menu a la Atacama today is porridge, porridge or muesli?" She held up the packs for him to choose from.

"Guess it must be porridge then," he smiled. "Really, you're a very different woman to any I know." He shuffled up his sleeping bag to the sitting position.

"Um, is that in a good or bad way?" she slowly stirred the porridge and handed him the pack.

"A good way. You're very independent and know what you want out of life that's cool." He took the porridge from her, leaning over on his elbow he placed it down next to his sleeping bag. "Try telling my family," She forced a laugh, "I suppose I am independent, perhaps too much so for their liking." She paused for a second catching his eye over their packs of porridge. A smile touched the corner of her lips. Despite him just waking up, hair scruffy and sleep in his long lashes he still looked hot. "I bet Miles was sorry to lose you?" Javier said searching with his plastic spoon for the last remains of the porridge.

"He'll find someone else a lot more suited to him than I ever was."

They rode side by side for most of the morning chatting about their lives. He found her great company; she was always upbeat unless they were talking about her family. She told him about her home back in London, how she'd saved every penny she had to put a deposit on it. He thought she was very young to have her own home at twenty-four. He showed her the different plants the Atacama played host to, he was very knowledgeable, and he was kind to her, she would be forever in his debt for this amazing experience they were enjoying together. The horses splashed along a river and through a narrow canyon where there was lush vegetation growing and tall Pampas grass gently wafting in the warm breeze. The horses stepped out of the river, water running off their well-groomed tails. The trail took them along a bank where they waved at other riders passing along the opposite bank on their own horses. "I didn't expect to see many people out here," Javier commented, "It's quite remote to be meeting other riders." He turned around to her, riding with his hand on Diego's back.

"It's just amazing," Dakota said, "I've never been anywhere like this before in my entire life it's just so beautiful and so unspoilt." She gazed around at the ever-changing rugged beauty that surrounded them. Javier lifted the reins and asked Diego to halt so she could ride alongside again. "Are you really enjoying it as much as you say you are?" He looked into her eyes; she could see doubt in his dark eyes. What if she hated it but was just saying she was enjoying herself because he'd gone to so much trouble? What if sleeping out had been awful for her? He was quite sure that hadn't been the case, but he had to ask. "Javier, I can't tell you how much I love this, riding along together through this incredible place. I'll be eternally grateful to you for arranging it and coming along with me when you could quite easily have booked me onto a tour with Al!" she smiled, distinguishing any doubt he had.

The horses walked on following an old road up and up and up until they reached what seemed like the highest place in Chile. They came to a halt and decided it was a good place to stop for lunch. Sitting on the sand with their backs against a large rock they'd come to the highest place for miles around and it rewarded them with the best view. They could look down and see how far they had travelled that morning. The river looked like a blue piece of ribbon snaking through the canyon far below and the steep road they'd just ridden along twisted and turned up the hillside. "Look how far we've come, look at the river, right down there all that way!" Dakota pointed at the tiny blue line far below. "It looks so tiny it's hard to believe it was coming up to the horses' stomachs and about twenty feet wide when we were wading through it earlier!" she said in complete amazement. "The road we've just ridden up is really steep though, we're really high up here but at least we get the best view for miles around," Javier said, "look, that's where we're going this afternoon" he pointed over to their right and she followed the line of his finger across the vast plain that was in front of them.

"Wow, it's just so cool." Dakota was loving everything; the trip so far had been way above her expectations. The Atacama landscape had been something she'd only seen fleetingly from her bike as she'd travelled along the road; to come out this far away from anyone, this remote really was the best way she was going to experience the desert. Lunch finished, they remounted their horses and rode onwards, down sand dunes out onto the road to cross it briefly and on the way Javier had shown her earlier, across more desert scrub land. There was not a sound to be heard apart from the horse's unshod hooves gently padding against the ground below. They rode together enjoying building the relationship that was starting to blossom between them.

The sun had started to fade, it was getting cool when they arrived at their second camp. Dakota took Diego's reins and lead the two horses into the small building where she unburdened them of their saddles and bridles and brushed them down removing the dried sweat. She heaped alfalfa into their stables, and they immediately tucked into the green stems. She carefully filled their buckets with water from the plastic container that Al had delivered the day before their trip. She emptied the cereal feed into the feed buckets in the stable area and dampened it down before giving it to them. She stood for a moment stroking the horse's necks and savouring the smell of the beautiful creatures who had made all this possible.

After the horses had finished their feed both of them looked settled for the night Dakota closed the building door behind her and went to help Javier collect wood for the fire. He had collected a large pile; she returned with her much smaller offering and added it to the heap. The fire was lit, and the dry wood was crackling and spitting before settling down to heat the small pot filled with water for their coffee. Dakota had brought two freeze-dried meals back with her from the saddlebags and placed them down next to the fire. "Are you okay with sausage casserole and I'll have the vegetarian version?" she asked looking to Javier for confirmation. "That sounds just great!" Javier leaned over and wrapping his t-shirt around his hand, he removed the now hot pot from the fire and poured the boiling water into the packets before handing them to Dakota. Dakota stirred the contents and closed the packets back up allowing them time to rehydrate properly before they tucked in. Still clutching the pot with his t-shirt, he poured water into their coffee, and they sat down on the sandy desert floor and drank.

"Isn't this just the best thing?" she asked warming her hands on the metal mug and gazing at the sunset, a big smile lighting up her features.

"It takes some beating" Javier replied, "sunsets are just something else out here" he commented then asked, "tell me about the bike." She glanced up at him from her pack of sausage casserole.

"The bike? Um, that one I'm riding around Chile is a hire bike, but I have one back home. I learnt to ride at seventeen on a much smaller bike, but I struggled with it, it was too small if you can ever get too small for someone my size. Anyway, I took my big bike test at twenty, the day I passed I went out and put a deposit down on a Harley and have owned one ever since. I love being free, putting on my leathers and off I go to wherever I want." She laughed and gently pushed against him with her shoulder. His heart skipped a beat, why was she having this effect on him?

"D'you ever get lonely?" she asked as if reading his thoughts.

"Sometimes I suppose I do. It was hard when Petra and I split up, we'd been together for years, but she changed when she moved away. It was for the best if I'm completely honest. Now I live alone I like just being able to get up and go and that's why I have the bike." She was watching him closely, listening to his every word as he continued "I learnt to ride when I was about eight and carried on from there. I've always had a trials bike because sadly one like yours isn't practical living out here but that doesn't mean I would say no if I was ever offered one" he added hurriedly.

"I found that out for myself, didn't I?" she laughed poking at the fire. He watched her gently stabbing at the embers with a stick, her eyes reflecting the red glow of the flames. "You're a very special person Dakota, I like you." The words were out of his mouth before he could stop them and he suddenly wasn't sure of the reaction he was going to receive. For a moment she stared into the fire and then she turned to him, a dark tendril of hair blowing gently across her cheek. She brushed it away not taking her eyes from his as she spoke.

"As are you Javier, and I like you too," she said, "Why are you staring at me like that?" She reached for his empty sausage casserole pack and he gently took her wrist as she leaned over. "Dakota you are the most remarkable woman I have ever met in my entire life, you truly are." He was overcome with the urge to pull her into him and kiss those beautiful full lips that were smiling at him and about to respond to his statement. "Probably the most *unusual* woman you've ever met!" she laughed. Javier gently released his hold on her wrist, she picked up her meal and continued eating the contents. "Wow it's really hot still." She blew into the pack and wafted it around to try and cool the contents, "I'm going to leave mine open for a minute or two longer to cool I don't fancy a blistered mouth for the next three days." She sat the bag down on the floor next to the empty packet she'd taken from Javier.

31

"Have you thought any more about your plans when we've finished the trek?" he tentatively asked.

"Sooner or later, I'll have to go back home. It took me a few days to ride up here. I want to go up to see Licancabur if I can then I suppose I will have to start the ride back to Santiago." Javier felt his heart sink. He knew it wouldn't be long after their return to San Pedro he'd have to say goodbye to her and watch her walk out of his life forever. He'd met a lot of people during his work and had to wave goodbye to them all. Some of the ultra-marathon competitors had returned a few times but most of them he never saw again. He didn't mind that, but this was different, he didn't want Dakota to be one of those people who walked onto the plane and out of his life. In only the few days since he'd spotted her sitting alone on the chair outside the bar, he'd grown to like her an awful lot, she was great fun, enthusiastic and kind. He had feelings for her he'd not felt for a long time.

Their meals finished; Javier poured them another cup of coffee. They lay on their sleeping bags looking up at the night sky. He pointed out all the constellations, showing Dakota each one as he spotted them in the night sky. She felt so happy lying on her sleeping bag on the sandy desert floor with this lovely man by her side. She stared up into the sky, "You are so lucky you know? You've no responsibilities, you can come out here and do this every night if you want to." Javier glanced over at her as she lay on her sleeping bag staring up at the sky. "I could but why would I want to come out here alone to look into the sky. It is only cool if you've got someone special to share it with."

"I'm here, will I do for now?" She asked.

"I guess so" he joked. "Okay, right last pee stop for tonight then I'm turning in." He got up and went off far enough out of sight to relieve himself. She undressed and clambered inside her sleeping bag and snuggled down inside unaware of how cold she had become she started to rub at her arms and legs to bring some heat to them. "Are you okay, you're shivering?" Javier had returned and noticed her vigorously rubbing her limbs inside the bag and the chattering of her teeth. He looked concerned.

"I think I just sat around star gazing for too long, I didn't realise how cold it had got since we started setting up camp" Dakota shivered.

"Do you want a blanket to put on top of your sleeping bag, Al keeps some in where the horses are bedded down, I'll go and get one for you if you want it?"

"No thanks I'll be fine in a minute. Just hope I don't need a pee in the night.... You know what, I think I'll make myself go now so I don't have to get up in the night." She hurriedly unzipped the bag and clambered out pulling her top on and leaving just her pants on the bottom half of her body. Javier looked away; it was only the same as seeing her in the bikini as he had done at the hotel the other day but somehow out here alone together, he didn't want her to catch him looking at her, he didn't want her to feel uncomfortable with him. A few minutes passed and she returned cleaning her hands with antiseptic gel she got back into the bag and zipped it up. "Damn freezing out there. Can't believe it when it is thirty-five degrees in the daytime and then minus something at night, damn freezing cold!" She rubbed her legs inside the bag to get warm. A short while later she was sleeping soundly.

Dakota woke with a start. She pulled herself up onto her elbows straining her eyes and ears to try and detect if something had come into the camp. Convinced she'd heard a noise she peered into the darkness but couldn't see a thing. She scrambled out of the warmth of her sleeping bag and walked over to check on the horses. They were happily munching on their alfalfa and didn't seem at all disturbed. She patted their necks, "You are good horses you two. Taking us far and away across the desert and looking after us. Two beauties you are," she crooned softly to them. Cherry whickered to her, and she smiled, "Dear Cherry, I'll think of you when I'm back home six and a half thousand miles away. Every day of my life I'll remember these special days with you, Javier and Diego," she whispered and then softly kissed Cherry on the muzzle. Leaving the horses contented with their alfalfa she closed the stable door and walked the short distance back to the camp. Javier was awake, "Are you okay?" he asked rubbing the sleep from his eyes with a clenched fist.

"Yeah, I woke up with a start and thought something might be around the camp, so I got up to investigate."

"What?" he suddenly exclaimed. Dakota looked over to him puzzled by his tone.

"What do you mean?"

"What if something had happened to you? What if someone had dragged you off and raped or murdered you or kidnapped you and I didn't know? Don't you think?" Dakota was shocked by his outburst. "Javier, I'm sorry I just didn't think, I'm sorry I've made you cross." She stood with her hands on her hips looking down at him in his sleeping bag. "I would appreciate if you do hear something you wake me up in future and don't take it upon yourself to go and investigate. I am here to look after and protect you!" He turned over and pulled the sleeping bag over his head, his side of the conversation was finished. Dakota sat down hard on her sleeping bag feeling cross with him for being so angry with her. She didn't need looking after or protecting, she was an independent woman, but inside she knew he was right. Of course, she should've woken him, but she'd slept out before and hadn't given it a second thought. Really, she should've given more thought to her own safety. She was in a foreign country and didn't know what sort of people roamed the desert at night anything could've happened to her out there and he wouldn't have known until he woke in the morning. Dakota knew she'd been stupid and tomorrow she'd apologise to Javier. She climbed back into her bag pulling it up around her ears to keep the cold out. She drifted off into a fitful sleep.

Chapter Five

The sun was shining high in the clear blue Atacama sky, it was already warming up by the time they woke the following morning. Dakota dressed and had poked the fire back into life with a stick she had taken from the wood pile. She then went off to attended to the horses. Javier woke and lay with his eyes closed for a while. He was feeling terrible for his outburst the evening before and didn't know how he could apologise to Dakota. She was after all a full-grown woman responsible for herself and quite capable of making her own decisions, but he would have been devastated if anything had happened to her. He wondered if he had spoilt the rest of their trip.

Javier dressed slowly and filled the small pot with water for their coffee and porridge. He shook, then rolled up their sleeping bags and put them back into their bags. Dakota returned from the barn with a spring in her step she was smiling and in a jolly mood. "Hey Javier, good morning, both horses are fed and watered and seem very happy with life at this very moment." She reported as she flopped down onto the rolled up sleeping bag. Things seemed different this morning, Javier didn't seem his normal self, there was an atmosphere between them, she needed to apologise and clear the air. "Javier I'm sorry about last night I just didn't think, I'm too independent for my own good sometimes," she glanced down at her hands. Her nails were chipped and dirty, a far cry from what they'd looked like when she'd had her office job she thought as she picked at them worried that she had spoilt things between them. "I hope we don't have a problem?" She looked from her hands to him watching her closely. His eyes were sad, his hair ruffled and scruffy and several days unshaven. He melted her heart. He was quiet, watching her picking at her nails, her face a little grubby and her hair was ruffled but she was the most beautiful woman in the entire world to him and he knew he was going to be in a lot of trouble when she went home. Javier expelled a sigh, "We don't have a problem, and it is me that should be sorry for going off at you." He handed her a mug of coffee and a bag of porridge along with a weak but apologetic smile. "Whoa, you know how to treat a girl, Javier!" She laughed taking both from him and placing them down on the floor to cool. "Can it be my peace offering?" he asked, "To show you how truly sorry I am?" He shuffled over to sit down next to her.

"There's no need for one, let's just forget it happened and I promise I'll not go off investigating if I hear noises again. D'you want me to wake you up next time if there is even a next time?"

"Yes, please humour me." He wondered how she could be so jolly, so forgiving when he'd spoken to her angrily and probably made her feel patronised.

They ate breakfast in silence. Javier extinguished the fire and Dakota groomed and tacked up the horses ready for the day ahead. She carefully put the saddle onto Diego's broad back wishing so much that this were her life every day. She longed to ride across the desert all the time with their horses and Javier by her side. He was an amazing and lovely man and along with their two beautiful horses they would have one great life together. But she had to remove the rose-tinted spectacles that were wedged well and truly onto her head, she had a life and home back in England, if only she could swap it with this one. She patted Diego and led him and Cherry to the camp. They packed what was left into the saddlebags and mounted ready for the trek to their next camp.

The horses walked on a loose rein, the mood had changed with their riders and the horses were quiet too. Around mid-morning they arrived at another river. "We're to follow this river all day now until our next camp tonight. Then we'll have a fresh water supply and somewhere to bathe." Javier held out the map in front of him balancing it on Diego's neck.

"That sounds good!" Dakota clicked her tongue and nudged Cherry on and into the river. The horse floundered through the gushing water and out onto the other side. They rode along the bank traversing the river at intervals when the bank disappeared and reappeared on the opposite side. Lunch time arrived later that day as they'd slept in longer than planned. They stopped by the river and let the horses graze on the small amount of grass that had sprouted with the moisture thrown up from the spume of the river. They ate fruit and finished the orange juice between them. Javier filled the carton with water and added water purification tablets. "We can fill our bottles from this one for this afternoon and then collect more water for our camp later. I might treat you to an extra cup of coffee tonight if you're good," he joked, "d'you think you can handle three coffees?" he turned to her whilst fastening the top on the bottle, careful not to spill any in the process. "I think I'll be buzzing if I have three so maybe I'll stick to two and water but hey, thanks for the offer!" Cherry stood as she packed her things into the saddlebag and mounted. "Come on lets make tracks."

The desert terrain was mixed. They crossed large areas of sand with dunes and then later passed smaller vegetated areas with animals grazing and pampas grass standing tall. The breeze blew up tiny cyclones of sand that danced around their horses' hooves as they plodded on towards the evening camp.

Making good time during their afternoon riding they arrived at the next camp by early evening. Dakota attended to the horses whilst Javier collected piles of wood. There was a good amount left around the site from the previous campers. Dakota washed down both horses at the edge of the river as they'd gotten sweaty throughout the day then gave them their alfalfa and water. She dampened down and mixed their evening feed. She loved looking after them, bedding them down for the night after they'd looked after their riders all day. As she walked the short distance back to the camp she called over to Javier, "I think I might go and have a wash in the river if you don't need me for anything?" She'd taken a towel from the saddlebag, and she was swinging it lazily in her hand.

"You go and make yourself beautiful for dinner," he replied, "I've collected the wood we need to get the fire going; I'll get the first pot on for the coffee and first course."

"Great idea!" Continuing to swing the towel she sauntered over to the riverbank and slipped off her clothes. She dipped a toe into the water, it took her breath away. It was freezing. If she fell in, she thought she'd probably die of shock! gritting her teeth hard to stop them chattering she waded in slowly until the water was up to her waist shivering violently as she took each step further into the icy abyss. Quickly she washed herself and rinsed her hair through in the water before scrambling out to her towel on the bank. That was certainly *not* how she'd expected a river in the baking hot desert to feel!

Dakota quickly towelled herself dry rubbing hard to bring feeling back into her frozen flesh. She dressed in fresh clothes she'd left on the riverbank by her towel. Kneeling by the side of the river, her teeth still chattering she rinsed through the clothes she'd been wearing, this would have to do, there were no washing machines out here, so the river had to suffice. Stopping off at the stables to hang the clothes over the doorway to dry she returned to the camp with the packs of evening meals and porridge for the morning. "You've got chilli con carne tonight with rice and I've veggie tikka masala. We've both got rice pudding for desert though, hope that's okay?" She handed the packs to Javier, and he ripped the tops and filled them with the hot water. He handed her a mug of steaming coffee in return. "You have a good bath?" he was giving her a cheeky grin, trying to smother laughter; he knew exactly how cold that river would've been. She was trying hard to hide how cold she still felt despite being out of the river's icy clutches and back into the heat of the fire and evening sun.

"You knew how cold it'd be didn't you?" She narrowed her eyes accusingly.

"Yeah. That water comes from the mountains, and you've seen what's on the top of Licancabur look!" he pointed to the volcano keeping watch over the desert, "Snow!" he laughed hard, doubling over with the effort, picturing her as she stepped into the unexpected freezing water. "Oh, I bet that took your breath away when you stepped into it!" his laughter was good, infectious, she joined in, finding it hilarious now she was out of it and warming up in front of the blazing fire.

"Well, it certainly woke me up, I thought I was going to die of shock when I was stood in it up to my waist, it was freezing! It most definitely made me ready for this coffee, thanks, I wish I had something a bit stronger to put in it though." She raised her mug to him. "Are you not having a bath in the river then?" she challenged. "I'll go down after dinner and have a quick dip, but I won't be in there long I can assure you of that!" he chuckled.

Javier disappeared along with his towel to wash in the river. Dakota cleared away their packs and put more water on for coffee. She felt sure he'd want a cup once he had endured the freezing depths. She added more wood to the fire, piling it on so the fire was really blazing and sat warming herself. As she sat staring into the flames, she couldn't help but wonder what her friends and family would think if they could see her now bathing in freezing cold river water, sleeping out under the stars with a stranger and riding a horse across the desert. Her friends wouldn't be surprised, and her family wouldn't be impressed, they would tell her she'd gone rogue and demand that she came home and found herself another brain numbing job and man to go with it. But that was another life away from this one, the one she didn't want to return to any time soon.

Dakota rubbed her hands slowly before the flames as they flickered eating up the dry wood. She piled on more and carefully removed the tin of water as it started to boil. She tipped the water into the mugs just as Javier returned to the camp. He was topless and was rubbing the towel hard into his thick black hair which was flopping over his brow. She glanced up as he entered the camp. Unable to help herself she gawped at the body he'd been hiding under his t-shirt. He was muscular and taught, his bronzed skin was glistening from the water he'd just bathed in. His face was adorned by three days stubble and with his shades on he looked almost God like as he strolled towards her still rubbing at his hair. She was unable to stop staring, her eyes were glued to the body of the man she'd only met a few days ago; who'd been sleeping next to her for the past two nights. Suddenly aware of what she was doing, openly staring and feeling embarrassed by her actions, Dakota quickly turned her gaze back to the coffee. "You didn't go in all the way then did you!" she teased smiling and squinting against the evening sunlight. "Here I made more coffee. Figured you would need it if you even dipped you toe in that river!" She handed him the mug and stole another glance at his physique. She'd noticed he had a good body; it was hard not to. He looked fit and strong, his muscles showed under his t-shirt as he worked but he was just something else half naked and dripping.

It was late, Dakota checked the horses one last time before unzipping her sleeping bag and snuggling down inside, it was so warm and comforting. Javier was by the river, rinsing out their cups and adding purification tablets to their bottles ensuring they'd be ready for the next morning. He dried his hands hastily on his t-shirt and returned to the camp clutching the bottles. "In bed already?" he asked looking down at her snuggled up in her bag.

"We can talk if you want to, I just wanted to be warm." She smiled at him from her makeshift bed on the Atacama floor, that beautiful smile from the woman he'd so quickly grown very attached to. Why had he been so stupid and opened his heart up to more pain? "What d'you want to talk about?" he placed the bottles between them.

"Whatever. I want to know more about you." She rolled onto her side and propped herself up on her elbow watching him as he went about his evening preparations.

"What d'you want to know, you know almost everything about me already." They'd talked a lot on the long rides across the desert, sharing things between them, things neither of them expected to talk to someone they had only known a few days about. They'd become very close without really knowing it.

Dakota sensed he didn't want to talk about himself, it made her think that things with his ex might still be painful. She changed the subject, "Tell me about Al the man who has kindly rented us his lovely horses, how long have you known him?"

"Ah Al, good old Al. I've known him years and years, since I was ten years old in fact. He was around when my dad wasn't, he looked out for me, and it never really stopped I suppose. We lost touch for a while when he got the horses and spent so much time out of San Pedro, then we met up again when I was supporting an ultra one time, he was supporting the same race with the horses. His horses could go places my bike couldn't. We camped together for a few nights, caught up on old times and things, I helped him with the horses, and he taught me to ride."

"Cool."

"Then the following year he called me up and asked me if I'd help him with the horses on the days my bike cover wouldn't be needed. There were a couple of days when they crossed salt flats and up small mountains where my bike couldn't go so, I rode the spare horse, and the rest is sort of history I suppose you could say. I don't see that much of him now because his horses are quite a way outside town, but we do bump into each other every now and again."

"That's such a nice story. The difference between us I suppose, I met most of my friends through work in an office no horses just computers. I'd love to live like you do out here it's just so liberating being free and doing what you want with your time" she breathed as she rolled onto her back to look at the stars above. "It can be very hard when the season is over. There's no way of making money other than tourists. I told you didn't I, my brothers and sisters wanted me to move to Calama to be close to them, but my home is here, I won't leave."

"A proper old romantic!" she laughed.

"No, I just love San Pedro and my job when the season is in full swing." He threw the piece of wood he had in his hand onto the fire sending sparks up to the sky. She looked over at him, "Are you okay Javier?" His mood seemed to have changed a little she sensed, he seemed sad.

"Yes fine. Are you?"

"I don't want to go home Javier; I want to stay here with you forever." She turned her head to look at him. He too was on his back looking up at the sky, he didn't turn his head to her. "You wouldn't like it here it's too far removed from your world, you'd get bored, and you wouldn't like me all the time I'm on my best behaviour right now." He sighed a tired and resigned sigh and closed his eyes. For a while she was quiet thinking about what he'd said then she whispered "But I wouldn't be bored, this is what I've wanted my entire life. I need freedom and this is it, you don't get freer than this."

"You're certainly spot on there!" he replied still with his eyes closed.

Dakota reached over to him and took his hand from where he was resting it on the top of his sleeping bag, "I won't ever be able to thank you enough for this time out here with you. I'll never forget you Javier and I promise you every single day of my life I'll think of you and all this, you have given me so much happiness in the few days I have known you." Javier didn't reply. He kept his eyes firmly closed afraid if he opened them his heart too would open, and he'd reveal his true feelings for her.

Eventually Dakota fell asleep, her hand relaxed its grip and fell to the desert floor.

He lay under the night sky thinking about how much happiness she'd brought him since they'd met. He knew he would think of her every day after she boarded that plane and flew back home, he'd miss her terribly. More than anything in his poor miserable life he wanted to ask her to stay, to make the life she wanted with him and ride the desert, to be with him on the races, to share his bed, his home and everything he had; not to return to England but he couldn't do that. He had nothing to offer her but a tiny one bedroom rented flat and his bike. He turned over feeling more miserable than he'd ever felt in his entire life and eventually sleep took him.

Chapter Six

Dakota couldn't sleep, she tossed and turned on the sandy desert floor. She woke early and lay watching the stars as they exited the night sky and gave way to the dawn. She attended to Cherry and Diego. They were now used to her and whinnied as they watched her approach, "Hello my lovely ponies I have your breakfast and fresh water for you." She filled the buckets and heaped alfalfa into their mangers from the store next door. Al certainly provided well for his horses, it was top quality fodder, and they readily tucked into it. The clothes she'd left on the door the previous night were still damp, she would pin them to her backpack, and they'd be dry before they stopped for lunch.

At the camp Javier woke. He sat up and looked around for Dakota, but she was not there. He knew she'd be with the horses. She loved those horses and was always fussing over them grooming, feeding and watering. He liked them but not to the extent she did. He was not feeling good having not slept well, he'd heard Dakota shuffling around in her bag, she'd had a restless night too. Javier knew he was in love with her, this beautiful woman who'd rode into his life and stolen his heart and would soon be leaving Chile and him behind taking his heart with her. In a few days he'd never see her again, the realisation made him feel miserable beyond all belief. How could he have let this happen? Last night she'd said she wanted to stay but he knew it was only the moment they'd been in. She wouldn't like a life with no money, big house or car. She wouldn't flourish out here. He knew his heart would be in broken again when she rode out of his life on that damn Harley.

"Hey you're awake! I'll get the fire going and do us some breakfast." Dakota chattered as she piled tumbleweed onto the charred embers of last night's fire coaxing it back to life. Carefully she fed the fire with small pieces of wood until it was blazing away. She placed the pot with the water over the fire and rolled up her sleeping bag to use as a seat. "Are you okay Javier you're not saying much?" Javier watched her from his sleeping

43

bag. She'd learned so much from watching him, she'd learned quickly how to survive out here.

"Fine." He rubbed at his eyes and ran a hand through his tangled hair.

She sensed he was not fine, perhaps he hadn't slept well or maybe her endless chatter was driving him mad. She handed him the muesli and coffee, "Horses are both okay this morning" she glanced at him over her mug, her brown eyes framed by those long thick lashes.

"That's good then!" he replied shortly.

"Are you sure you're okay?"

"Yeah, sorry, I just didn't sleep very well last night, and I'm still tired." He sighed knowing he couldn't tell her the truth, how he felt about her.

"I didn't either." She took the cups, rinsed and packed them into the saddlebags.

"Come on you'll feel so much better once you're riding through the desert on Diego with Cherry and me keeping you company." Off she went to collect their horses. She returned, she looked so beautiful standing with her hands on her hips, a horse in each hand and smiling her stunning smile, her hair was blowing back from her face in the early morning breeze. She was ready to go. He scrambled up, brushed the sand from his jeans and took Diego's reins giving her a feeble smile. "Let's go!" He swung his leg over the saddle, taking up the reins and led the way.

Dakota brought Cherry to a halt. "Javier, can we stop for a minute?" She called. He stopped,

"What's wrong?" he asked turning to look behind him. She was putting her now dry clothes back into the saddlebag. He quietly watched her moving around on the back of her beloved Cherry like she had been born there. "Okay I'm finished now." She took up the reins and handed him the water bottle, "Want a fill up?" He took it from her and filled his bottle.

"Just about enough to last until lunch. Good job we're still following this river." He pulled out the map and spread it out in front of him on Diegos neck. "We're next to the river until this afternoon when we start to move away from it back towards Al's again." He packed the map away and nudged Diego into a trot. They covered a mile or so at that pace and then slowed to walk.

It was so hot; they didn't want to tire the horses out too much. "Shall we do a lunch stop over there on that outcrop?" Javier pointed up a hillside at a small pile of rocks jutting up towards the sky. "Yes, looks good to me" she replied, shielding her eyes with her hand. He turned to her, he was wearing his shades, the same ones he'd been wearing when he'd turned up at her hotel and found her on the sun lounger and when he'd returned from the river the night before with water running off him like some God. They made him look hot, damn it he was hot, but she wasn't going to tell him that. He still seemed to be in a strange mood, maybe he hadn't slept well like he said or maybe he was getting fed up with her company. She hoped that wasn't the case, she'd become very attached to him and the thought of going back to England and leaving him was one she was trying to push out of her mind.

They sat on the rocks looking out over where they had just ridden. They could see for miles and miles as they'd been able to do on previous days. Al certainly knew how to pick lunch stops she thought taking a large swig of water with her food. Tomorrow their trek would be over, she would be back at the hotel and he in his lonely flat.

Javier was so angry for allowing himself to have such strong feelings as he did for Dakota, he was in a foul mood, and it was not lifting. He was trying hard to hide it, so she didn't see how he was feeling, he was trying to make the most of their last day together. "When are you going to go back home to England?" he asked staring off into the distance. Shocked by the abruptness of his question Dakota looked over to Javier wearing a slight frown. She had been over this, her plans and wondered why he was asking her again. "I want to see Licancabur but I'll have to think about making tracks back home soon I suppose. My savings won't last me for ever" she laughed, a forced laugh. She was only too aware at some stage she was going to have to make the biggest decision of her life and decide just what she was going to do with the rest of it. "Are you busy when we get back to San Pedro?" Dakota asked.

"Don't know yet, I'll have to see a few of my friends and acquaintances, see what's happening I guess." He slowly munched on his cereal bar staring out into the vast Atacama and avoiding looking at her.

"Are you really okay Javier?" She moved over the rock they were sitting to him and put her hand on his jean clad leg. She could feel the muscles under the denim.

"Not right now Dakota, I don't want to discuss it." He turned his eyes to meet her gaze, she could see her reflection in his shades, but she couldn't see the sadness and despair that was in his eyes, hidden behind the darkened lenses or she'd have understood. She thought he was being moody and spoiling their last day together.

"Right come on then, we have more miles to travel before we spend our last night under the stars." She jumped up from her seat on the rock and quickly started packing the food they hadn't eaten into the saddlebags. She collected the horses from under the only tree for miles around and mounted. She nudged Cherry into a trot and off she sprang across the sandy desert floor.

A few miles along she slowed again to a walk and Javier caught up with her. She'd wanted to stay out of his way she wasn't happy with him for being moody with her on their last full day on their trek. It was okay for him; he could do this anytime with anyone he wanted, and God alone knew he must have a stream of women queuing up to come out here and be alone with him. She'd wanted to live the experience, and she'd loved every minute of it, now he was spoiling it, it just wasn't good enough. "I didn't think you were going to slow down," he commented as he finally caught up and pulled alongside her and Cherry, "She can certainly set a pace!" He said nodding his head towards Cherry. "I'm pissed off with your mood Javier and that's why we've kept out of your way!" Dakota snapped. The change in her took him by surprise.

"Oh, um, okay, I'm sorry for being a bad-tempered sod." He cast his eyes downwards.

"So am I. I'm sorry I dragged you out here against your will; that I'm boring you to death with how much I love it, I'm sorry Javier, sorry that I know I'd love this lifestyle, and you don't, in fact you come across as hating it!" She yelled at him then choked up with tears. "Now look what you have done, you've made me cry!" Cherry stamped her food, nodding her head up and down

46

as if agreeing with her rider. Dakota turned her away and walked ahead leaving Javier and Diego standing staring and shocked by her outburst. "Dakota please don't be like this," he caught up with her, this was all his fault, how much he'd upset her, how it was breaking him, "I'm sorry I really am if I upset you!" But it was too late. His words didn't mean anything to the distraught girl on the strawberry roan horse at his side. He looked at her, what he'd done. Tears streaming down her dusty cheeks, under long lashes her eyes brimming unable to see the way ahead, her chest was heaving with the sobs he'd caused but still she and Cherry continued onwards refusing to look at him, not wanting him to see what he'd done. "We can go back to Al's now if you can't handle this Javier, I looked at the map at lunch, we can take a short cut back, you can go home, and I'll go back to the hotel and that'll be the end of it all." She snivelled wiping her tears with the heel of her grubby hand. "That isn't what I want, and I think you know it" he brought Diego to a prompt halt. Cherry stopped a few paces ahead, but Dakota refused to turn to face him. She was angry with herself for crying in front of him, for showing weakness and being emotional. She couldn't look at him, she knew she was powerless to control her feelings for him any longer.

"Dakota, I need to be honest with you," he spoke quietly to her back, pouring out his heart and the feelings he'd been harbouring for what seemed an eternity but in fact was only a few days. "You know I'm in love with you, don't you?" He spilled the words he felt were sure to end what had been a magical few days, now it was too late, he knew he had to tell her his true feelings because she was leaving anyway. Staring at her back, her long dark hair cascading down to her waist and feeling a fool for admitting his feelings to someone he'd only known a week and was so far out of his league. How could he ever have let himself do this, to spoil what could've been a great friendship if he hadn't been so stupid?

"What?" she turned to look at him. He could see streaks of tears down her cheeks. "You heard me," he replied softly.

"Are you being serious?"

"You know I am." Diego moved the few paces forward to stand next to Cherry. He gently nuzzled his friend, aware of what was happening between their riders.

"Your foul mood is because *you think you are in love with me*?"

"I don't think, I *know* I'm in love with you."

She wiped her tears on the back of her hand and down her jeans. "For God's sake Javier why didn't you say anything to me before now? Why have you let things come to this? Don't you realise I have feelings too?"

"I know you have feelings Dakota, I'm so sorry that I've hurt them, that I've spoilt this trip for you, what must you think of me?" he felt terrible.

"Not just feelings Javier, feelings for you, surely you must've realised how hot I think you are, and I mean *seriously* hot so please don't treat me like this, I'm not a child you know!" She scowled. Their horses fed up with what was going on between their riders started to walk on. Dakota let them, not ready to continue any further conversation with him until he had time to process what she had just said.

The afternoon sun was fading fast as they reached their final camp on the trek. Dakota took both of their horses as she had done every night. She sponged them down and then led them to their stable. The alfalfa was already in their mangers, so she topped up their water buckets and tipped their cereal feed into the buckets Al had stored there. She picked out their feet before closing their door and walking back to the camp.

They'd not spoken all afternoon; the atmosphere had been very tense between them. Dakota was angry with herself for letting down her guard and getting upset. Now he knew the extent of the feelings she had for him. She'd not confess to being in love with him, as he had done to her. How could he be so sure in such a short while and *why* did he feel the need to tell her? He'd said a number of times she wouldn't like living out here and she wouldn't like his lifestyle. She knew she'd love both, she craved someone like him and a life like this instead of house and job and shopping that seemed to be her life in England. Javier had done all he could to try and put her off having a life in San Pedro, then gone and confessed his love for her. She sat away from the camp staring at the horizon and trying to sort her feelings out in her head. She was confused, thoughts and emotions whirling around inside her pretty head. The warm touch of his hand on her shoulder brought her back to reality, she turned to see Javier had brought her a mug of coffee. "Dakota I'm so sorry I really am," he watched her closely from behind his shades speaking softly to her, "I shouldn't have told you how I felt I'm sorry."

"I don't understand you Javier," she took the mug from him. "You do your best to tell me how much I'd hate it here and I wouldn't be able to adapt and then you drop a bombshell like that. What goes on with you?" she questioned.

He took her arm and effortlessly pulled her up from where she was seated and into his arms. Before she could stop him, he was kissing her with a passion she'd never felt before in her entire life. He pushed his tongue into her mouth searching for her response, holding her so tightly against him as he ran a rough calloused hand through her black mane of hair. She felt her knees go weak; a thousand tingles run over her skin, her nipples hardened against him, and she thought she was going to faint. The kiss lasted a long time then he held her tightly against him. She buried her head in his chest, she could smell him and the aroma of horses on his t-shirt. She held onto him feeling breathless and excited, her heart racing, what had just happened? Whatever it'd been she hadn't wanted it to end. Finally, after what seemed an eternity, he stepped back and let go of her. "Come back to the camp?" He took her hand and led her back to where the fire was burning and the little pot for the water was bubbling away.

They sat close together on Dakota's sleeping bag talking and drinking coffee. The mood had lifted, and things were better. "Look, I know I'm stupid, I shouldn't have allowed myself to have feelings like these for you, you are way too good for me, you're amazing. In all my years and all the people, I've met I've never known anyone like you." He reached for the pot and poured more hot water into his mug. "You're like a force of nature, you turn up here out of nowhere on your huge bike, you wander around San Pedro like it was your home. Next thing you want to stop out in the desert sleeping under the stars, no tent, nothing. I have never known anyone, man or woman to be like you in my life!"

Dakota cocked her head and looked at him quizzically. "Is that a bad thing then, that I know what I want?"

He leaned over and gently stroked a strand of hair back from her face. "No, it isn't a bad thing it's just that you're so different to anyone I've ever known and that's why I find you so attractive" Javier continued, "You're not bothered about clothes, getting dirty, washing your hair and shopping like the women I've known, you are just unique." He shuffled along to be closer to her. Placing his coffee cup down he reached for her face and held it in his dirty hands before kissing her with a tenderness she'd never felt. He was melting her heart with his every word. "Now I need to know how you feel?" His dark eyes met hers holding her gaze. A smile touched Dakota's lips lighting her face in the fading light, he wondered for the one hundredth time how he was ever going to be able to say goodbye to her. "You're hot Javier; I like you a lot, do I need to say more?" She confessed, remembering how she'd felt when he'd appeared after his dip into the river, the glistening drops of water on his taught muscular body but it wasn't just that, it was the man who'd ridden beside her all this time, who had taken time out of his life to show her the wonders of the desert, the relationship that had developed between them and he'd been kind to her.

"What is hot? And why did you decide to tell me your feelings earlier?" He asked.

"Um, hot means er, sort of sexy?" she felt embarrassed, hot had always been her word of choice never having to explain the meaning to anyone before now, "And because you were acting out and you made me cry. I was angry and frustrated; I didn't want our last day out here to be spoilt. I didn't know what I'd done to upset you, the atmosphere between us wasn't good."

"Wasn't it?"

"Damn it, are you so thick-skinned Javier that you didn't even notice?"

"So it seems" he smiled making her already pounding heart skip a beat. She leaned over to him and ran her hand through his thick black hair before removing his shades. She studied his face, he was so good looking she wanted to stare at him forever, to get lost in those eyes would be heaven. Now, in her heart she knew their relationship had moved on, progressed to a different plane, they'd covered so much ground and it'd only been an hour. They'd been very honest with each other. She did have strong and passionate feelings for this man, but did she trust her judgement after the nightmare that'd been Miles? How could she ever have been so wrong about anyone she wondered. Javier was so different to Miles - he was the man she'd been waiting for since before she even knew it and that realisation frightened her. Quietly she whispered to him. "Everything about you, what you believe in and what your life is all about attracts me to you. You're everything I want, what I *need* in a man Javier, but you say I'm wrong. What makes you so sure you know what I want out of life?" He looked up and into her eyes, she couldn't help but notice there was sadness in them. "You live in a rich country; you have a nice house and a well-paid job. I live in a one bedroom rented flat with a motorbike, that is all I have. Some months I have no money. What do I have that you find so appealing, please enlighten me?"

"It's because you live like that, you're not obsessed with money. You're so genuine. Life out here is so *real*." Javier took her small hand in his.

"What d'you want me to do?" He asked her gently caressing the back of her hand. "Whatever you want to do Javier, you're a free man and I'm certainly not going to tell you what to do with your life or your feelings for me."

"I'm only too aware you'll be returning to England soon," he paused, "Let's see how the rest of your stay works out and we can talk again, rethink things?" He sounded positive.

"Rethink what exactly?"

"How things are going to work out for us."

Dakota was relieved to hear his words. She'd never have pushed him into a decision regarding their very new relationship, but she knew she wanted to be with him at whatever cost and they'd just have to see how things worked out. It was a very new and tender relationship; time was what they both needed. "I won't be going anywhere in the next week" she told him as he continued to stroke her hand. She leaned back against his warm and solid body feeling safe in his arms as they sat by the fire. She closed her eyes feeling happy and secure with Javier.

That night they slept close in their sleeping bags. Javier held her close to him all night, she slept the best sleep she'd had in what seemed a lifetime.

Chapter Seven

Their last night under the Atacama stars gave way to a day where the sky looked pale. The vivid blue that had greeted them in previous mornings had given way to grey and there were a few clouds drifting across the skyline. Dakota woke to find herself locked in Javier's arms almost stifling in the heat of her sleeping bag. She gently prised herself from his grip and rolled away onto her side. She had thought long and hard about their conversation before falling asleep. Realising she really did want the man as well as the lifestyle, now it'd be up to her to prove it to him and herself that she could take up the challenge of life in Chile.

Dakota pushed herself out of the bag leaving it in a crumpled heap at her feet. She took a large stick and poked the fire back to life. Javier yawned and rubbed his eyes and leaned over and took her arm in his rough hand. "Come here you!" She allowed him to gently pull her over to him. He rolled her onto her back on top of her crumpled sleeping bag. He wrestled off his own bag and kissed her softly to start with then the passion and intensity of the kiss increased, she could feel her heart start to race in her chest as he ran his hands through her tangled hair kissing her with a growing passion. She felt powerless in his clutches, this was going to go where she thought it might have done last night and she was unsure what to do about it. Her breath was coming in small gasps as he continued his seduction. She closed her eyes and felt his hands caress her, he was so gentle, she was totally helpless, not wanting this to end but then it did, this was not how he wanted it to be for her, for their first time together and he stopped. "I don't want our first time to be like this Dakota, I respect you too much." He'd wanted to take her there and then on top of her sleeping bag out in the desert under the grey rolling sky. She rolled from under him feeling disappointed but also a little relieved. She'd wanted him more than anything in that moment, she would not have stopped him had he continued but he was right, the middle of the Atacama Desert wasn't the right place for their first time together.

"Are you okay?" he asked wondering if he'd done the right thing.

"Yes, you're right Javier, this time yesterday we were just friends, if this is to work out, we're not to rush it." She was still feeling breathless and highly aroused. "I know and I'm sorry. I wasn't trying to rush things I just got a little carried away, I've had a beautiful lady in my arms all night in case you hadn't noticed."

Dakota pulled on her jeans and dressed before going to check the horses. She needed to calm down. Her heart rate was through the roof, she had to walk away from something that perhaps would've taken only five seconds longer and they would have been making love on the desert floor. It would have been very passionate. She'd wanted him; she'd wanted him to take her right there and then on their crumpled sleeping bags out in the remote wilderness that is the Atacama Desert. She'd wanted to feel him inside her, for him to take her to paradise but it hadn't happened. She knew it would also have completely changed their dynamic and it was too soon.

When Dakota returned to the camp Javier was dressed and in a jolly mood. "Here, I made coffee and breakfast this morning for you. Don't ever say I don't know how to treat a lady." He handed her a mug of coffee in one hand and her packet cereal in the other. "I have no doubt you know how to treat a lady, Javier." She reached up, holding onto her coffee and cereal and kissed him softly on the lips. He tasted of coffee.

"Today we ride back. Shall we go out tonight for a nice change and not have packet food or have you developed a fondness for it?" she asked.

"Going out sounds good to me." He rolled up his sleeping bag, tidied up the camp then opened his porridge and started to eat, "I'll miss this porridge though!"

"Really?"

"No, I'm joking but it would be good to have pizza, and a beer later don't you think?" He looked up at her, his hair flopping over his eyes, his unshaven face and his cheeky smile. She knew she couldn't walk away from him; she couldn't leave him here in San Pedro and board that plane back to London. She was going to be facing a lot of trouble and heartache, but what lay ahead, her life with him was going to be worth it. "Yeah, I certainly miss beer out here, but I will also miss Cherry and Diego. They've carried us for miles and miles and not put a foot wrong despite us being rubbish at riding." Her heart felt heavy with the prospect of having to say goodbye to the horses.

"Speak for yourself, I'm not rubbish!" he threw his head back and laughed.

They were both very accomplished riders; Dakota had been quite impressed by Javier's horsemanship skills; Al had taught him well.

By mid-morning they'd arrived back at the stables with Cherry and Diego. Cherry gently nudged at her rider as she stroked her soft roan nose. She could feel the horses' whiskers against the back of her hand, she reached over to pat her neck. "These horses are truly incredible," she told Al. "They haven't put a foot wrong for the whole five days and they've been a real joy to look after." Al smiled at her taking the reins from her hand he led the horses into the stable block. Afterwards, they sat on chairs drinking coffee and chatting to Al, telling him all about their trip. "Sadly, I think I'm going to have to think about giving all of this up soon," Al told them, "I'm just getting too old to go out riding across the desert all the time with tourists and having the four horses to look after, picking up feed orders and mucking out every day. I want a quiet life at home with Catalina now I'm getting old, and I need to retire, enjoy what time I have left."

"What will happen to the horses if you give it up?" Dakota spoke, her mind working overtime.

"They'll probably be sold but I'll be so sorry to see them go they've been remarkable horses and a real joy to look after and work with. I'll make sure they go to good homes." Al stared into his coffee cup, Dakota noticed how sad the old man looked and felt sorry for him. He'd had the horses a long time and to have to sell them, send them off to new homes would be an incredibly difficult decision for him to have to make.

After saying their goodbyes, they started up their bikes. Riding back to San Pedro the road was busy; they had to focus their attention on the traffic. Dakota's mind kept wandering back to their time out in the desert and how much she'd enjoyed it, way beyond her wildest expectations and it had also been incredibly intense. The time had helped her sort things out in her head, to decide what she was going to do with the rest of her life. She hoped more than anything that things would work out here in San Pedro with Javier.

"I'll meet you at the bar at seven tonight then?" Javier asked shuffling his bike around in Dakota's hotel car park. "Are you sure you'll be okay until then, you won't miss me too much will you?" His cheeky smile, his eyes shielded by the dark glasses and his teeth so white against his tanned skin. Dakota was overwhelmed by how much she was attracted to him; he looked like a film star sitting on his scruffy bike with his shades on. Swallowing hard she replied, "I have to sort out my stuff and get some laundry done at the hotel or I'll have the Atacama in my clothes forever," she laughed, "I'll see you at seven." She blew him a kiss and he rode off down the dusty street.

Sitting on his sofa in his tiny flat Javier gathered his thoughts. What a crazy few days it had been out in the desert. They'd gone off into the Atacama for five days, a leisurely trek to enjoy what the desert had to offer, he was her guide. They'd shared so much, talked of many things, things he'd never have spoken to anyone about yet to her it had been natural. Everything had been so good; nothing had been forced between them. Then he had fallen in love with her. How crazy could five days actually be? He'd no idea how things were going to work out with Dakota, and he was still struggling with believing a woman like her would even look at him let alone want a relationship with him. She was here, with him for now, but for how long? How long before she got fed up with Chile and him and decide to return home, to leave him here heartbroken? He couldn't understand his feelings; the intensity of the love he felt for her. He placed the coffee cup down on the work surface and started to unpack his bag.

Dakota scuffed her boots on the loose gravel as she crossed the hotel car park to her bike. She unfastened the panniers and emptied the contents out into a plastic bag before unloading at the hotel laundry. Returning to her room she showered and made her way outside to sit out on the sun lounger by the pool. She lay back in the sunshine and closed her eyes, her thoughts were instantly with her family back in London. Should she call them? She hadn't been in touch since she left England, but the truth was, she'd come to Chile to get away from them, she didn't want to call and be on the receiving end of their anger. No, she wouldn't bother calling not just yet anyway. Her phone remained turned off in her bag.

As Dakota dozed in the sun, she turned over events of the last five days in her mind, the five days they'd spent in the desert. That time out in the vast wilderness with the horses and Javier had been pivotal in her life, she understood now. She'd always remember those days. Although trying to fight admitting it to herself, she had fallen in love with a Chilean man whose life was so completely different to hers. How could she have allowed herself to fall head over heels for someone so soon after meeting him, it just wasn't what she did? She desperately wanted to make this work for them both. She knew he'd been lonely; he had a lot to offer her as a partner and was in so many ways very similar to her, wanting someone to love and share the rest of her life with.

It was six-forty when she closed the hotel room door behind her and started the walk to the bar where they'd agreed to meet. Hands stuffed into her jean pockets Dakota smiled at everyone she met along her route. She felt happy and relaxed. At the bar Javier had already bought the beers and was sitting outside at the table where they had first met in what seemed an eternity ago. "Hey you're early!" He stood and kissed her on the cheek then he pulled her back to him and kissed her on the mouth. "Wow, you *have* missed me" she declared staggering back from his passionate embrace.

"More that you'll ever know pretty lady!" He was dressed in a white linen shirt and jeans, Dakota thought how handsome he looked, her heart ached. His tan more evident against the white linen of his shirt.

"But I thought I'd bugged you the whole time we were out there, and you were getting thoroughly fed up with me?"

"What d'you mean?" he looked puzzled.

"I thought I annoyed you with my endless chatter?"

"No, you didn't annoy me. I just couldn't understand your enthusiasm for the place, but you never annoyed me," he frowned. "I'm sorry for upsetting you yesterday, Dakota." He looked down at his hands and picked at his now clean nails as he spoke. They were the hands of a man who worked hard for his living.

"Please let this work between us," she whispered taking his hand in hers, "I so badly want to be with you, I know I've only known you five minutes, I can't quantify my feelings, I keep trying to fight them but what's the point of doing that, life is too short?"

"I want it to work too but I'm struggling to get my head around the fact that you find living out here so cool. I know I've told you countless times but it's so hard making a living here. This is such a poor country in comparison to where you come from." He flagged down the waitress who had appeared outside and ordered another beer and handed Dakota the menu.

"So, what happens now?" he asked.

"I don't know Javier but I'm here for another week so let's just see how it goes. I can't change my whole life on the flip of a coin, and I don't want us to rush into things then have regrets." She listened to herself speaking the words, but she knew she'd already rushed into things, there was no going back from here.

After their pizza was finished it started to get dark, they took a slow walk back to the hotel. "Are you coming in for a night cap?" she asked turning to face him and letting go of his hand.

"Yeah, that'd be cool. D'you think we can drink it by the pool on the loungers?"

"I don't see why not there won't be anyone out there now," she added "Do you want a whisky?" He nodded, she went into the bar and ordered then followed him around to the pool area with the drinks. They sat on the loungers and looked up at the night sky. "I wish we were back out in the desert with Cherry and Diego," she whispered up at the sky, "I felt that was home."

"You are one crazy lady Dakota. How can a desert the size of the Atacama be home to you?"

"I don't know," she said not taking her gaze from the star-studded velvet laid out above them, "but I'd love to stop out just one more night."

He looked over at her. "Really, but we only just got back?"

"I know. I'll be alright in a few days just ignore me."

He leaned over and kissed her. She could taste the bitter whisky on his lips. "I will never ignore you," he said taking her hands in his. "Now tell me, what are your plans for tomorrow beautiful lady?"

"I don't have any at the moment" she replied.

"That is good because I do so, please be ready for ten and I'll pick you up on my bike."

"Okay I'll be ready where are we going?"

"All will be revealed tomorrow." he stood brushing down his jeans before pulling her to him. He kissed her standing by the pool in the darkness of the cool Chilean night. She thought she would burst with happiness standing there in the arms of her handsome lover in the place she was going to call home.

"See you tomorrow then" and he was gone into the night.

She walked back to her room in a bubble of happiness. She undressed and got into bed pulling the covers up to her chin. She fell asleep quicker than she'd anticipated and dreamed of the desert.

Javier walked back to his flat. One day soon he would bring her to his flat and show her what he was worth. He felt sure afterwards she'd go back to England and not return to him. He wanted to be wrong; he wanted to be wrong more than anything. He unlocked the door and walked into the small kitchen to get himself a glass of water. Sitting on the sofa he glanced around at what he'd made for himself in the thirty years he had been on the earth. It wasn't a lot. He could only imagine what she had back home, her own four bedroomed house and a bike like the one she had arrived in San Pedro on. He knew what people from rich countries owned, he had supported enough of them through the races and had heard their conversations too. He felt incredibly miserable convincing himself she would leave him sooner or later and go back to the big house and boring job. Why was he allowing himself to drag it out? He did not know the true feelings Dakota held for him inside her heart.

Chapter Eight

Dakota stood in the car park of the hotel her hands firmly planted on her slender hips, her legs slightly apart gazing at the volcano in the distance as it towered out of the desert floor and up to the sky. Already the sun was beating down but there was still snow visible on top of Licancabur. The volcano looked majestic against the blue of the Chilean day, visible from anywhere in San Pedro.

Dakota heard Javier's bike in the distance. She felt excitement at the thought of seeing him again. "Hola lady," he smiled, "You look more beautiful today than I've ever seen you. How can that be possible?" he asked tilting his head and giving her one of those gorgeous smiles he was so good at rolling out.

She smiled raising an eyebrow "You know flattery will get you nowhere, but it's probably because I've finally managed to wash all the desert sand off my body and out of my hair?" She walked over to him swinging her helmet in one hand and placed an arm around his neck. She pulled him closer to her and kissed him. She could feel his body, hard, warm and strong against hers arousing her slightly. "You are so hot you know?" she whispered to him and planted a soft kiss on his cheek.

"Oh, pretty lady, don't you start that, or we'll never get out of here!" He stroked her cheek so very gently with the tips of his fingers feeling her soft skin beneath them. She looked beautiful. He turned away and turned the bike around so Dakota could clamber on behind him. She put her arms around his waist pulling herself close to him. She breathed in his smell and closed her eyes as the bike sped off.

Just over an hour later they were standing at the base of Licancabur gazing up the slopes to the snow-covered cap at the top. Dakota had never seen anything like it and was in awe as she stared up at the volcano. "It's amazing, awesome, look at the sheer size of it. It is a hundred times better than I ever imagined it be." They gazed up to the snow that covered the top. "I wish we could've gone to the summit of the volcano" she said, "but I guess you have to be super fit and have way more time than we

60

have to get up there and back in a day." He laughed at her, the thought of climbing the steep slopes was far from his agenda, he knew very well how tough that would be for them.

"You certainly need a whole day and yes, you need to be fit to climb up and down the slopes, there's no path, and it's loose rock," he added, "come on we haven't finished yet." He reached for her hand and led her back to the bike.

"Where are we going now?" she asked surprised there was going to be more to the day than she had expected. "Get on lady, it's another surprise!"

It was mid-afternoon and they were stood at the edge of a massive salt flat. As far as they could see was rough white salt. The glaring sun was reflecting off the surface making them both appreciative of their shades. "This is awesome, Javier, I can't believe such things exist" she turned to him her face alight with wonder, "Can we walk across it?" she asked.

"Not all the way, well not today it is nine miles across from here to where it ends, and we don't have the right kit for it" Javier explained.

"Can we walk a little way and then back again?" She pleaded squeezing his hand tightly. "Sure, you lead the way." Javier relented, stood back and held out his arm for Dakota to step onto the path in the salt flats.

Walking on the rough surface of the salt flats was tough going. Neither of them had dressed for it and after only a couple of miles they decided to turn back. "It's just so cool!" Dakota had her hands in her jacket pockets looking down at the salt as she spoke, taking great care where she was placing her feet. Javier laughed at her. "Why are you laughing at me?" she frowned.

"You're just so enthusiastic about everything it's so refreshing," he hugged her to him and kissed her temple, "Come on let's get back, it's getting late."

They walked back, stumbling over the spiky hard salt to the bike. She scrambled on behind him and off they sped. Dakota could feel the hot wind rush past her, flicking her hair and blowing into her face, she closed her eyes enjoying the feeling as they rode along the smooth tarmac. She wrapped her arms tighter around Javier, resting her head on his back. This amazing man who she was clinging onto had made the last week of her life just brilliant. Each day he'd make sure she enjoyed to the fullest. Despite thinking she'd go back to England without him he never tired of making her happy. A silent tear slipped down her cheek; she didn't want this to ever end.

Javier stood in his shower. He rested a hand against the tiles just letting the jet of water wash over his tired body, rinsing away the remains of the shampoo from his thick mop of hair. He'd invited Dakota for dinner the following evening. He was deep in thought, planning the menu. On his way home he'd stopped and bought some beers. He'd tidied the flat and tomorrow he would clean everywhere until it was spotless. Unable to quash the feeling she was going to leave him once she saw how little he had, he'd made the decision to invite her sooner rather than later. He knew in his heart that tomorrow would be decision day, quite possibly the last time he'd see her. His mind went over the day they'd just spent together and what great time they'd had. All the time he spent with her was fantastic. *She* was fantastic and he wanted her in his life so badly it was eating him up inside. Stepping out of the shower Javier hurriedly dried himself and dressed in jeans and a white cotton shirt. He fastened the buttons leaving a few at the top undone. He collected his keys and wallet and closed the flat door behind him.

Back at the hotel Dakota stood in her shower feeling incredibly sad. She knew why Javier had invited her to his flat the following evening and it hurt her. He'd admitted his feelings for her, he told her he loved her but still he thought she'd leave him once she saw where he lived and what he didn't have to offer her. After spending all that time together in the desert, all those conversations he *still* didn't understand her. Still, once tomorrow was over and he saw she did still want him he'd stop this. She rinsed her hair and applied conditioner. She wanted to ask him to stay the night with her, but she understood she needed to go to his for this dinner he was preparing and put his mind at rest before they could consummate their relationship. She rinsed the conditioner from her hair and wrapped it in a towel. She dried herself and padded into her room, the intended outfit already laid out on the bed. She pulled on her jeans and a blouse. It had been the only blouse she had brought along with her thinking that t-shirts and vest tops would suffice most of her trip. She fastened the buttons and ran a comb through her soaking hair.

Javier was already in the hotel bar when she walked in. Standing with his elbow propped on the bar he looked sexier than ever in a white shirt and his jeans. Her heart skipped a beat, she smothered a smile knowing how much she would enjoy ripping that shirt off and taking advantage of the body, she knew was beneath the white cotton. Quashing the thoughts, she strolled over to him. He turned and smiled at her, "You look gorgeous," he reached for her and pulled her to him kissing her on the mouth, "absolutely gorgeous."

"You don't look too bad either!" she whispered taking her drink. "Come on let's go and sit at our table in the restaurant where we can talk." They sat on opposite sides of the scrubbed wooden table. She watched him over the menu unable to take her eyes from him, he was just so easy to look at. "Why are you staring at me?" he caught her glance and raised a questioning eyebrow. "You look so good you are worth staring at" she replied casually pushing her hair back behind her ear she reached for her drink. "Hey lady, I'm not a sex object you know?" He laughed and reached over the table to take her hand "You know I can't stop thinking about you?" fixing her gaze with his dark eyes.

"Then I hope you realise how serious I am about you?" She replied. He dropped his eyes and studied the menu for a few minutes longer before deciding. "Right, I'm having steak, I think. Have you chosen what you want?"

"I'm ordering vegetarian chilli." They handed the menus back to the waitress and ordered more drinks. "My sister called me before I came out," Javier casually mentioned, "to see if I'm okay, check up on me I guess."

"And are you okay Javier?"

"I couldn't tell her about you."

"Javier, I know what you're doing. I know where you are going with all this, I'm not about to leave the best thing that's ever happened to me, when are you going to get that into your head?"

"What?"

"*You*. I'm not leaving you because you think I'm going to once I've been to your flat and seen what you don't have as you keep telling me. D'you think I'm that shallow that all I want you for is material possessions and not love?" Her face was flushed, she could feel herself getting angry with the man she so badly wanted to trust her.

"You're just so different to me. You need to see what you're letting yourself in for Dakota before you make any decisions about staying here or even getting involved with me." She stood up pushing the chair back, scraping it on the wooden floor. "Don't you think I am already involved with you Javier; shouldn't you have thrown this wobbly before now? It's a bit late now, don't you realise how I feel about you? I've just about had enough of this," she turned knocking her chair over and stormed out of the restaurant. "Please cancel the order we've just made," she barked at the waitress on her way out. Javier jumped up from his chair. "Dakota don't do this please I'm sorry." He scurried out after her.

Out in the car park she turned to him, there was something he had never seen before in her eyes which made him take a step back, "Come on Javier lets sort this out once and for all. I'm fed up with wasting time going round in circles." Dakota stomped out of the car park and into the road outside. There she turned to him aware that she didn't know where she was going. "You lead the way I don't know where your flat is."

He stood before her, his arms open, eyes wide and a lost look on his face "What?"

"I don't know where you live so you lead the way. We're going to yours and we are going to sort this out now. I'm not pissing around any longer and wasting my time. If you think I'm going to leave you after tomorrow night let's do it now, why waste another day going around in circles like this? Let's just damn well get it over and done with, I can't stand this Javier, it's killing me." She stood with her hands on her hips, her eyes flashing with anger. Her dark skin was flushed, her hair was hanging round her face still damp from her shower, but she looked so sexy he couldn't hide his arousal. "Okay." He led the way to his flat.

Dakota followed him up the steps behind the shop. He took the key out of his pocket and unlocked the door. Standing back, he let her in first. She stepped inside and looked around at his home, the place he'd lived in for years. The small kitchen diner and the lounge with the worn sofa and small TV set. There was a rug on the floor covering the aged floorboards. She slowly walked into the room and took in the atmosphere, she looked at the beautiful prints that covered the walls, the thin curtains, she entered the small but very clean and adequate bathroom. Lastly, she ventured into his bedroom. It was furnished with old furniture but had been very tastefully done. The bed linen co-ordinated with the curtains and the whole place was clean if a little untidy. "Well, what do you think?" he asked cautiously studying her, trying to gauge her reaction. She turned around to face him. "Are you really expecting me to leave you now that I've seen where you live, your home?" there was a profound sadness in her voice.

"I don't know. I didn't know what to expect if I'm honest." Javier felt ashamed. How could he even have begun to think she would be like those people he'd met in the past – Petra, the woman he'd been engaged to even? This was Dakota, she was different to anyone he'd ever known. More than anything, five days alone in the desert should've shown him that, made him realise she wasn't materialistic, she was a good, honest person and that was why he loved her.

Dakota walked back into the lounge. "Honestly Javier you could've tidied up a bit." She bent down and picked up a beer bottle from the coffee table and handed it to him. "I did, I would've made a bigger effort if I'd known you were coming tonight" he protested looking sheepish.

"Okay well you'd better tidy up for tomorrow night then, don't think I'm sitting amongst old beer bottles to eat my dinner!" Relief flooded over him, and he laughed. Her mood had changed, and she was still here. "I love your flat Javier," she spoke softly stroking his clean-shaven cheek, "I can't understand why you would think I wouldn't?"

"It's very small and everything in it is old."

"But everything in it is loved and well looked after. Why d'you want new stuff it doesn't last, and it goes out of fashion so quickly. Your flat is just like you, unique and beautiful." He blushed at her kind words, he cast his eyes down to the rug on the floor flicking the edge with his booted foot.

"You're the beautiful one Dakota, you are as beautiful inside as you are on the outside and I'm totally in love with you." He confessed.

"So, I'm still invited for dinner tomorrow then?"

"I'm more worried about dinner tonight," he replied, "As you cancelled our order at the hotel!" She'd forgotten about that in her haste to get to Javier's they hadn't eaten. "Shall we get something from the shop downstairs, and we can cook up here together?" she said excitedly.

"Okay what d'you fancy?"

"You!" She grasped his shirt pulling him to her, "I fancy you Mr hot Chilean man!" She kissed him and he kissed her back, it was filled with passion consuming them both, all the worry and angst was gone, in its place was hungry lust, it filled the room, was all around them. She ran her hands under his shirt and over his hard muscular body. She could feel him tense under her touch as she kissed his neck and ran her hands over his back. He stood locked in her grasp wanting to rip her blouse off and enjoy the soft skin that lay beneath, but he was a gentleman, but he didn't know how much longer he could remain one! She stopped and stepped away from him red faced and breathing hard. "Wow, I don't think we'll get dinner tonight if we carry on like this," she straightened her blouse and pushed her hair back behind her ears. "Come on let's eat." Still recovering from their moment of passion they descended the small staircase at the back of Javier's flat and walked into the shop below. Dakota picked up two bottles of wine and a steak with salad and some bread. She paid for them. "I was going to treat you to dinner tonight anyway, so I'm getting these" she took out her money and handed it to the shopkeeper who was openly intrigued by the woman Javier had suddenly appeared with. "Javier, are you going to introduce me to your friend?" he asked revealing a blackened and crooked smile as he took her money. "Dakota this is Ruben my landlord and local store owner. Ruben this is Dakota the woman who has stolen my heart." Ruben's eyebrows almost disappeared into his hairline. "Stolen your heart? About time someone did you've been on your own too long!" he winked at Dakota and handed her the change. "Yeah, thanks for reminding me of that!" Javier smiled at him.

"Well, it's very nice to meet you Dakota d'you live here?"

"No, I'm on holiday at the moment but things could change." She shook his hand, and they left with the groceries.

As they sat at the small table in the kitchen eating their dinner Dakota spoke "Ruben seems nice?"

"He's okay. Very convenient having a shop downstairs" Javier joked raising his wine glass. "To us" he toasted their new relationship and Dakota felt he was at last starting to come round to things. "Are you okay with everything now?" she asked. "Dinner was great!" he replied as he cleared away the dishes and put them into the sink. "I didn't mean dinner," she said tentatively, "I meant are you okay with me being here or do you still think I'm going to walk out on you and catch the first flight back to London?" She followed him into the kitchen eager for his response. He moved over to the fridge and opened the door retrieving the wine bottle from inside. "We'll have to see, won't we?" He replied light heartedly as he refilled their glasses and moved to the lounge. "Really you still think I'm that shallow Javier?" Dakota probed.

"I don't think you are shallow at all I just know people from England are on the whole very rich compared to Chilean people and I've met people who've looked down their noses at what we have and how we live." Dakota was amused by his statement "And you think I'm like that?"

"No, I don't but I had to be sure. I know you're not like that you are a wonderful person who is genuine and just beautiful in every way."

"Careful you are going to make my head big with all this flattery" she smiled.

"You see, even now you are joking with me!"

"That's the way I am Javier, I have a sense of humour that sometimes upsets people. I hope it doesn't offend you?"

"No, you don't offend me I just find it hard to understand at times." She lay on the sofa with her head in his lap and her feet up on the sofa arm. She'd removed her shoes, and her socks had holes in, but she didn't care, she was here with him in his home, and he didn't care either.

It was eleven-thirty and Dakota was starting to fall asleep on the sofa. She struggled to sit up. "Hey, I'm falling asleep here I need to go back to the hotel." She rubbed her eyes and swung her legs back to the seated position. She pulled her shoes on. "You can stop over if you want to?" he offered. She smiled to herself; this was great progress. "Thanks Javier and thanks for a lovely evening but I need to collect my laundry tonight, so I'll go back to the hotel." He was disappointed. He'd wanted her to stay, things were going to be fine between them he knew that now. "Just give me a minute and I will walk you back to the hotel," he stood and smoothed out his ruffled shirt before pulling on his shoes. "Okay I'm ready now."

Outside the evening was cool but not as cold as it had been in the desert. It was quarter to twelve and there were still people around in the town. Laughter and joviality and music from the bars could be heard on every road. They walked slowly along the road with their arms around each other holding each other close. "Are you happy Javier?"

"Happier than I've been in a very long time." Dakota remembered telling him the exact same thing just a few days ago as they'd camped in the Atacama. "Are you *really*?" she probed squeezing him tightly against her slender frame.

"Immensely." He patted her hand. She knew this man was going to drive her crazy but even knowing that she was not going to let him go and she hoped with every fibre of her being that he felt the same way about her.

They stopped outside her room, and he pulled her to him. She stood in his arms for a long time and then he leaned down and kissed her good night before leaving her for his return trip home. It was a tender kiss unlike the one they'd shared earlier that night when she had so badly wanted him to take her on the freshly laundered duvet that adorned his bed.

Dakota let herself in and opened a bottle of water before crawling into bed and mulling over the evening they'd just spent together. She'd been flattered by his introduction of her to Ruben telling him that she had stolen his heart. Would he have said that in all honesty if he'd thought she would leave him after he'd taken her to his flat? She didn't think so, he'd been much more relaxed once they'd started to cook dinner together. He had hurt her, presuming she was like everyone else he'd met, thinking she was a materialistic person, but they were from such different cultures, different backgrounds, he didn't really know her in the real world after all. She knew her feelings for him where true, she loved him more than she had ever loved anyone, and it had only been such a very short time. She'd never been so sure of anything; she wanted a life with Javier in San Pedro and for that to happen she was going to give up everything she had in England to be with him.

Chapter Nine

Dakota was deep in thought; she was making plans. She'd been thinking about Diego and Cherry and dear old Al and, had remembered late the night before that Al had mentioned he wanted to retire. Dakota knew she had to get a job in San Pedro that would grant them an income when Javier didn't have much work, and she was contemplating the idea of buying Al's business and taking up the Atacama treks herself. She'd need to sell her house in London or at least rent it out for the short term until she got herself sorted; she could use her savings to buy the horses. She'd have enough money and even some left over. Her mind was working overtime but first she needed to speak to Al.

She slowly stirred her coffee lost in the idea of riding Cherry around the Atacama every summer, showing tourists the unspoilt beauty of the desert. More planning and researching would need to take place, she'd need to learn what looking after four horses in the desert would entail. Should she speak to Al about it or Javier first she wondered. If she spoke to Javier, she knew he'd try to put her off, he'd persuade her to think about it, to live out here for at least a year before jumping into anything big. She didn't want to do that; she wanted to show him she was committed, to be working, have a way to earn an income and to have a job she'd really love for a change. The other worry was if Al decided to sell the horses to someone else in the meantime. Her decision made, Dakota quickly swallowed the dregs of her coffee and left the restaurant.

At the hotel reception Dakota enquired about horseback tours around the Atacama and was handed Al's name and number. She called the number scribbled on the scrap of paper the receptionist had given her with trembling hands. The phone rang six times then Al answered. He was pleased to hear from her and, after a brief discussion summarizing her ideas, he agreed to meet at the barn outside of San Pedro where his business and horses were based. He gave her directions to the barn; she assured him she'd be able to find her way.

Just over half an hour later Dakota was standing in the barn stroking Cherry's nose and chatting to Al. He agreed he had wanted to sell his business but had realised since he'd miss the work and the horses. Dakota listened to his worries and concerns before speaking. "If you're not wanting to sell up, I quite understand," she smiled as she spoke gently to the old man. "But if you wanted someone to take out the rides during the busy season then maybe I could help out and help you with the horses too?" She raised her eyebrows eagerly awaiting Al's response. The old man thought for a while rubbing his greying stubble. "That'd be something I could work with. I'm quite able to take the feed and water containers out and muck out the stables but I find it hard all the riding and caring for the horse's day to day" he explained, "Grooming four horses and getting three people up and ready for a day's riding can be very testing and I'm getting too old for it." Dakota studied the man who was sitting in the barn with her. She didn't think he looked too old but who was she to question his reasons. "I'd be more than happy to do a few weeks trial for you if it involves following maps that are as well detailed as the one you gave to us? A bit of flattery never hurt anyone she figured. Al smiled, his eyes twinkling mischievously. "You really want to do this don't you?" he chuckled.

"I do. I loved it out there riding around for five days and I'm sure I could be a great asset to you and if you thought it wasn't working between us then I'd understand and look for something else." Dakota knew it would work. She would do everything within her power to ensure it did, to secure them an income and her a job she was going to love.

"And what does Javier have to say about this?" She realised he knew they were in a relationship. "Erm, well I haven't exactly told him yet, you see it's complicated."

"You'd best sit down and tell me all about it then." He patted the seat beside him, and she sat.

Al had just made coffee; he poured her a cup and handed it to her. She took the coffee and poured her heart out to the old man. "I don't know if you realise, we are sort of in a relationship?" she cast a sideways glance at Al.

"Um, I didn't think you were when you first arrived here, but I sensed an atmosphere between you when you brought the horses back, there was something strange going on between you both, I couldn't quite put my finger on it" Al said slowly sipping his coffee.

"We sort of got it together out in the desert, that's where Javier declared his love for me anyway." The coffee was incredibly strong, but it was fabulous.

"Javier did *what*?" he was astounded.

"In a way he did yes. You see the thing is I really want to stay out here I absolutely love it, but he thinks I'll hate it when I realise how tough things are."

"Um, well it's all fine now at this time of the year, but it is hard in the winter when there are not many tourists around, he's right about that."

"I understand that, but he's really worried, he thinks he has nothing to offer me, he doesn't understand that it's *he* I want, not a big house or a fast car only him, I love him Al." She stared down into the coffee cup fighting an urge to cry.

"D'you have anyone back home, a boyfriend or something?" Al asked watching the young woman next to him studying her coffee. She was stunning, she couldn't be single surely. "I did have someone but that ended a while back. I was single until I met Javier," she swilled around the black liquid in her mug and then her gaze turned to Al. Her dark eyes pleading with him, "How can I make him understand Al, can you give me any advice?"

"I don't think you can Dakota, I think you need to live out here and prove to him that you're serious about both him and the lifestyle if you're sure in your heart this is what you want. He'll get better in time, understand you're here for him and not what he can provide for you," he paused for a second and then continued "It was hard for him when his fiancée broke it off, he's still struggling with it. She is probably the reason he thinks you'll leave him. She moved to Santiago enjoying all the trappings life could offer her, then left him saying that she was fed up with him always being poor, he couldn't provide the lifestyle she had wanted and got in Santiago. He was in a terrible state for a very long time."

"His fiancée? He didn't tell me they were engaged!" She frowned. It didn't matter to her, it was in the past, but it was something he hadn't wanted to talk about, and she hadn't pushed him. He'd tell her in his own time of that she felt sure. "My advice to you, young lady, is to go back and talk with Javier about all this. Come and have a few days riding out and looking after the horses then see if it's still what you want. I'd be more than happy to have you work alongside me, it'd be a real pleasure, and I'd get to see more of Javier." She felt grateful for Al's advice. Dakota finished her coffee handing the mug back to the old man. "Tonight, I'm going to his flat, he's cooking us dinner I'll bring it up then, see what reaction I get." She gave him a big smile, hugged him and shook Al's hand. He walked with her to her bike, she pulled on her helmet and mounted, firing the machine into life she waved to Al and rode back to San Pedro. Dakota felt pleased with the progress she'd made so far. She'd made the first steps to her new life in Chile with Javier. She'd have a job and be able to contribute to their finances. Hopefully it would also stop Javier worrying so much!

The sun was once again baking down on another hot afternoon in San Pedro. Dakota was in her room doing the maths, trying to figure out how she'd be able to survive on the money she'd earn working with Al. Despite her earlier enthusiasm about getting the job, reality had set in. Ideally, she'd wanted to buy the business but if she worked for Al, she would at least earn a wage and the money she had intended to put into the business they could use to live on for at least the first winter if things got tough and they were careful. She was excited but also a little worried, what would Javier have to say about her being so impulsive?

Dakota had brought only one dress with her to Chile; she wore it that night for her official dinner date at Javier's flat. Her hand was shaking as she put on make-up, she struggled to fix her jewellery her excitement was so great. Finally, she closed the hotel door and strolled along the streets of San Pedro to the flat. Lifting her dress, she climbed the steps and tentatively knocked on the door. He opened it and stood gaping at the vision before him. She was wearing the loveliest floral dress with a plunging neckline which revealed her cleavage, it was incredibly flattering to her figure, she wore a slick of lipstick and had mascara on her lovely long lashes. Her hair was combed back and shone in the evening sunlight. He didn't speak, he didn't move he just stood with his hand on the door staring at her. "Javier, are you going to let me in?" She asked slightly amused by the expression he was wearing. "My *God* you look gorgeous." He stepped back to let her pass. She smiled a coy and flirty smile. "Come here" he pulled her to him. She let him. He took her face in his hands and kissed her and then kissed her again. She could feel his arousal pushing against her and it excited her. She wanted him, she ached for him, and she knew he wanted her just as much. "You look lovely you really do, lady, you are just so *damn* sexy, what d'you see in a man like me I just don't know." He let go of her, they stood in the kitchen both slightly breathless, "Have you seen what you look like, in that dress! Damn good enough to eat, come here!" again he started kissing her.

"You mean I look like a *woman* instead of a biker? Are you seeing me in a different light now I have a dress on instead of jeans?" she laughed at him.

"I suppose that's what I mean." He walked over to the sink and finished drying his hands on the dishcloth that was in his hand when he'd opened the door to her. Dakota's gaze followed him. "I made pizza I hope you don't mind?" He handed her two glasses and poured wine out of the fridge. "I'll put it on now and then it will be ready in about fifteen minutes is that okay for you?"

"Yes, that's fine, I'm really quite hungry" she replied handing him his wine glass and lifting hers to her lips. Javier stood with his back against the cooker assessing her. He could tell there was something bothering her, something she wanted to tell him, she just didn't seem quite her usual self.

"What's the matter Dakota, is there something bothering you, you don't seem your usual chatty self?" He tilted his head studying her, waiting for her to respond. "I've got something to tell you over dinner, but it can wait for now" Dakota walked over to him and grabbed the dishcloth pulling him away from the cooker and closer to her. "You know you mean the world to me; you do know that don't you Javier?" She whispered softly to him.

"Yes, I think so." He was confused, unsure of where the conversation was going.

"Okay!" was all she said.

Dakota set the table whilst Javier busied himself sorting salad and poured more wine. She felt comfortable in his flat with him, preparing dinner together. This was only the second time she had been to his home, but she already felt safe and happy there. Once the dinner was on the table they sat down to eat. "What were you going to tell me earlier?" Javier asked forking salad into his mouth.

"I went to see Al today"

"Al?"

"Al with the horses, I went to see him this morning."

"Why would you go to see Al?"

"I've been thinking. Al mentioned he wanted to sell up and retire and I was thinking about what I'm going to do if I stay here so I went to see him, and we talked things through, came to a mutual agreement."

"But I thought you were thinking about going back home in a week?" Now he was confused.

"I was but then I got thinking. I have enough money saved to buy Al's business presuming he doesn't want a ridiculous amount for it, so I went to talk to him to discuss things." Javier's eyebrows were raised but he didn't speak he pushed another mouthful of pizza into his mouth and listened as Dakota continued. "Anyway, he doesn't want to completely retire but he does want someone to help with the horses, to take the tourists out and about, he said that's what he's struggling with. So, we spoke about it, and he has offered me a few weeks trial to see how we get along together and if it works out I have my summer job and have not spent any of the savings I have stashed away."

"So you think you can live off your savings over the winter if you decide to stay?"

"Javier, *I am* staying. I'm not going back to England I want to make my home here and if we work out all the better but if we don't, I'm still staying here do you understand what I'm saying?" He beamed at her.

"That's the best news I've heard all day," he said through mouthfuls of pizza. "The best news I've *ever* heard in fact, you're staying here despite me telling you how hard it is in the winter when there are not many tourists around and you've still decided here is where you want to make your home!" He was delighted.

"Yes, Al told me it was hard too, but I want to live here. This is the life I want, and you are the man I want to share it with if you'll have me?" She glanced up from under those lovely lashes at him, how could he not want her. "I'm so happy you've come to that decision I just can't tell you." He reached for her hand over the small table. "I think it's a brilliant idea you work with Al. You'll both get along so well, and you'll have the horses and the desert, and we'll be together when we're not working." She could tell he was brimming with excitement over her plans. "And if the winter is hard and we don't save enough to get us through then we have my savings to use as a backup plan."

"No, I'll not use your savings Dakota, that's for you if anything goes wrong and you need to go back home."

"Javier this will be my home with you here in San Pedro. I'll keep enough money back in case I need to fly back to England in an emergency, but the rest will be for us and our life together here.

Chapter Ten

Dakota lay in bed staring up at the cracked ceiling unable to sleep but feeling a great sense of calm. Javier was quietly sleeping beside her. They'd shared a beautiful evening together discussing plans then he'd told her about his broken engagement. She'd told him she already knew. He'd been sorry for not telling her sooner. She'd told him it was fine; she had known in her heart he'd tell her when the time was right. Then as the sun had gone down, he had made love to her. His seduction had started in the kitchen after they'd finished washing up. The kissing had started with tenderness but had quicky bloomed into lust as they'd taken it into the lounge and onto the sofa where clothes had started to be removed. His seduction had ending in the bedroom where he'd taken her to heights she never knew existed. It'd been hot and frenzied and incredibly intense but had been worth the wait, the best sex either of them had ever had.

Now she lay against his chest feeling relaxed and fulfilled listening to his heart beating and wondering if the rest of their lives would be like this. She hoped so. Now she was aroused for the second time that night. Slowly she ran her small hand over his smooth chest tracing the outline of his nipples then downwards feeling his defined stomach muscles, tracing the outline of his stomach button beneath her fingertips. Further her fingers explored, down to where she took him in her hand. She felt him start to harden in an instant. He stirred next to her and opened his eyes. "You want some more pretty lady?" His smile, seducing her in a heartbeat he ran his warm hands over her naked breasts making her arch towards his touch. "What do you think?" She gasped feeling shivers like small electric shocks running through her body as caressed and fondled her, working her like putty in his hands. She moved in to kiss him on the mouth, neck and chest. She threw back the cover and he gasped as she mounted him. Feeling him enter her she rode him gently at first and then harder. His rough hands on her hips, she gained momentum until she felt him start to tense as he exploded inside her. She threw her head back and a small scream escaped her lips, her jet-black mane tumbling down to her waist she took everything he had to give her, then it was over again.

The following morning Javier was awake first. Dakota was still sleeping soundly so he got up and made her coffee and breakfast. She woke and realised he wasn't there. She reached for him wanting more of what they'd shared together the night before, but he was gone. She turned over and pulled off the covers. Naked, she walked into the bathroom and showered before dressing in last night's clothes. Javier was busy making scrambled eggs and toast in the kitchen. "Hola lady," he kissed her cheek, "did you sleep okay?"

"Sure, slept like a log once we'd had our early morning workout." She mumbled. Wearily she pulled out a chair out to sit down at the table. He placed the eggs and coffee down in front of her. "Better than freeze-dried which is the other option!" He too pulled out a chair and sat opposite to her and tucked into his food. "Are you happy?" She asked as she picked at her scrambled eggs with a fork.

"Yeah, very happy." Dakota could see he was. He seemed a very different man to the one who'd been insecure and worried about her leaving. He was relaxed and moved around the kitchen dishing food onto her plate like she'd always been there. She smiled to herself. "I love you Javier" She hoped he knew just how much.

"I would hope so, I'm a good devout religious boy and I wouldn't expect anything else from the woman who'd just shared my bed and taken advantage of my innocence" he teased.

"You were not very devout last night if I remember rightly!" She smiled and forked more of the eggs into her mouth, washing them down with coffee. "I do love you." Unsure why she felt she had to tell him a second time. His eyes met hers and he held her gaze for just a few seconds.

"You know I love you, don't you?" he replied, "you've made me so happy since you appeared here barely over a week ago."

"I can't believe we've only known each other that amount of time, it's mad how fast things have developed between us." A week was a very short time in the real world to get to know anyone let alone have the feelings she was, and to have shared his bed but they had shared their lives together out on their adventure where they had eaten, slept and ridden beside each other day and night for five days.

Dakota had returned to her hotel. Javier sat in his lounge reliving the previous evening. He'd known the minute he saw her he'd have to make love to her that night; she looked gorgeous. Their love making had been incredible, beyond anything he'd ever imagined, she'd been demanding, and he'd given her everything. She'd worn him out, but he'd loved every minute of it. Lying next to her, watching her sleep, he knew he wanted her to be with him forever. He would've been devastated if she'd gone back to England, but he couldn't be the person to ask her to stay, that had to be her decision. She'd gone to see Al about the horses, he'd been so pleased Al had offered her a job. Al needed the help and if she wanted to stay, she needed a job. She'd turned up at his flat, told him of the job offer and her decision to stay in San Pedro with him. Now he had to speak to Ruben about something he wanted from him and then he had an afternoon's work to get on with. As he had kissed Dakota when she was leaving the flat that morning, he'd arranged to meet her in her hotel later where he hoped it would be the last evening she'd spend in the hotel before moving in with him.

"Javier that is the best news I've heard this week!" Ruben offered his hand and Javier shook it hard, "I'm so pleased she makes you happy you absolutely deserve it!"

Javier smiled broadly; his happiness was hard to hide. "Thanks Ruben, are you sure it is okay with you?"

"Absolutely and I hope it works out with the horses for her she seems a really nice woman from the one time I actually met her!"

"She is a lovely woman; I love her so much. I'm just not sure how we're going to work all this with visas and getting her things over from England."

"Just enjoy what you have now and don't worry about all that," Ruben told him, "It'll sort itself out."

Dakota was sitting on her bed, her head in her hands. She was pondering how she was going to tell her parents she wasn't returning to England. Sooner or later, she was going to have to call them and let them know. She hoped she'd be allowed to stop in Chile, but she'd put on her visa she was only in the country for a few weeks. She wanted so badly to be with Javier, she needed to be with him, but they'd only met a few days ago and everything was just so crazy. How could she be so much in love with someone she'd only known a matter of days? She had known Miles for a long time before she arrived at the decision she loved him, and it'd been months before they'd slept together. Why were things so different with this man?

Making the decision to work with Al had been a good idea it would give them time apart and Dakota time out in the desert with her beloved horses. She reached for her water bottle and took a long drink. She would do her trial with Al first and make sure she made the grade before taking the plunge and calling her family. If she didn't have a job out here, she'd have to go back to London and sell her house before she could return to the man she loved. After all, her family had only expected her to take a holiday not to call them and say she wasn't coming back!

Al was more than happy to hear Dakota could start with him the following day. He had a booking for a couple who wanted to ride out for the day then the following day he had another couple who wanted to camp out overnight. Dakota could ride out on both treks and learn the ropes with him then, if they were both happy, the following week she could take out a longer ride on her own or with minimal supervision from Al. She was looking forward to riding again and was thinking she would need to stock up on freeze-dried food and electrolyte tablets for the treks out in the desert when it would be very hot.

Javier sat opposite to her at the table in the hotel. His arms folded on the wooden table smiling and shaking his head in disbelief. "So, I start tomorrow!" she said smiling her best smile.

"Well, that's good to hear," he reached for her hand across the table and gave it a squeeze, "So what are you going to do about living arrangements, have you given it any thought?"

"Not decided yet but I was going to speak to Al about how many nights he thinks I'll be out in the desert."

"Erm well, I hope you don't mind but I have taken the liberty of speaking to Ruben, and he agrees with me."

"Agrees with you about what?" Dakota looked puzzled.

"He agrees that it would be a good idea if you were to come and live with me in the flat if you can bear it that is and if I promise to make an effort to be tidier?"

"Really, do you really mean it Javier, you think it's a good idea for me to move in with you this soon?" He looked into her eyes; she knew it was a great idea, but she didn't want him to feel he had to ask her to live with him because she had nowhere else. "I think it is going to be great, that is if you can manage to live in a shoe box?" he laughed but it was the laugh of a man who knew she wouldn't mind the size or how shabby his flat was.

"Javier I'd love to come and live with you but are you absolutely sure it's what you want?"

"Yes, I am positive it's what I want. We won't see much of each other in the summer months, we'll both be working but I want to wake up with you beside me every morning when we can be together. So, the real question is when d'you want to move in?" he flashed her a cheeky smile and made her stomach somersault. "This is happening so quickly my parents would have a meltdown if they knew about it." She thought of what they would say, her smile started to fade, she realised sooner or later, she was going to have to speak to them and it looked like it was going to have to be sooner because they'd be expecting her back home any day. "When d'you want me to move in?"

"How about tonight," he said, "I want to wake up next to you tomorrow, the next day and every day for the rest of my life." He gave her hand another squeeze. "Lady, I hope you feel the same."

She smiled at him, his hand feeling rough against hers, but she didn't mind. They were his hands, the hands who could work her like putty in his bed. "I have all my stuff here and my bike. I'll have to sort out a smaller bike for me to ride to Al's and take that hire one back or it'll cost me a fortune." The endless list of things that needed to be done had made her realise she was going to be very busy. "Would you mind if I move in tomorrow night after I've finished my day with Al?"

"Sure. I've got some work on in the morning, but I'll be around when you get back. Come round when you're ready, and I'll make dinner."

The fading light from the window cast a shadow over the small table Javier and Dakota were eating their last meal together at the hotel. The bottle of wine they'd ordered to toast their exciting future together was open in the wine cooler on the table. Dakota's heart was filled with a mixture of happiness, love and anticipation for the huge adventure that lay ahead for them. Javier had resigned himself to the fact he was going to spend the rest of his life living alone, he never thought he'd find happiness again and he would never have gone looking for it. This woman, this beautiful woman had ridden into his life and turned it upside down and now he couldn't be happier.

The following morning under a pale sky Dakota checked out of the hotel for the last time. She'd become friendly with the reception staff over her short stay and a few of them knew Javier, they'd seen her ride off into the desert with him and him dropping her off and picking her up. They'd also seen the change in the woman who had arrived in San Pedro just over a week ago. The man on reception this morning had been very friendly and helpful to her, he asked her to pop by and keep in touch with them. She'd promised to do so and passed over her key and credit card.

She stepped out of the hotel into the car park and to her bike for the final time. She rode straight to Al's barn where Cherry, Diego, Nico and Juan were waiting for her. Al showed her around, where the saddles and bridles were kept along with the grooming equipment, the feed store and the order the feed was stored in. Al was very particular, and she liked that. She quickly got to work grooming all four horses, getting them tacked up and ready to go before the customers had even arrived. The couple they were taking out could ride well and were English speaking, so they had a very enjoyable day chatting and riding, they had a few canters and a gallop across a flat plain. Al was clearly impressed with Dakota; both her horsemanship and how easily she chatted away to the strangers, the couple left a large tip for her. She was pleased with her first day's work and felt happy as she removed the saddles and bridles from the horses and put them back into the tack room. Al had cleaned out the stables and prepared their alfalfa and hard feed before they'd left that morning so once the horses were groomed, they were stabled for the night. Al's barn in San Pedro was only a short distance away from the town. He explained to her, on longer rides they sometimes finished up at the barn where she and Javier had hired the horses quite a long way out of town, but he didn't keep the horses there unless he could stay with them, it was considered too remote, and he worried in case anything should happen to them.

As Dakota and Al had worked that morning, she'd recalled her conversation with Javier, and now they were moving in together that very evening! Al had been delighted to hear the news, at last his friend was moving on with his life, he liked this woman who'd come to share it with him very much. The old man waved goodnight to her, and she rode her bike across the small town to Javier's. Already she knew San Pedro so well, she'd no difficulty finding his flat in the maze of roads that made up the town.

Dakota stood at the top of the steps outside Javier's flat with her small bag of clothes. Standing in the open doorway Javier was smiling broadly at her, "You don't need to knock, this is your home now!" He was brandishing a wooden spoon, and she thought she'd caught him starting their dinner. He hugged her hard against him. He could feel the swell of her breasts beneath her vest top and took a breath, letting her go he went back to the cooking. "Are you okay today lover?" she asked stroking his stubbly cheek with her fingers.

"It's you lady. You make me hard the whole damn time!" She tried to smother her amusement with her hand. He adjusted his jeans, "What's so funny?" he asked.

"You're so funny Javier. We can work on your hardness later if you'd like?"

He shot her a cheeky grin. "Oh yes! now I'm starting to feel better," he continued adjusting his jeans with one hand and stirring their dinner which was bubbling away in a pan on the hob with the other. "You go and unpack, then I want to hear about your first day in a proper job since your arrival here in the cowboy capital of Chile." Javier was preoccupied stirring the chilli.

"It certainly is a proper job, and I really stink. I'm going to shower after I've unpacked my stuff do I have enough time before dinner?"

"Sure!" he was peering down into the bubbling pot on the hob.

Dakota unpacked her things humming happily to herself as she folded her clothes into the drawers in the bedroom. She glanced around at what was now home, *her* home. She thought about her house back in London. She'd bought a vast four-bedroom detached house expecting one day they'd have children or at least they'd have Nina's children to come and stay with them. She expected Miles would've moved out by now so the house would be standing empty. In her heart she wanted to sell it, but her head told her to keep it for now just in case she needed to go back. She wondered what Javier would have to say if he saw her house back in England. He'd probably have a wobble about how much it'd cost. He didn't understand what life away from Chile was like nor did she want him to. This was her home now in San Pedro, this flat in the middle of the town with the man of her dreams in the kitchen cooking dinner for her.

She stepped out of the shower her body steaming from the hot water and dried herself on one of Javier's very tatty towels. He'd made dinner, so she hurriedly dressed and popped downstairs to get wine from Ruben. "Ah hello, the new lodger has arrived" he smiled showing his decaying teeth as she entered.

"Hello Ruben," she said selecting the wine. "We're celebrating our first night together in the flat." She put the wine on the counter and handed over the pesos to pay for it. Ruben smiled again, "I hope you'll both be very happy in the flat," he took the money and handed her the change, "I'll be seeing you quite often then I can assume?"

"Well, I'm working with Al, you know, Al with the horses?"

"Yes, I know Al alright."

"I'm taking rides out for him, so I'll be around some days and not others depending how long the rides are out for and if we're camping."

"I see, so you ride then, have you done it a lot?"

"I've ridden for many years, and I love the horses and the desert so to me it is my dream job, and it helps Al out as he is wanting to take life a little easier these days."

"I wish you good luck with everything and I hope it works out for you; Javier deserves to be happy and you do too." He handed her the wine, and she walked back up the stairs to her new home.

Dinner was vegetarian chilli. Javier's cooking skills were not brilliant, but he'd tried, and she was impressed he'd tried something new to him. After all, it was only just over a week ago he said he would never eat anything but meat! After dinner was finished and they had cleared away the pots and pans Javier had strewn around the kitchen they relaxed on the small sofa with the window open listening to the town passing by outside. Dakota leaned back against him and closed her eyes. If anyone had told her six months ago, six weeks even, this was the path her life would take she would never have believed them. If anyone had told her she'd be living with someone she'd only known a week and a half she would not have believed them either. But this was the person she was, impulsive and everything spur of the moment. She had wanted to find someone to spend the rest of her life with and she believed that person was Javier.

Chapter Eleven

Two weeks had passed in Javier and Dakota's new life together. Al had made the decision Dakota was the woman for the job. He was thrilled with how she handled both the horses and his clients. She'd followed the maps clearly and had kept to the timetable. The first few times she had ridden out he'd met her each night at the camp in his truck bringing with him alfalfa and water for the horses. Now at the end of week two he was taking the alfalfa out during the day and leaving her to sort the horses and riders out. There'd been one occasion when Juan had been startled and his rider had fallen off. Dakota had caught Juan and remounted the rider who was a little shaken but otherwise unharmed. She'd worked out for herself Juan and Nico were not a good mix and had remedied that by riding Juan herself leaving her dear sweet Cherry to take the more novice riders in safety along with her friend Diego.

Sitting on their bed, staring down at her phone Dakota had made the decision it was time to call her parents. Her trial period with Al was over, she had a permanent job and somewhere to live. She wouldn't tell them she was living with Javier just yet, the news she wasn't returning home would be enough for them to take in. Javier was out at work; he wasn't due back until the following day. Dakota called the number. It rang seven times before anyone answered. It was her mother. "Hello?"

"Hi Mum, it's Dakota."

"Hello Dakota, how are you?" Her mother replied rather briskly. Something was wrong she could hear it in her mother's voice. "I'm fine thanks, how are you and Dad doing?"

"Where are you Dakota, we've not heard from you in such a long time?"

"I'm in Chile Mum, I told you where I was going when I left, why?"

"You need to come home." She could hear her mother's voice start to shake.

"Mum…."

"Your sister is very ill Dakota, she has leukemia"

"What? I've only been gone four weeks and Nina has leukemia?" Dakota was stunned. She didn't know what to say, her sister had been fine four weeks ago when she'd left for Chile.

"She passed out at work and was taken to hospital, that's where it was picked up on the tests that they ran while she was in there. She'd been very ill with that cold she had before you left, it just wouldn't go and then there were the bruises." Dakota remembered Nina had been ill for a while with a cold that just wouldn't seem to clear.

"Bruises?"

"Karl told us she was always covered in bruises, and he'd been worried about her for ages. She told him she'd get herself checked out but then this happened, and the doctors told us that was a sign of the disease."

"Oh my God, is she going to be okay?" Dakota's heart was pounding hard against her rib cage. "The truth is we don't know, it's acute, we just don't know. We've tried to call you many times, but your phone was turned off, we had no idea where you were."

"I've been here in Chile the whole time, and I did turn my phone off." Dakota felt sick to the pit of her stomach. Her family had been trying to contact her and she'd been so wrapped up in her new life with Javier, she hadn't even given it a thought let alone turned it on. Now it was too late, her sister was lying in a hospital bed somewhere in London critically ill.

"Of course, the decision is yours if you come home or not but we don't know if she's going to make it." Her mother's voice was broken by teary outbursts.

"Mum, I'll call you back, give me some time and I'll call you later today."

Dakota sat on the edge of their bed; her mind was in turmoil. If she went home, she'd have to stay until she knew if her sister was going to be okay and if she wasn't, she'd have to stay with her until it was over. Nina was in hospital, and it was acute, she knew that wasn't good at all. She was going to have to go home and act like the good daughter she should have been rather than the useless and selfish one she'd turned into. She was going to have to pull off a pristine job of hiding things from her parents about her new life in San Pedro.

Dakota managed to catch the next flight to England from Calama. It would take her at least a day to get back with the flight times but she would be back in London in two days' time. She tried Javier again on his borrowed mobile but still there was no reply. Knowing she had no choice; she would have to leave him a note explaining what'd happened. He would panic as soon as he read it and convince himself she wasn't going to come back but she could only hope he'd gotten over all that by now. Al had been very understanding and had told her not to rush back, he'd managed alone this long and would manage until she could sort things out in England. He'd wished her well.

The following morning Dakota was on the flight from Calama to Santiago. She'd not managed to reach Javier despite calling him over fifty times. She was desperate to talk to him about what had happened back in London with Nina, she didn't want to just leave without him knowing why she'd gone. Dakota prayed he would understand why she had to leave so quickly. She'd asked both Ruben and Al to speak to him, to explain her plight and she would return to him and their new life as soon as she could.

The next day she was back in London and by her sister's bedside in the white and very clean hospital. Her mother and father met her outside the ward and now they were all gathered around Nina's bedside staring down at the pale and weak young woman swathed in white sheets. "She fainted at work, and they thought to take her to hospital, or we would probably still not know to this day that she was ill." Her father explained. Dakota looked down on her very thin sister as she slept stroking her hand and silently cursing herself for being so selfish. "The doctors won't tell us what they're thinking which only makes us fear the worse," her mother added. "Are you stopping with us or has Miles moved out now?" She added as an afterthought.

Dakota didn't look up from her sister as she answered her mother's question. "I have no idea I haven't spoken to him since I left but if I can I'll stop there." Dakota hadn't thought to see if Miles had moved out, she'd just jumped on the first plane to England. She still had a lot of her things at the house and didn't think it would be a good idea to stay with her parents. She knew sooner or later they would start on at her about her job, Miles and everything else they could find to throw at her, it wasn't the right time to start an argument with Nina being critically ill. She'd just turn up at the house and hope he had gone.

That evening she sat in her house staring out across the road at the houses opposite to hers, they all looked the same as her house in row upon row of sandstone. How different this was from her home in San Pedro. She wondered what Javier would be doing now, she felt lost without him and incredibly homesick. She tried again to call his number.

Dakota lay in bed feeling frightened, cold and very alone. She desperately wanted Javier beside her. She needed him to hold her, to tell her it would all be okay even though she knew it wasn't going to be. She reached out across the space in the bed where, in Chile he would have laid but he wasn't there he was six and half thousand miles away in San Pedro. She slept fitfully and woke late. Realising it would be very early morning in Chile she tried him again and finally she managed to get an answer. "Javier it's me, oh God I'm so sorry I had to come away without seeing you I'm so sorry." She gasped and then tears came.

"What's happened? Al and Ruben told me your sister is ill is that right and it might be life threatening. I'm so worried Dakota, you just left."

"She has leukemia and she could die. The doctors are not being forthright with us, nobody seems to know what to expect it's awful I wish you were here." She sobbed trying to hide her guilt from Javier, wanting more than ever to reach out and hold him next to her to smell him and to taste him on her lips. She wanted to run her hands through his hair, for him to hold her against him and comfort her and make all this go away but all she could do was sit on the bed and cry.

"Dakota my love *please* don't cry. I wish I was with you too my pretty lady please don't be upset you must be strong for yourself and your sister and your parents too. I love you so much I know you'll come back to me." Javier knew he had to be strong for her. He knew she was in a very bad place and needed his support.

"You do? Promise me Javier, promise me you are not just saying that" Dakota sobbed.

"You will, won't you?"

"Oh Javier I really hope so." She didn't know what the next few weeks were going to hold in store for her. The one thing she had not accounted for was just how incredibly guilty she'd felt coming back home, the realisation of just what she'd put her family through the past few weeks especially Nina.

"Dakota, I know you'll come back, this is your home now." Javier was trying to convince himself as much as Dakota that she would indeed return to the Atacama and the man who loved her unconditionally. "Al said Cherry is missing you, but Juan isn't." He tried to lift her mood and Dakota laughed through her tears. "Why isn't Juan missing you, he wouldn't tell me?" Javier asked.

"Juan is a very naughty boy and takes advantage of people who are slightly nervous or apprehensive, so I've started riding him and he isn't too keen on being bossed around." She explained to him smiling through her tears at the thought of the horses with Al. "I miss you and the horses. It seems like you are a million miles away from London and all this."

"Six and a half thousand not a million miles" he said, and she laughed again, he was doing a good job of cheering her up.

"Listen I have to go I can see my mum is trying to get hold of me."

She hung up and picked up the call from her mother. "Dakota, we need to get to the hospital as soon as possible Nina has taken a turn for the worse and the doctor has called us to be by her bedside." Dakota's mouth went dry, her heart thundered in her chest, and she started to shake. "Okay Mum, I'll meet you there." She jumped off the bed and ran down the stairs. Her heart was pounding, she knew these would be the last few hours she would ever spend with her sister, with Nina. The end of her life was near, and she'd done nothing but bring grief and sadness to her sister in the last few months. How could she ever forgive herself? She didn't deserve the happiness Javier had brought her. Dakota grabbed her bag and ran out of the door. Her bike was in the garage. She pulled up the door and started up the bike. It roared into life as she turned the key in the ignition with trembling fingers. She moved onto the road before accelerating off in the direction of the hospital.

Nina had indeed taken a turn for the worse. Dakota didn't think it was possible she could look any worse than she'd done the day before, but she did. She was unconscious and looked very frail. She'd arrived before her parents and had taken the chance to try and speak to her sister alone. "Nina, dear Nina can you hear me? Please open your eyes if you can hear me, it's Dakota." Nina didn't respond to her sister's voice. Dakota felt someone beside her and turned to see it was Karl Nina's boyfriend who she'd desperately wanted to marry as soon as Dakota had married Miles. But that'd never happened; Dakota remembered the terrible argument they'd had before she left. Nina had blamed her for everything including the reason she wouldn't be allowed to marry Karl. Nina had been furious with her about it all and they hadn't spoken since.

Karl put his arm around Dakota's shoulders. "I'm scared I'm really scared," he whispered to her, "I think she is going to die." A tear rolled down his stubbly cheek. Dakota turned and hugged him, "Look we just don't know what's going to happen." She tried to comfort him with what seemed like stupid and meaningless words knowing they were not true. They were all too aware of what was about to happen to Nina.

Dakota's parents arrived and bustled into the room staring down at the skeletal shape of their youngest daughter as she lay still as the dead under the white sheet. "She looks worse than she did yesterday" Dakota's mother said with a trembling voice. She took Nina's hand in her own and stroked it. A nurse entered the room along with a doctor both wearing sympathetic expressions. "May we speak with you all outside?" The doctor gathered them outside Nina's room and closed the door. "I'm afraid Nina has taken a turn for the worse. She's not been conscious for a while now; her tests have shown she is not responding to treatment. I want you all to prepare yourselves for the worse I can't say how long she has but I anticipate it won't be long now." Dakota put her hand up to her mouth, her mother started to cry, and Karl gasped then also started to cry. Dakota put her arm around him trying to comfort the poor man. Nina had been his life; he'd loved her so much. They'd been together for years and now she would be so cruelly taken from him. Dakota felt terrible for everything she'd put him through. If it hadn't been for her leaving Miles, then Karl would've been quite possibly looking down on his wife. She may even have borne him a child then at least he would've had someone to comfort him through the long dark days that lay ahead. Dakota had ruined it all for them. Her grief was suffocating.

At Nina's bedside her mother and father were comforting each other. Dakota was still standing outside the room, and she spoke quietly to the doctor. "Can we stay with her until the end please?" she asked.

"Of course you can, you can stay as long as you like." He opened the door and let her back into the room. The family huddled around Nina's bed and stopped with her until her life passed from her body at one-thirty the following morning.

Chapter Twelve

It was a cold and overcast day in May. Dakota, Karl and four undertakers carried the coffin that contained Nina's body into the church carefully placing it down on the wooden trestle. They stepped back from the coffin alongside the undertakers and took their seats on the front pew along with the rest of the family.

The service was brief and very well attended. Afterwards Nina was carried to the churchyard and buried alongside her grandparents. Dakota felt sick. She'd barely eaten since she'd arrived in England two weeks ago. She was engulfed in grief and guilt because of how she'd left things with her sister, now Karl was alone in life without his beloved Nina. Dakota stood motionless, staring down into the hole, at the coffin that contained her sister. Her lip started to tremble, and yet more tears made tracks down her pale and drawn face.

At the wake Dakota drank too much wine. She didn't want to circulate, to talk to people, she wanted to go home and be in the arms of Javier. She longed for him to hold and comfort her and tell her it would all be alright, but she knew it wasn't going to be so for now she had to endure the pain of losing her sister alone. Her parents had made the presumption Dakota was going to stay in London, that her holiday was now over. She hadn't told them she was returning to Chile permanently. She'd made the decision to sell her house and had instructed the agent to put it on the market without a sign outside so her parents wouldn't see her house was for sale. Dakota had felt despicable, lower than low and deceitful at hiding this from her family, but she couldn't cope with their grief and her own right now. She'd made arrangements to put her furniture into storage until things were finalised in Chile. Perhaps she'd get it shipped over or perhaps Miles would want it, she didn't want to think about it. Miles had appeared at the funeral, but Dakota didn't speak to him. She'd been polite enough but had avoided him afterwards at the wake. Her parents had been pleased to see him and thanked him for coming. They'd even suggested that Dakota meet him for a drink once the funeral was over perhaps in the hope that they'd reconcile, and she'd change her mind about marrying him. She didn't have the first idea of how she was going to explain herself to them. Her life was quickly becoming a deceitful mess.

Once Dakota was back at her house she called Javier. She felt so relieved to hear his voice she thought she would cry again. "Hey, my pretty lady, how was today, I have been thinking about you all day!" She crumbled at the sound of his voice wishing so much he was beside her and she could just spend the night being held in his arms. "Hey, I miss you my lovely man, I miss you so much it hurts." She spoke trying to hide the rising tide of tears from her voice.

"How did Ninas funeral go?" Javier asked.

"It was tough, very tough but it's over now and I need to break the news to my parents I'm going back to San Pedro."

"And I can imagine that isn't going to be easy. I wish I were there to support you. Will you stay a while in London after you've told them?" He asked hoping for both their sakes she wouldn't. "I'm hoping to leave the day after tomorrow, so I'll be back soon. I have absolutely no idea how they're going to react and I'm really dreading telling them Javier. I feel so guilty for being deceitful, but I can't cope with all the arguments that are going to come after I break the news. I need to leave telling them as late as possible so I can just get on the plane and come home to you."

"They're going to be really upset Dakota, they've just lost your sister and that's only natural, they won't want to lose you too." Dakota knew that and she didn't need Javier to point it out to her. She'd endured a huge battle with her conscience finally deciding she was going to back to Chile and if Nina's death had taught her anything then it was that life was too short, and she had to live it whilst she could.

"How are the horses doing?" she asked changing the subject. "Have you seen Al?"

"Al came over last night for a few beers, he was asking about you he's missing you more than the horses are I'm sure of that."

"Tell him I'll be back soon. I love you." She rang off with a heavy heart. Tomorrow she was going to have to tell her parents about Javier and her life in San Pedro.

"*What* did you just say?" Her father standing with his hands on his hips and a furious look plastered across his face boomed across the room to his only daughter. "You are going back, but you only just got here for God's sake?"

"Dad I'm relocating to Chile as soon as I can. I've put the house on the market and I'm leaving on a flight tomorrow." Her mother started to cry; huge sobs escaped her heaving chest. What a mess she was making of things, there was no telling them, they didn't want to hear what she had to say. "We thought you'd come home, you were back for good, to stay with us and make things up with Miles?" Her mother's tone couldn't have been any sourer as she sat on the velvet sofa, her handkerchief clasped in her hand glowering at Dakota. "Mum why do you think I went? I can't be the person you want me to be I'm a free spirit, and I won't marry Miles, he isn't the man for me!" Dakota stood in the middle of the room. No matter how hard she tried her parents were not seeing her point of view. She was losing the battle. "What will you do in Chile?" her father asked with a glowering red face, "Have you really thought about this, no, I bet you haven't, you've done a typical Dakota thing and run into this headlong with no thought about your actions haven't you, you stupid little girl?" he spat.

"I've met someone. He's a local man and I love him more than anything. I've got a job in San Pedro, and we live together." "My God girl, you were only out there a couple of weeks, and you're living with someone, a stranger. Are you just a common tart?" Dakota was shocked, her eyes widened as he continued, "And what sort of job have you gone and got for yourself dare I even ask?" He was furious and spittle was escaping his lips as he spat each word. "I help a friend taking horse riding treks out into the Atacama Desert. Some are day treks and some up to five days." Her father looked horrified and disgusted at the same time. "A friend? How can you describe someone as a friend when you've only known them five minutes? I suppose you'll have great career progression in that role, won't you?" He bellowed at his oldest and now only child. Dakota stared down at the pattern on the Axminster carpet that had been in that room longer than she'd been on the earth. She was fighting back tears. "Dad, Mum, when will you realise, I'm twenty-four years old. I stopped being a little girl when I was eighteen, I'm an adult and what I do, who I love and where I live is my business. I would love it if you were behind me in my decision and were there to support me, but I will do it regardless. Just because I live in San Pedro it doesn't mean that I don't think about you or love you any the less." Dakota sniffed and dabbed at the tears running down her cheeks with the cuff of her blouse. "That is just *typical* of you, thinking only of yourself. Hell, if this local man means so much to you then go back tomorrow and *don't* bother coming back. No need to worry about us we'll be fine without you." Her father wasn't going to give up. Dakota walked out, she closed the door behind her and left. She'd hoped things wouldn't end like this but that had been naive of her, she should've known she would get that reaction. Her parents wanted her back home and married to a man she didn't love. They wanted her to be respectable and have children. Unfortunately, they had just buried the daughter who would've done all that for them. Dakota knew she wasn't going to win; she felt deflated and empty, there was no compromise now her parents had banished her back to Chile and into the arms of Javier without their blessing. Wiping fresh tears from her face with the sleeve of her leather jacket she climbed onto her Harley and rode back to her lonely house.

The next morning Dakota was at the airport checking in for the flight to Madrid. It didn't seem five minutes since she'd been standing on the same spot returning from Chile, now she was going home, back to San Pedro and Javier, keeping her fingers crossed for residency. The flight didn't take long, soon they were touching down in Madrid. Her second flight from Madrid to Santiago was an overnight flight. Dakota lay back in her chair and covered herself with the airline blanket. She couldn't sleep. She kept turning things over and over in her mind; how she'd left things with her parents wasn't how she would've liked. It was the worse timing ever to tell them about Javier, her life in Chile and her plans to leave England for good. News of her house sale had been what'd sealed her fate. Closing her eyes she was torn; her life was with Javier now in San Pedro but that left her elderly parents without both Nina and her. She was going to give them time, a few weeks to calm down and then she'd call, try again to get them to see her point of view. Eventually sleep came for the last few hours before her plane landed in sunny Santiago. Dakota spent the day walking around the airport waiting for her connecting flight and thinking about Javier. She couldn't wait to be with him again, to return to some sort of normality. She was going to have to try and bury the pain of her relationship with her parents, she was going to have to find a way of moving on or it would destroy her.

It was past eight o'clock that evening when Dakota's plane arrived in Calama. Javier had borrowed Al's truck and was waiting at the airport to collect her. He was shifting from foot to foot, hands in his pockets, feeling nervous. She walked through arrivals and out to the road where he was waiting. As soon as he saw her standing on the tarmac her hair all dishevelled and at least 10lb lighter than she'd been when she'd left his heart melted. She looked terrible; he'd never been so pleased to see anyone in his life. "Dakota my lovely, lovely lady" he mumbled into her hair as he held her tightly against him. She stood with her face buried in his chest and cried. Tears of sadness for Nina, of sorrow for the parents she'd left in London, for Karl who would probably never love again and for Javier, the man she loved more than she loved life. "God, I've missed you so much," she sobbed into his linen shirt, soaking it with her tears, "I never want to be away from you again." He hugged her tight against him, she felt safe in his arms.

Javier picked up her bags and slung them into the back of the dusty old truck. He climbed in beside her and smiled but it was full of pity then he reached over and kissed her properly. "I can't begin to tell you how happy I am to see you, that you have come back." He put the key into the ignition and let off the handbrake without turning his head to look at her. She slouched in the seat.

"Left to my parents I would still be in London. They didn't want me to come back, I've been read the riot act back there I can assure you!"

"What does that mean?" He looked over at her his face a picture of confusion. "It means that they're furious with me; I made the decision to put my house up for sale and that only added fuel to the fire."

"You're selling your house?"

"One thing being away from you made me realise and that is I don't want to ever have to do it again. Two weeks without you was hell. There's no need for me to keep my house in England I'm not going to live back there again. I just have to keep everything crossed I get residency here." She smiled weakly at him and rested her hand on his thigh as they pulled out of the airport and onto the road back to San Pedro.

"It sounds like you've been to hell and back in those two weeks. I'm so glad to have you back home." He smiled and patted her thigh with his rough tanned hand. She had missed those hands, those rough, calloused and yet such tender hands when they held her and caressed her. "Being away from you has been the hardest thing. Being out in the desert with Al for a few days at a time is fine but I can't be away from you for two weeks!"

Back at their flat Dakota was slowly unpacking her bags. She'd stuffed them full of clothes from her house. Javier had been to collect wine from Ruben's shop. "She's back then the woman in your life?" Ruben enquired handing him the change.

"Yes, she's back and changed, it's not good Ruben, her parents have really made her incredibly miserable, and I think she has a lot of guilty feelings about her sister's death. I hope she never goes away again!" He replied pushing the coins into his jeans pocket and collecting the wine. "So do I, it's made you a miserable so and so! You really like her, don't you?"

"It is more than that Ruben, I absolutely adore her, she's my life, I don't know how I ever managed before she came along. We've only been together a few weeks, but it feels like a lifetime. We're just so easy together."

"No falling out then upstairs?"

"No. I don't think I could ever have asked for anyone more perfect for me than Dakota is. She is just something else."

Ruben smiled showing his bad teeth, Javier had the look of a teenager in love. He was glad his friend was happy again.

Upstairs in the flat Javier poured out two large glasses of wine and handed one to Dakota. "Here's to us and life in San Pedro!" He raised his glass to hers. "To us," she repeated, "and life in San Pedro." They sat huddled together on the small sofa his arm around her shoulders pulling her close. She closed her eyes, rested her head on his shoulder and drank in the comfort being with him gave her. Later she told him everything that had happened whilst she had been back in England, she was exhausted, and grief stricken. It was to be expected with all that had gone on in her life in such a short time frame. Whilst they talked Javier filled her in on what had been happening in San Pedro. Al had instructed Javier to let her have as much time off as she needed, he understood grief only too well. He hoped she would return to him and the horses when she was ready.

That evening they made love. It was slow and tender, he was gentle, and she cried. Afterwards he lay awake gently stroking her long dark hair and she slept soundly next to him for the first time in weeks. Not a single day had passed since she'd arrived in San Pedro Javier hadn't thanked God for her. Dakota was unaware he visited the old church in the square almost daily, said a silent prayer then crossed himself before leaving and carrying on with his everyday life. That night as he lay in bed with Dakota sleeping beside him, he knew their life together was about to change again.

Dakota was fretting about her transport to work. "I don't have a bike to get to work on now, I had mine picked up by the hire company. I need to think about what I'm going to do!" She stressed as they sat in bed eating breakfast. "Oh God, I should've done it way before now." She was cross with herself for forgetting to organise anything when her hire bike had been collected.

"Don't worry about it I can take you to work." He replied casually.

"But what about when you're at work, what will I do then?" she spluttered angry for not sorting it out before now. "Hadn't thought about that." He frowned, "let me speak to a few friends I have who might be able to point us in the direction of a bike or two. It won't be like that one you arrived on though," he warned her, "a lot more desert worthy than that piece of kit!"

"I can cope with a crappy bike if you can fix it up for me?"

"Leave it with me" he winked as he leaned over the bed to collect her empty plate and mug.

It was not as hot outside now, Dakota wondered how she'd managed in the cold month of May back in England. She'd had the central heating on full and it had still been cold. Back in San

99

Pedro the temperature was around twenty degrees, and it felt comfortable. Soon it would be winter in Chile but even then it wouldn't be as cold as it was back in England. She stood with her arms folded across her chest watching as Javier was giving the trials bike a full mechanical check over. The owner hadn't used it for five years and wanted to get rid of it; he wouldn't be riding it again aged seventy-eight. It started easily enough but ran very badly. Javier had assured her he'd be able to sort it out in a few days. She handed over the money to the seventy-eight-year-old man and became the new owner of the battered trials bike. Dakota wasn't used to riding bumpy little bikes and would need to get used to it quickly she realised as she tried to steer the frisky little machine back to their flat. She had a feeling she'd quite possibly be on the floor more than in the saddle in the days ahead as she tried to master the bike.

Chapter Thirteen

Cherry spun around in her stable and whinnied her delight as Dakota rode into the yard. Al had made coffee, and the aroma met her as she removed her helmet and walked around to the stables. Al had made a start on the mucking out and the wheelbarrow stood half full outside Cherry's stable. The old man hugged her hard and then they sat and chatted for a while and drank the coffee Al had made before saddling up Cherry, Diego and Juan to take out a couple on a half a day ride in the desert. Dakota was pleased to get back to work. It was a welcome distraction from the grief and guilt she'd been feeling since Nina had died. Sleepless nights and feelings of terrible sadness hit her hard at every opportunity. How she wished with all her heart things had not ended badly between them, but they had and now she had to get on with life. Now there was no going back, she had to learn to live with the guilt. Dakota told Al everything that'd happened in London. He listened to her without interruption. "You need to make it up with your parents you know, they were hurt from the death of your sister now they will be sitting at home regretting how things were left between you!"

"I know I need to talk to them, but they're not interested in anything to do with Javier. They think I'm wasting my life in a no-good job shacked up with a poor man with no prospects in life. They don't even want to meet him and get to know what a lovely, kind man he is. They think I am a stupid little girl." Dakota whined.

"But they will love him once they meet him, they'll understand why you're here."

"No Al, they'll never understand. To them I'm one huge disappointment. They wanted me to be married and have kids by now. I even disappointed my own sister because she wanted me married so my parents would allow her to marry the man of her dreams. Now he's back in England, lonely and has nobody to love. I feel so terribly guilty for that d'you understand Al?" Tears started to choke in Dakota's throat. She swallowed hard trying to

101

regain her composure. "But you wouldn't have married Miles to make your family happy surely?"

"No, I wouldn't but with me not marrying him it had a sort of domino effect, everyone was hurt because of my actions. I don't think they'll ever forgive me."

"Of course they will, you are their daughter they *have* to forgive you!"

"Well then it won't be for a long time. I need to give them a good few weeks to calm down and then I'll test the water, give them a call and see what they have to say."

"But you will at least try and speak with your parents?"

"Yes, I will of course. I don't like leaving things like this."

The couple arrived at the barn for the ride out, Dakota left Al to finish the mucking out and got the couple mounted up, adjusted the stirrups and girths on Cherry and Diego. Dakota rode Juan who was pushing his luck and trying his best to be naughty and upset the other two horses. They rode out further than the usual half a day ride. The couple were on their honeymoon, and both had horses back in Texas where they lived on a ranch. Dakota enjoyed taking people out on the rides that she could talk to and get along with, this couple were great company and told her all about their ranch, the horses and cattle that lived there and how many staff they had working for them. Dakota was amazed, she couldn't imagine running something the size of a ranch.

The sun was beating down as they rode through the desert stopping every now and then to admire the views and take photos. Dakota lifted her face to the heat feeling the soft very gentle breeze tease at her hair and play with the tumbleweed around their horse's feet. She breathed in the smell of the desert a mixture of sand and fragrance. *This* was home!

They returned to the barn by early afternoon. After waving off their clients, Dakota and Al took the alfalfa and water around to the stables at the camps out in the desert. The track was bumpy and dusty, tumbleweed blowing under the truck. Dakota thought how much she preferred riding this route on horseback rather than in Al's battered truck. During the trip he drilled her on how much fodder to leave in storage, explaining how much to leave for a five-day ride so each horse would have ample feed and wouldn't go hungry. Al was a very knowledgeable man and

Dakota enjoyed being in his company. He also enjoyed teaching her the ropes, handing down his knowledge and happy knowing all he had worked for wouldn't be sold to a stranger. Al always referred to Dakota as his adopted daughter to their clients and when he was home at night with his wife Catalina.

At the stables Dakota groomed the three horses making sure that their manes and tails were tangle free, brushing out the debris that had got tangled up in their tails as they'd trekked through the desert. She filled their feed and topped up their water buckets. Tomorrow she was going to be on her own, Al needed to go and buy more alfalfa for his stores. Dakota would be in charge of the horses and any bookings that came in. At present she didn't have any rides to take out, there were no bookings but that could change by the morning. She finished brushing the yard and tidying away the mucking out forks then waved to Al to let him know she was off back home. She kick-started Javier's bike and rode off, leaving a cloud of dust spewing out behind.

Javier had been busying himself with domestic chores for most of the day. He'd worked on Dakota's new bike hoping to fix it, but she would have to take his to work again the following day. He needed to do more to the bike; the parts hadn't arrived to allow him to fix the problem. Dakota wasn't used to having bikes fixed, she'd always been fortunate enough to buy new or nearly new depending on the model she'd favoured at the time. She would never have admitted that to Javier, she'd instead asked him to teach her how to repair her bike in case she was ever stranded so she would be able to get back home. He'd spent the following day showing her the basics until she felt confident that she would be okay should the worse happen.

Dakota always carried her phone now just in case her parents were to call, Al would often call her if he needed anything when she was at work, but she knew Al had been testing her to see if she was up to the tough parts of the job; part of the test had been if she would return to San Pedro following Nina's death and when she did, she realised she'd passed his test. Dakota knew Al would be starting to take things easier now, allowing her to take over from him. She felt comfortable knowing he'd always be around if she needed him, but she was independent and would try her hardest to manage alone.

Javier had cooked pizza for dinner and served it with salad. Dakota now considered herself a fully-fledged local and was now drinking local tap water. She poured them a glass to have with dinner and flopped down in the chair exhausted. "God I'm tired, I think everything is starting to catch up with me," she muttered, "I can hardly keep my eyes open!" she rubbed at her temples with grubby fingers. "We can have an early night if you want to?" Javier suggested.

"Yes, I think I might have a shower and turn in for the night. I'm on my own tomorrow, Al is off to fetch feed for the horses."

"So, you're in charge then? He must trust you!" Javier chuckled as he handed the plates over. "I think he does trust me. I really like him; I know I passed his test when I returned to San Pedro. Maybe he thought I'd stay in England, and he'd have to find someone else to help him out?"

"He hoped you'd come back almost as much as I did, I can assure you of that," Javier told her as he piled salad onto his fork. "He missed you helping him out even though you'd only been with him a few weeks."

"Really?"

"Yes really. He was concerned your parents would persuade you to stay. I think he was worried about me too if you had decided not to return to San Pedro."

"You didn't think I would stay though, did you?"

"I hoped and prayed you wouldn't, and, in my heart, I knew you'd come back but some days it was really tough, I would convince myself you were not coming back."

"Javier!"

"I know. But you're here now with me and I'm so pleased you are." He flashed her his best smile then reached over and squeezed her hand. She glanced down at his hand, ingrained with oil from fixing her bike, covering her freshly washed one and smiled.

It was three in the morning when she woke. She turned over to see he was sleeping. She reached over and gently stroked his chest with the back of her fingers. Sleep wasn't going to return to her that night, too much was whirling around inside her head. As she lay staring up at the ceiling, she contemplated what her life would be now had she not met Javier at the bar that night.

She would've returned to London and always wondered what it would've been like to live in Chile. He had given her everything. He loved her beyond doubt, he was kind, and he respected her. She thought about her parents and the conversation she'd had with Al the previous morning. It would be too easy to just leave things and let them go on as they were, but her parents were grieving too, and she knew she'd have to offer the olive branch and repair the relationship at some stage.

Dakota pushed the sheet back and padded across the aged floorboards to the kitchen. She poured herself a glass of water and sat at the small table turning things over and over in her head. In the doorway Javier appeared. His hair was sticking up and he was rubbing his eyes and yawning. "Can't you sleep lady?" He looked concerned.

"No, I'm worried about things, and they all seem to surface in the middle of the night, going round and round in my head." She smiled weakly at him. She'd lost a lot of weight, was now almost skin and bone. Javier was increasingly worried about her. He poured himself a glass of water and pulled out the chair to sit opposite to her. "What are you worried about?" he asked.

"Stuff with my parents and Al and are we really going to be okay?"

"Your parents, you know you'll sort out. You just need to give them time to calm down, to realise you're an adult and doing what you want with your life." She looked up into his beautiful dark eyes, the eyes of the man she loved with everything she had, the man she wanted to be with for all time. She could feel her lip start to tremble, the all too familiar tears start to well up in her eyes, she closed them, but they fell under her long lashes and down her cheeks despite her best efforts. Javier took her face in his hands, wiped her tears away with his thumbs, searching for her eyes to meet his, "My beautiful lady, why are you worried about us, and what's this with Al?" She lifted her eyes to meet his, tears continued to steam down her bony cheeks and onto the table.

"I want what we have between us to work so much Javier, but sometimes I worry. I don't know what'd happen if I had to leave here what if I don't get residency?" He held her gaze,

"I'd move to England with you that's what'd happen, but you *will* get residency, you have a work visa now you have your job with Al and you should get the temporary residency visa any day now."

"But your whole life is here in San Pedro you told me that yourself. That's the reason you didn't move to Santiago or Calama with your family so how could I ever expect you to leave everything here and go to England, Javier?"

"You're more important to me than San Pedro, Dakota. There's no way you would leave here without me by your side unless it was something you wanted." Dakota was moved by his admission, she'd worried so much about getting residency; if it wasn't granted, she'd have to return to England and that would be the end of them or so she'd thought. "And what is worrying you about Al?" Javier continued.

"I don't want him to sell up and I feel he'll do that soon. If I'm out of a job, I'll be in trouble with my visa."

"I spoke to Al when you were away, and he told me if you stay with him, he'll not sell the business. He didn't have anyone who he trusted, who wanted to help him out with the horses before you came along, that's why he was considering selling up and retiring. He said he's happy taking the feed and water round and doing some of the hard work, but it was the riding all day then having to sort the horses out as well as the camp and the customers that was getting too much for him. You seriously don't need to worry about things with Al." Dakota smiled weakly at him. "Thanks Javier, thank you for putting my mind at rest about everything." He always managed to have the answers, to put things right and make her feel the world was good again. "Come on let's go back to bed or it'll soon be time to get up." She collected their glasses and took them over to the sink then followed him back to bed. Javier held her against him, his arms encompassing her, making her feel safe again and she fell asleep. It was the sun spilling though the thin curtains that woke them the following morning.

Chapter Fourteen

Things had gone on for long enough between Dakota and her estranged parents, it was obvious they were not going to call her and offer reconciliation, so she was going to have to offer the olive branch to them she had decided. Sitting on their bed with her back against the headboard she stared out of the window off into the distance, her phone resting against her ear. Her mother was on the other end. "Are you and Dad coping Mum, I know it's been a while since we spoke, but I wanted to give you time to calm down, I wondered if I gave you some time, you could start to see things from my view." She added.

"You mean with Nina's death?"

"Yes, of course but also my return to Chile; you and Dad being angry with me about my decision."

"In case you hadn't noticed Dakota, we lost your sister a few weeks ago and we're too busy dealing with the grief of her loss to be worrying about what you're up to chasing around the desert with some rough fellow you've only just met!" Dakota was not one bit surprised to hear they hadn't calmed down and were still angry with her. "Mum, I think you're being a little harsh on me. I was there when Nina passed away as well as you and Dad. She was my sister as well as your daughter and I'm grieving her loss too? I rang to see how you are and hoped we could go some way to repairing our relationship!"

"I think you need to grow up Dakota then think about repairing our relationship. You've pushed your father and I to the edge with your stupid idea's. You've been selfish and not taken our feelings into account at all. We're getting older you know; we were expecting you to marry well and set a good example to Nina. We want grandchildren, but I don't suppose you are going to provide us with any and if you do what use are they going to be living in Chile?" her mother spat down the phone. Dakota closed her eyes, she felt increasingly frustrated but tried to hide it, "I've only been with Javier a few months, but he is the kindest most genuine person I've ever met. He doesn't have a lot, but I don't care. He loves me and treats me well. What more can I ask for?"

"Indeed, my child, what more can we ask for but you get back here and marry a decent man who was kind and genuine and would give you a family!" Dakota knew she was referring to Miles. He'd been making a habit of calling round to see how they were managing after Nina died, he was also waiting for Dakota to return despite her parents telling him she was living with someone in the Atacama Desert. He had smiled wryly and told them whatever Dakota did would never surprise him.

Dakota was staring out of the window with unseeing eyes. Her phone on the bed beside her. She had tried for an hour to talk to her mother, but the call had ended badly, she wasn't surprised, but she was incredibly frustrated by her parents' inflexibility. Her mother had said if she were not prepared to come back and do the decent thing with Miles who, she said, would still have her back, then they didn't want to hear from her again. She was devastated, her call had expected to find they had calmed down and realised she was their daughter, and her happiness mattered but it seemed their status in the community mattered more. She knew they blamed her for Nina not being able to marry Karl because she hadn't married. It was their wish; the oldest daughter should marry first. If it was anyone's fault Nina hadn't married Karl, then it was theirs and their damn stupid ideas! Dakota wondered if the feelings of shame and guilt she felt would ever leave her. She felt lost; she didn't know what to do but she was certainly not going to give in to them and return to London. Did her parents really want to cut off all contact with her after all they had been through? Were they so angry with her they blamed her for everything even for not giving them grandchildren? Dakota had thought at one time she might have children with Miles, but it hadn't taken her long to figure out it wasn't going to happen; children certainly hadn't been anything she and Javier had discussed in the short while they'd been together but now all this had come to light, and she felt evil. She buried her face in her hands and cried.

Dakota heard Javier's bike pull up outside. She was glad he was back home tonight, that had been part of the reason she'd chosen to call her parents. She knew there was a good chance it would go badly but Javier would be home to talk about it with her. She heard the sound of his footsteps on the metal steps outside and hurried to open the door and welcome him home. He stood before her clutching his backpack. He had a smear of oil on his face, his dark shades were pushed back into his black mop of hair, the dust from the desert on his unshaven skin, he was wearing his old dirty jeans and his black ripped t-shirt. He was wearing his cheekiest smile, and she had never seen him look sexier. She squealed and pulled him inside, standing on tip toe she kissed him frantically, running her hands up and inside his t-shirt, over his firm muscular body, now familiar with every dip and hollow of it. "Wow lady, I think I need to work away more often," he gasped when she finally let him go. "What a cool welcome. You okay?" He dropped his backpack on the floor and took her in his arms. "Yeah, just had a bad call with my mum. I'll tell you about it later. Come and sit down and tell me what you've been doing for the last week." She pulled him into the lounge where he collapsed onto the sofa. She handed him a steaming mug of coffee and sat astride him running her hand through his dirty hair as he recalled the events of the previous week where he'd been out supporting an ultra-marathon staged in the desert.

Over dinner Dakota recalled the conversation she'd had with her mother. Javier was shocked and disgusted. This was not something that would happen in his culture, family was important. He felt sorry for Dakota, she'd tried hard to reconcile with them, it had taken a lot of courage to call them and offer the olive branch, but they'd thrown it in her face. She sat across the table from him at the bar where they'd first met all that time ago now and she looked drained. "Your mother perhaps needs more time to come to terms with things. It's only been a few months since your sister passed away, that isn't long in the grand scheme of things."

"I know it isn't, but I thought it 'd be long enough for them to miss me being around and to wonder how I was doing. They just didn't want to know."

"You're such a good and wonderful lady Dakota I'm sure in time they'll miss you that's why I'm convinced if you give it another couple of months then call again things will be different.

They may even decide to call you before then." Javier was being cautiously optimistic. "Javier, these are the people who gave me life, who brought me up, I can't believe they're being so cruel to me now."

"Has Miles been back on the scene by any chance?" Javier asked raising an eyebrow. She told him about his visits to her parents. "Well, if he keeps appearing then your parents are going to be permanently reminded of how wonderful he is and what sort of lifestyle he has to offer you, things I don't. I suppose they'll never get any better until he finds someone else and stops calling by."

"I know, and you're right that is the reason, but I don't know if he will stop visiting them; even if he'll get back into the dating scene if he thinks there's a chance I'll go back to him."

He squeezed her hand and smiled over his bottle of beer making her heart skip. Everything she'd done, given up, sacrificed and turned her back on since she'd met him had been worth it. Even though her family were making things tough for her Dakota knew it had all been worth it, she had Javier.

They walked home hand in hand back to the flat. Javier unlocked the door and led her inside. "Are you ready for bed?" he asked.

"I'll sit up for a bit it's still going round in my head you know?"

He poured them strong coffee and they sat and chatted more about the race and then the horses and Al. Dakota had taken out a three-day ride that week, it'd gone well. Juan was starting to understand that she was the boss, and she thought they were at last becoming friends. She told Javier Juan would never be as good a friend as the lovely Cherry, but he was starting to know his place in the team and had only tested her once during the three days. Dakota had taken a new route for the ride. Al had given her the map; it had been a testing ride over a lot of rough ground and river crossings. The three clients who had been with her had been exhausted at night, they were covering around twenty miles a day on the horses. After they'd returned to the yard the clients had left her a very large tip, she had been a good guide and looked after them so well, heated their packs of food and made coffee for them each night as well as looking after their horses as they

110

had been too exhausted after the days riding. Javier smiled, she was chatting away excitedly about the trek, the people she had met and the tip she had been left. Afterwards he took her to bed and made up for the week they had spent apart.

Dakota hummed to herself as she finished hanging out the washing and readied herself for her journey to the barn. "Are you coming home tonight or are you off for a few days I can't remember?" Javier scowled and scratched his head. He was standing in the kitchen in his shorts, his hair a black mess on top of his head.

"I'm back tonight, I'd have reminded you if I wasn't coming home." She kissed him holding him against her feeling his warmth and wishing that she had more time so he could make love to her again as he had the night before.

Dakota arrived at work where the horses were waiting, their heads over the stable doors calling to her. She parked her bike; Al had not yet arrived. She put on the coffee and fed the horses. Whilst the horses ate their breakfasts, Dakota hummed to herself as she mucked out. Once finished she took the horses outside, tied them up and started to groom. Nico and Juan were trying to bite each other, she sighed knowing she was going to have to move them, Juan was a troublemaker at times. Her main task for the day was to ride the horses out, loosen any stiffness they might have after spending the night in after long days out in the desert. Her plan was to ride Juan and lead the other horses. Time was ticking away so she saddled him up. There was still no sign of Al, perhaps he was running late. Dakota decided to head out without him. She mounted up, took hold of the other three horses lead reins and set off into the desert. The sun was beating down from a perfect blue sky. There was not a cloud in sight and despite how things had been left with her parents she felt happy. The worries with her family were temporarily forgotten, the horses strode out through the sand onto a quiet track. It was silent, the only sound was the horses' hooves gently padding on the sand. She breathed in the aromas of the desert, the smell of the crisp vegetation under the horses' feet and fresh air. Half an hour later she was at the river. The horses dipped their heads and drank. She watched the river flowing by with its icy cold waters that had come from somewhere up in the Andes off to the ocean where it would eventually come to an end. A smile touched her lips, she remembered the day she had bathed in the same river weeks ago now when they had been on their trek.

At the barn Al was busy with his truck. "Hola, I'm sorry I missed you this morning, I hope everything was okay here?"

"Hola Al, yeah all was okay here. I mucked out and groomed and took them for walk to make sure everyone was good from yesterday. Some of that terrain was rough on their legs, I asked the riders to dismount and lead the horses over rather than ride." She scrambled down from Juan and started removing his saddle and bridle.

"That was good thinking, it is getting worse out there. The problem is, that is a good three-day route, I think I'll have to look for another one that's a bit easier on the horses." The horses were returned to their stables after Dakota had checked them over then she and Al shared coffee and sat and chatted in the sun. Dakota usually stayed at the barn whilst Al did the delivery chores, she preferred riding over the desert to being shaken to pieces in his truck but today she went along. She filled the water containers from the river whilst Al mucked out the stables they had been using for the last few days.

It was late when they arrived back at the barn. The horses were put to bed for the night then Dakota rode home. Javier was taking the washing in when she pulled up around the back of their flat. She waved up at him letting him know she was back then hurried into Ruben's shop to buy wine. Wearily she climbed the steps back to the flat. "Hey Javier, have you been doing pink jobs today?" She joked watching him as he carefully folded and put away the washing. "Yes, because my lady has been looking after those horses again!" He leaned in to kiss her, "I've not made dinner tonight, we're doing something different" Javier proclaimed. "Oh?"

"Just give me a minute." He called from the bedroom as he hurriedly put the remaining washing away. She sat at the kitchen table wondering what he was up to. "Right then, you will need your sleeping bag, change of clothes and wine."

"What?"

"Sleeping bag, change of clothes and wine. I've got the freeze-dried food, and towels so don't worry about those."

"What are we doing?" Dakota walked into the bedroom to follow Javier's instructions.

"We are having dinner in the desert and a sleep out," he announced feeling very proud of himself for thinking up the idea, "under the stars!"

Dakota's face lit up with delight. "Brilliant! That is just a great idea Javier!" She squealed grasping a bottle of wine in each hand, her sleeping bag and clothes stuffed under one arm. "Go and get your bag then and we'll have to go on both bikes, we won't fit it all onto either bike but at least you have one suitable for the desert now!" She certainly did have one suitable for the desert but she would still have preferred her Harley to the Honda, but it did the job and she had just about mastered it.

The fire spat and crackled at their feet as they sat huddled together eating the freeze-dried meals trying to get warm. They'd finished the first bottle of wine, and it lay discarded in the sand ready to be packed away when they were turning in for the night. The wine was being consumed from metal mugs that had been intended for coffee. Camp was next to a river on part of the desert that was unknown to Dakota. Javier had asked Al for a secluded spot close to the river where he could take her for the evening. Al had laughed, telling him that she was probably fed up with the desert now she was sleeping under the Atacama stars for at least one night a week and sometimes as many as five. Javier understood her well, he knew that wasn't the case, he'd wanted to do something different for her to cheer her up, she had been quite depressed lately with her sister passing away and her parents still refusing to have anything to do with her. Al told him she could take the following day off, so Javier had planned to take her across the desert on the bikes for the day. He knew she would love it.

Later they bathed in the river together laughing and splashing each other. It was cold but not as cold as the first time she had stepped into the river all that time ago. Perhaps now she had become more accustomed to it. As they clambered out, he looked over to her standing dripping wet and naked by the riverbank shivering and laughing at the same time. She had never looked so lovely and vulnerable. He wrapped her in his towel and held her against him. She could feel his breath against her quickening as he started to gently kiss her and rub her with the towel getting her dry and warm again. She lay down on the sleeping bag still shivering but now with anticipation as he mounted her slowly kissing her mouth, neck and breasts, teasing her nipples with his tongue and making her ache for him. She opened her legs, wrapped them around his waist and he slipped easily inside her, she ran her nails down his back; it wasn't gentle, it surprised him, he pushed himself deep inside her, slow but hard and she gasped, he pushed hard again and she smiled up at him, she liked it, he continued, slow to start then building speed and momentum. He was pumping fast and hard, she was pulling him into her with each movement, wrapping her legs tighter around him, they had never made love like this before and, as they reached their peak, she screamed into the night sky and dug her nails into his firm buttocks.

They lay under the velvet night sky the stars twinkling like small diamonds. They made love on the sandy floor of the Atacama Desert many times that night. It was free, exhilarating and full of heated passion. Much later when they had finished, she lay cradled in his arms feeling the heat from his body and as she listened to his breathing she fell to sleep. Later the wind picked up and threw sand and tumbleweed around the camp. They did not wake.

Chapter Fifteen

Javier woke early and lay with Dakota still in his arms. He thought about the night before; the most incredible sex they'd ever had. Just thinking about it made him harden. It had been so very real out under the starlit sky. She had just been incredible, he had never known anything like it, he was happier than he'd ever been in his entire thirty years. He knew he wanted her to be with him forever, she was his soul mate, his life companion. He glanced down at her sleeping so peacefully in the breaking dawn. Her long dark eyelashes framing her sleeping eyelids, her black hair tumbled over his arm in tendrils. He stroked it gently and remembered the sad and dark days he'd endured before she had come into his life on that warm and sunny April evening. It seemed so long ago now but really it wasn't. His memories of the two years he had been alone in his flat drifted into his mind. Yes, he'd met people with his work but there had been nobody like Dakota. Petra, the girl he'd been engaged to had been a huge mistake. He had known she was materialistic, and she had been in love with him but not like this. She had gone to Santiago and found love and fortune leaving him far behind in the Atacama without a second thought. Now he had Dakota, and she felt like a part of him. She loved him and life in San Pedro for what it was good or bad, easy or hard. He knew in his heart he would always love her.

Javier understood it had been hard for Dakota when her sister had passed away and now her parents were being difficult too. He knew she wouldn't be bullied into doing what they wanted but he also didn't want the rift between her and her parents to grow. He knew she hadn't been sleeping at night, that she was wracked with guilt and the sorrow of losing Nina. He too felt guilty for taking her away from them but then he loved her more than anyone could ever imagine so surely that made up for it? If her parents ever decided to come to Chile and meet him, they would understand how much he loved her. His thoughts drifted and he wondered if he and Dakota would ever have children together, something he had never thought of before now. If they did have any, he would make a promise to them that he would never insist they marry anyone they didn't love. He would do his very best to make sure they had happy lives and were brought up in a happy family as he had been.

Dakota stirred in his arms and turned away from him. He didn't let her go he just held her closer, her curves fitting his. Things had just got better and better for them after she'd moved into the flat and was earning money too. She'd been happy after Miles had agreed to buy her house, now they had financial stability, money to keep them over the winter. She hadn't really cared who had bought it; just as long as it was sold, and the money was in her bank account. He never asked her how much money she had, and she had never told him. Javier was a proud man and wanted to provide for them as much as he could, but he was also aware she was very independent and wanted to work.

Dakota sat up looking around at the desert and the smouldering fire. She smiled at Javier, yawned and stretched and clambered out of the sleeping bag completely naked. She collected more wood and put it onto the fire before returning to her warm sleeping bag and cuddled up against him. She was cold and he was warm. She wrapped her legs around him slowly and seductively pulling him closer to her. She could feel him tense against her, she reached down and found him hard. Gently she worked him, caressing in her small hand until he grabbed her hand and took control, throwing her onto her back, she laughed as he scrambled to mount her, holding her hands over her head he ran his tongue around her bullet hard nipples driving her into an ecstatic frenzy, she arched into him, wrapping her legs around him, pulling him into her deeper and deeper, harder and harder he thrust, she gasped as they reached their climax, somewhere close by a bird rose up from the bush alarmed by the noise, squawking as it flew high and away from the lovers on the ground below. They lay breathless on their backs staring up at the blue sky. "You are some man Javier, you know that?"

"Yeah, I know, all the women tell me so," he joked. "They can't get enough of me didn't you know?" He propped his head on his elbow and gazed down at her as she stared up at the frothy white clouds dancing across the early morning sky. "Can't say

I'm surprised really," she replied casually, "especially if you seduce them first with your coffee!" she giggled.

The fire was roaring Dakota pulled on her underwear, t-shirt and jeans adding the little pot with the water to the heat. She rolled up her sleeping bag and sat on it eating her rehydrated freeze-dried porridge. This had become such a normal part of her life now. "I'm so happy I could burst; you've made me the happiest woman alive Javier; I hope this never ends." She spooned porridge eagerly into her mouth. She had worked up quite an appetite.

"Obviously I knew I was good, but I didn't think I was *that* good!" was his cheeky reply. She playfully slapped his arm. "Don't joke with me, you know what I'm saying don't you?"

"Yes, you want to marry me!" he glanced over at her wearing the cheeky smile she loved so much.

"No, just that you make me so happy being the man you are."

"You *don't* want to marry me?"

"Don't be silly, I'm trying to be serious and tell you how I feel about you. With all the stuff going on with my mum and dad you've been brilliant, I really appreciate everything you've done for me!" She looked over at him taking a mouthful of coffee.

"I love you Dakota, I'm sorry that you're having to go through all that grief with your parents. I'm sorry it's because of me and our life here but you know I love you so very much I can't let you go if your parents like it or not!"

"I don't want to go I want to stay here with you forever," she finished her porridge and collected his packet from him, "I need to get back to the horses soon." She started to pack up the camp readying herself for the trip home.

"No, no, no lady, Al has given you the day off at my request," he said, "the adventure didn't stop at last night, I'm taking you on a bike tour of the Atacama today if you're up for it?" "Really?" She glanced over her shoulder to see if he was joking but she could see he was being serious. "Really!"

"Of course I'm up for it, come on let's get sorted out here and we can start riding, it will make a change from riding a horse!" She scurried around the camp packing up all their belongings and shoving them into their backpacks. She doused the fire with water from the river and then mounted her bike. Javier watched her, in awe at how much she had learned, and this had all become second nature to her since the trek they had embarked on back in the early days. "Are you ready? Lead the way!" Off they rode across the baron and sandy desert floor blowing up clouds of sand dust behind them.

The sun was searingly hot beating down on their skin. The desert was so quiet, not a single sound could be heard. The slightly fragrant smell from the plants close by was pleasant as they sat and ate lunch. Javier pulled out a heap of energy bars for them to snack on. "Do you remember that day when you were horrible to me, the last day we were out in the desert, we sat on a rocky outcrop eating lunch?" Dakota was lying flat on the floor, her boots by her side, arm over her eyes looking up at the clouds passing slowly by. She loved the desert, everything about it and with every visit she found more things to like and learn about. She reached for the fragrant bush and picked a tiny piece off rubbing it around in her fingers. "I remember very well, and I remember how bad I felt after I'd upset you." Javier watched her playing with the small stick in her fingers. He had never forgiven himself for upsetting her so badly on that ill-fated day. He remembered how she had cried, and he'd not known how to deal with it, with her. He had seen her cry so many times lately, her sister's untimely death and the treatment she was receiving from her mother and father. All so alien to Javier.

"Do you remember you told me you were in love with me?" She mused still twiddling the stick around in her fingers.

"I do!"

"Are you still in love with me?" She asked casually.

"Dakota, I can't believe you have to ask me!" She glanced sideways at him and grinned, "I'm teasing you," she said, poking his arm with the stick.

"You are one bad ass lady, you know that?" Javier poked her arm in return.

"So you tell me, but you are one bad ass man too!" He reached for her arm and pulled her to him. They sat with his arm around her shoulders finishing their small lunch of bars and water. "Are you truly happy with me and our life together?" Javier asked on a more serious note. Dakota looked at him questioningly. "Of course, I'm happy with you and our life together. You've

118

changed me for the better, I love it here with you, I want my life to stay like this forever just you, me, the horses and Al."

"What about the rest of our friends?"

"Okay some of the people we meet when we're out but not all of them."

"Are there any bad points to life with me?" He asked tentatively.

"None that come to mind no. It isn't as hard as you told me it would be but then I knew you would dramatize it all up to try and put me off staying here!"

"I didn't dramatize at all. It's easier with two of us living in the flat and two incomes yes, I agree. I didn't want to mislead you; make you think it was some idyllic lifestyle, and it scare you off when the going got tough." Dakota stood and brushed off the crumbs and sand from her legs. "Come on let's get going" she held out her hand and pulled him up from the rock.

Back at the flat that evening they lay on the bed resting as the dinner cooked. Dakota's hair was wet and lay in tendrils around her shoulders making the bedding damp. She didn't care. She was studying Javier who lay on the bed with his eyes closed. She studied his thick eyelashes and slightly crooked eyebrow that was hiding a scar. She looked at the dark stubble appearing because he had not shaven that morning when they'd been out in the Atacama. His skin was perfectly taught over his firm muscular frame, there was not an ounce of fat under his tanned skin. She slowly ran her fingers over his chest and down his stomach and then back up again. He opened one eye, "You want a quickie before dinner?"

She smiled at him, "No I would rather have one after dinner." She slowly kissed his cheek feeling the stubble prickle her lips. "Right, I'm going to dish up the dinner now are you coming?"

"Lady, you drive me crazy yes I'm coming!" He sat up quickly and pulled on his t-shirt. Dakota was secretly disappointed he was covering himself up.

Dakota had cooked Javier steak and chips, one of his favourites as a thank you for the time they had just spent together. Loading a piece onto his fork he remembered something he had wanted to ask her during their time out in the desert but had forgotten with all their frolicking. "You know I have another race to cover in a few weeks' time. They've asked for horse cover too as there will be areas that'll be difficult to get to with my bike." He glanced up at her over his steak, she was holding her wine glass watching him. "Do you want to speak to Al about it or shall I ask him?"

"What are the details?" Dakota liked the idea of working alongside Javier.

"Six weeks' time so mid October about 100 competitors taking part in roughly six marathons in seven days across the desert. If you come, we'll need to camp out at night. We'll need food and water for the horses so Al will have to give vehicle support for the horses' provisions. Will you speak to him and see what he says he might want you to do it or he might just say no."

"I hope he doesn't say no I'd love to do it. Will I see you every day?"

"Yeah, and every night camping out with our delicious, freeze-dried menu to choose from!" Javier chuckled.

"I'll speak to him tomorrow. How many horses do they want to cover, one for me and one spare as a recovery horse I would think?"

"Yeah, that's usually how it works. Speak to him tomorrow and let me know what he decides. If he says no, I'll have to let the organisers know we can't get horse support." Life with Javier was never dull. Now she had leapt from taking rides out to being offered a seven-day full time job alongside him. She really hoped Al would let her cover the race.

"It'll be cold you know in six weeks' time, we are still only mid springtime, are you sure you want to do it when it is about eighteen degrees in the day and freezing at night?" Al warned her over coffee the following morning. "I really do want to do it Al, please say yes. I can take Cherry and Diego with me?"

"Of course, you can if you want to do it, if you are absolutely sure you are up to it, I just think Javier hasn't told you the full story, it'll be cold, and it can be very difficult terrain for the horses. You spend a long time in the saddle and on your own with only the horses for company, you will be following the race in walk most of the time."

"Great." Dakota was brimming with excitement.

"Seriously?"

"Seriously. Is that a yes then Al can I go with Javier and take Cherry and Diego?"

"It's a yes Dakota but don't say I didn't warn you. It's a good job you two are on personal terms and can sleep together you'll need to do it to keep warm. It is spring but don't let that fool you into thinking the weather will be warm, I suppose he need me to do motor support, take all the food and water round to the camps for the horses, has he said anything to you?"

"Yes, he told me to let you know the horses would need feed transporting and water to the camps at night would that be okay for you to do, do you mind?"

"Yes, that'll be fine. You know these people pay really well. It will be a good earner and if you enjoy doing it there are quite a few races like this every year although we don't get asked to cover them all sometimes they use other people with horses and sometimes no horses it just depends on their set up really. What they pay me will keep the horses and Catalina and I fed over the winter!"

"Wow that's great and if they book us again then it will feed you all for longer."

Al shook his head, "You are certainly the right woman for that crazy man of yours, you're both as bad as each other," Al laughed leaning over to top up her coffee cup, "I'll have to take you through the routine, but I think it is a good idea if you are absolutely sure you're up for it."

"Do *you* think I'm up for it?" Dakota's excitement was infectious, and she made Al chuckle. "I certainly do, I wouldn't be letting you take the horses if I didn't think you were capable of doing this." Dakota felt assured, both Al and Javier had confidence she would be suitable for the job. She rode her bike home that night her heart bursting with excitement.

Javier had been busy doing his pink jobs as Dakota called housework. She thought he was a wonderful house husband; he kept the house spotlessly clean, he didn't mind washing and ironing although he told Dakota she was clearly much better at ironing than he was. Dakota had taken on most of the cooking as it was not Javier's forte. The joy of having a man who had lived on his own she often thought to herself as she rode the couple of miles home at night to a tidy house. Miles had expected it all to be done for him and wouldn't lift a finger unless he had to. He had thought pink jobs were not on his remit and had offered to pay for a cleaner.

"Hola beautiful lady," he kissed her cheek. "Did you get a chance to speak to Al today about the race?"

"Sure, I did, and he said yes," she hugged him, "I'm just so excited about it all I can't wait for it to come round!" Javier smiled; he was pleased she would be coming along; it would be an experience for her if nothing else.

"It'll be great and if it all goes well, they'll probably book you again. They pay well this company, they look after us, so we will have money in the bank after we finish! We could go out for a nice dinner when we get back as a treat and a nice change from all the freeze-dried meals we'll be eating over the week."

"Al already told me he'll have enough money to feed the horses over the winter, which is great, at least he won't be worrying about that, he said he'll show me the routine, what I'll need to do each day and how far behind the last competitor I have to ride." Javier glanced over at where she was standing in the kitchen, she was brimming with excitement. She would be riding for seven days and one night through the desert that could be quite cold at times as well as incredibly challenging, they'd be camping out at night when it would definitely be very cold, and she'd have to look after the horses as well as themselves when they'd been out riding for hours at a time. She was embracing the challenge, and he felt incredibly proud of her.

Chapter Sixteen

Dakota was on the second attempt at reconciling with her parents. Several weeks had passed since her last effort. Her father was on the phone with her this time. "We don't see things the same way as you do Dakota. You just up and left when Nina died, you didn't give us a second thought, you couldn't wait to get back to your piece of rough in Chile. Your behaviour has caused us great embarrassment, how you've handled things with Miles was quite unforgiveable and now this *man* who you've taken up with in the middle of the desert for goodness sakes, what do you think you are some sort of nomad?" She could tell he was angry and all she seemed to do was make things worse despite her best efforts. "No Dad, I'm doing what I want to do. I'm an adult, this is my life to live how I see fit. I don't want to grow old and have regrets and if I'd married Miles, I would have deeply regretted it. I can't be the sort of person who stops at home and brings up the children."

"I don't know why not, plenty of other women manage to do it why are you so different?"

"I don't know Dad but I am. Please understand or at least try?" Dakota pleaded with her father but to no avail.

"Your mother is in pieces do you know that? Do you realise how much you've upset her with your antics?"

"I don't think that is completely true, is it? For a start she's devastated because of Nina's death as we all are and I'm just getting the blame for it all as per usual."

Dakota was starting to lose her temper. She was fed up with being held responsible for everything that went wrong in the family. "It is fairly obvious we can't have a decent conversation together, so I think it is best if I hang up now and leave you to get on with your life in Chile with this man of yours as he seems to mean more to you than your own parents!"

"I want to sort things out with you both I don't want things being left like this." Dakota pleaded with him.

"Then you need to do the decent thing and come back home, and I suggest you do it sooner rather than later!" her father instructed.

"No Dad I'm not coming back home and that is final." She knew she had lost the battle. "Then this is the end of the conversation. I have nothing else to say to you. We don't want to hear from you again until you change your mind, leave that man and get yourself back to London." And with that her father ended the call.

Again, as she had done weeks previously Dakota found herself sitting on the bed, her phone in her hand wondering how she was ever going to find common ground with her mother and father. She felt frustrated and angry. Why were they behaving this way? Why wouldn't they accept Javier? Why had it been so easy for them to cut her out of their lives? She threw her phone across the room; it bounced off the wall and landed face down on the floorboards. Javier appeared in the bedroom doorway holding a mug of coffee for each of them. "Hey, beautiful lady, are you okay?" He could see she looked troubled.

"Another dreadful phone call with my dad this time," she told him, "They have told me not to bother contacting them again unless I leave you and Chile and return to London, can you believe that Javier?"

"Oh no Dakota I'm so sorry. Do you want to go back to London, just to sort things out with them?" How long were her parents going to keep treating her like this he thought to himself, she was so keen to try and mend the relationship.

"They mean go back to England for good not a trip to sort things out with them!" She said retrieving her phone from the floor. "I'm sorry you're having such a tough time both with them and here with me too." He set the coffee mugs down and sat on the bed with his arm around her.

"It isn't tough here with you it's great. I love you Javier that's why I don't want to go back; I want to stay here with you and the happy life we have together. I just can't understand why they don't see that and feel happy for me?"

"I really thought they would calm down over time, but it doesn't look that way, does it?" He felt sad for her.

"No, it rather looks like I'll just have to learn to live without them as part of my life now they have made their feelings very obvious." She stared down at the floor, biting her lip, they would not make her cry again, she had spilt enough tears over them and now it was going to stop.

Dakota had made dinner, but she wasn't feeling hungry. She picked at the food and pushed it around her plate with her fork. Javier watched her as he ate, she was really worrying him. All this business with her parents was taking its toll on her. Dakota cleared the plates away and retrieved two glasses from the cupboard. She poured wine for them from the bottle in the fridge and they moved into the lounge and collapsed onto the old sofa. The windows were open, and they could hear people laughing outside. Dakota felt as though she would never laugh again. Inside she felt bitter, twisted and resentful towards her mother and father. "Come her lady," Javier gently pulled her over to him and held her tight. She loved the feel of him against her. She loved the smell of him and how gentle he always was. He instantly calmed her just by holding her in his arms. She closed her eyes. She would never leave him no matter what her parents put her through. He was her soul mate.

"Am I worth all this pain and heartache?" He kissed the top of her head.

"A million times over Javier," she mumbled into his t-shirt, "I am never going to give you up, *never,* so they're going to have to either get used to it or be true to their word and cut me out of their lives."

Javier stared up at the bedroom ceiling thinking about the woman by his side. The pain she was going through and there was nothing he could ease or mend for her. He felt guilty for being with her, but he knew she loved him as much as he did her. She was everything to him, his entire life and although the choice to stay would ultimately be hers he hoped she would always be with him in San Pedro. Both their lives had changed so much since that first meeting. She had now gained residency, and she had her job with Al and the horses. They were both so happy together; he'd told his family all about the amazing woman who had ridden into his life. They had been thrilled for him and couldn't wait to meet her; he must arrange something soon they had insisted. He was a changed man and for the better since that day she'd arrived in the dusty little town on her big red bike.

Dakota woke feeling much more positive. She had made breakfast and had arrived at the decision that her parents were over six thousand miles away and they were not going to affect her life in Chile. "Come on lazy bones it's time to get up. What are you doing today?" she asked a sleepy Javier as she tried to pull the duvet from him. He grabbed it, pulling it back over himself, "Hey, what are you doing lady?"

"Come on, its time you were up Javier."

He pulled a face, "I'm going to sort out our food and stuff for the race. It's not far away now, I want to get things together, so it isn't a crazy rush at the last minute." He rolled over "I'll get up in a minute, not just now." She kissed his cheek and picked up her keys from the bedside table. "Your breakfast is on the table when you do decide to get your ass out of bed. I'll see you later." She closed the door behind her and ran down the metal steps to her bike.

Al was at the barn busying himself with jobs, sweeping and shovelling stuff into the wheelbarrow. He'd already got the coffee on; the strong smell greeted her as she arrived. The horses whinnied their welcome, she removed her helmet shaking her hair loose and hung it on the handlebars. She strode over to where Al was busy sweeping. "Hola Al, is everything good with you today?" she asked.

"Hola, Dakota, everything is fine thanks, are you?"

"Yes, all good. Javier is starting to get stuff together for the race today do you think we need to go through things regarding the horses?"

"It was my plan for today funnily enough, yes we can do." Al handed her a steaming mug of coffee which she took gratefully. "I'll just pop the feeds in then we can make a start." Putting the coffee down to cool a little, she walked round the stables distributing buckets of feed for the eager horses then took her place on the old wooden stool with her coffee to chat to Al.

Al laid out the plans; all that would need doing for the horses and her to be safe and well. "I'll have to drop off feed, water and alfalfa for each night. The organisers will need to give me the route they are sending the competitors out on, so I know where to make the drops."

126

"Okay I'll ask Javier for that when I get home. He does have a couple of maps and route books spare he has been using to show me where we will be going and the sort of terrain we'll be crossing."

"You will need to keep the spare horse saddled up at all times in case you need to rescue or recover someone from the race. Make sure they have a head collar on under the bridle so you can lead them when the recovery is mounted."

"What about first aid kit and the likes?"

"You'll carry a small one for the horses but if you need more or you need to collect a replacement horse then you'll have to send Javier so I can arrange it for you. The route the race organisers choose is usually around San Pedro. They need to get back so their vehicles can refuel. As long as I know roughly where you are on the course I can come out with another horse." Dakota hurriedly scribbled down notes as Al talked through everything making sure she was clear on all his detailed instructions. "Please be careful Dakota, it can be dangerous *very dangerous* with the rocks and steep inclines and slopes, you will really have to have your wits about you at all times."

"Javier has already marked on the map any danger spots. I am planning on dismounting and walking the worse bits and lead Cherry and Diego."

"Some bits you will have to stay mounted, you won't be able to walk and lead both horses. If at any time you think it is too much for you or the horses let Javier know and I will pull you from the race." The old man's face was serious.

"How will they be supported though if they are expecting us to do it and then you pull out our support?"

"They'll manage I can assure you of that. They will not want you to risk yourself or the horses, they are good people running this race, you will get on with them. But please, promise me, you and the horses come first Dakota, I can't stress that enough."

"Of course, Al, and thanks for letting me cover this race I really appreciate it. I know it's a huge thing in terms of you trusting me to do it being so new to the job and a massive responsibility for me having the horses to look after and watch out for." She was only too aware of the responsibility on her shoulders, and she didn't want to let Al down or disappoint him

127

or Javier. This was her chance to prove herself. "Right, mucking out duties next and then I think I will ride out for an hour or so if that's okay with you Al. Are you joining me today?"

"No, I need to collect more feed and stockpile some alfalfa for the race. Javier is right it isn't far away, and two weeks will soon be upon us."

Dakota rode out for a couple of hours. She ventured across the river and off into the Atacama wilderness leading three horses, she was riding Juan. The race was going round in her mind; would she manage without having to ask Javier to help her? Would the horses be safe in her care? What if she let Al down? What if she disappointed Javier? He had been brilliant; he'd talked her through the route and explained in detail the tricky sections. She would have to be on full alert for the entire time, that would be difficult if she had to make a recovery and remove a competitor from the course. Javier had gone into great detail showing her where the roads were, where the check points would be on the course. These would be the places where the recovered competitor would be collected by a member of the medical team and her job would be done. She would then have to rejoin the race behind the last competitor.

Javier had been busy visiting the shops purchasing freeze-dried food and supplies he knew they would need. He had a first aid kit which he kept fully stocked for emergencies and he bought a few additional pieces he thought Dakota might need. He was looking forward to the race with her being a part of it too it was going to be more than just work, he would see her at night, and they would be able to sleep under the stars again. He knew she was looking forward to that very much. He did have some concerns; this could be dangerous for her and the horses; he would never have mentioned it to her if he hadn't seen first-hand how capable she was on the back of a horse.

Javier pushed open the door. Ruben was behind the counter stocking shelves; he was pleased to see him. "Hola Javier, how are things with your lovely lady these days. I don't see her around much?" he asked.

"Great, just great. You know she helps Al with the horses and the treks? Well Al is letting her cover the race that's on in two weeks, so I won't be working away without her. This time she will be coming along with me."

"Man, you have got it bad! Does she like sleeping out under the stars when it is freezing cold at night? Have you warned her about how cold it gets out there?"

"She loves it, Ruben. I know you'll find it hard to believe but she is just amazing, we're both looking forward to it." He collected the electrolytes Ruben had been saving for him and passed over the pesos to pay for them. "Here are your tablets, have you got enough for both of you?"

"More than enough. Don't think we will use many, but it is just in case it gets really hot."

"I wish you both the very best of luck with the race but I'm sure you'll be in here again before you go. Be sure to let me know how you get on won't you?"

"Sure. And thanks for these" he waved the tubes of tablets at Ruben as he left to return home to the flat.

Chapter Seventeen

Dakota sat on an impatient Cherry listening carefully to the race briefing. She was grateful it was in English. The race organisers were going through the daybook, what the terrain and weather had in store for them for day one of the race. The distance would be twenty-eight miles of sand, rock and everything else the Atacama had in store. Check points would be every five to seven miles depending on where they could set them up. There would be a doctor at each check point with a vehicle in case anyone had to be evacuated. Dakota was introduced and her role explained to the competitors. Cherry stamped her hoof and threw her head up and down; she was eager for the race to start.

At eight o'clock that morning the race started. Javier was already several miles ahead of the bulk of the racers, his role was to ensure the race leaders were supported. Dakota waited patiently until the last competitor had crossed the start line then Cherry sprang into action. Diego plodded alongside quite happily. The sun was out but it wasn't very warm. Dakota wore a long sleeve shirt, and a fleece was safely tucked into her saddlebag should the weather get colder. At the second check point some ten miles into the event Dakota stopped to water the horses and walked, leading them both for a few miles to give Cherry's back a rest. The last competitor was quite slow, she was conscious she didn't want them to feel as though she was hurrying them along. She walked far enough behind to keep them in sight and shouting distance should they need her.

At the third check point the person she had been following pulled out of the race. It seemed they had been nursing an old injury and walking on the sandy desert floor had proven too much, she made the decision to abandon the race. Dakota remounted Cherry who was only too pleased to have a couple of miles to trot before they caught up with the back of the race. The terrain underfoot was getting worse, it was hard work for the horses floundering up and down sand dunes. Dakota dismounted for the second time and lead the horses across the dunes.

It was six o'clock that evening when she finally rode into the first camp of the race. Javier had sorted out where they were going to sleep and had fetched the fodder for the horses. She was glad to see him, he jogged over and took Diego from her. "Hola, how was race day one out in the Atacama then?"

"Great, but it's tough. I need to water and wash these two." She patted Cherry.

"I'll help you, I don't need to wash my bike down" he joked, leading Diego to the river. Dakota sponged their sweaty backs and necks and let them drink from the fast flow. She led them into the river and let them stand knee deep for a while. "I want to cool their legs off a bit we have done a lot of climbing up and down and I don't want anyone getting heated tendons," she explained to Javier. "And we don't want Al having to come out and do an emergency swap over."

Horses sorted and fed Dakota sat by the fire drinking coffee and eating the freeze-dried meal Javier had prepared for her, "It's so good having you here with me," he continued shovelling food into his mouth as he spoke, "I get lonely sometimes out here when I'm on my own. It's different when you've got someone to camp with like when Al comes along." He thought for a minute, "Hey, what about if I help you with the horses if I'm back to camp first?" He raised his eyebrows.

"That would be a massive help if you don't have anything else you need to do." Dakota was exhausted and secretly worried; it was only day one and she had walked a lot to save the horses. She hoped day two might be a bit easier.

The following day was Monday, the second day of the race and it was easier. After the race briefing Javier took off again at top speed racing across the desert with the front runners. Dakota took her place at the back. Day two was only twenty miles. The terrain flattened out after lunch, and they were walking on tracks which were proving much easier for the horses. Dakota walked between the two check points leading the horses and giving Cherry's back a rest. Tomorrow she would ride Diego and lead Cherry. They crossed through the river at places where it was deep and fast flowing. Dakota watched as the competitors crossed before she, Cherry and Diego plunged into its icy depths. She wondered where Javier had crossed, this was way too deep for his bike to negotiate. Same as the previous day, Dakota watered the horses after ten miles at check point two. The organisers were kind to her, the offered her water and snacks at each stop and asked her if she needed anything. Javier had been right when he'd said they were good people who ran the event. After the horses were watered, she took her place behind the last competitor on the course. That evening she learned three people had abandoned the race due to injury. She couldn't help but wonder how many would be left at the end of the seven days when they finally crossed the finish line.

Dakota rode into the camp at the end of day two; Javier was there waiting to meet her. "End of day two only five more to go!" He grinned up at her his shades shielding his eyes from the late afternoon sun. "How did you find the river crossings?" He asked.

"Scary, very scary. They were really fast flowing and deep. I was glad that Al wasn't here to see us negotiate those!" She handed Diego to Javier who led him to where they were camped for the night. They removed the saddles and bridles, and Dakota brushed off the sweat marks as they tucked into their feeds. "These two are so good you know; you'd think they'd been doing this all their lives." She continued to groom, brushing the undergrowth from their tails. "They never put a foot out of place and just go wherever you ask them. That river was deep, they just jumped in and got on with it."

"They've been well trained. Al has been doing this for years, I know he bought all his horses from a guy who trains and treats them well. I think Juan might be the exception to the rule!" He laughed as he busied himself. She was glad she hadn't had to bring Juan with her. At least Cherry and Diego got along together and were very trustworthy horses, the very horses you needed to support a tough event like this.

Javier recalled the events of the day he'd endured at the front of the race. His job was to ride ahead and make sure the racers at the front knew where they were going and to make sure they got there safely. He had to radio the organisers when one of the competitors had broken his ankle getting his leg caught between two rocks and falling over. The poor man was now being seen to in hospital, his race was over, and he would have to return home without his medal. Dakota filled him in on life at the back of the race and how slow it was. It was nice walking through the desert on the horses but sometimes she had to stop for quite a while if the competitor wanted to rest at a check point. They ate their meals and drank coffee before Dakota did the final check on the horses and turned in for the night.

She had been asleep for about two hours when the noise of the camp woke her. She wondered how people managed to sleep with generators and cars driving in and out all night. Trucks were back and forth for hours, she eventually drifted off before dawn broke over the Atacama Desert. Javier was already up and dressed, he handed her porridge and coffee. "I filled your water and dropped a few electrolytes into it so if it tastes funny that is what it'll be, don't go washing the horses off with what's left in your bottle or they'll be sticky," he warned. "You okay for today?" She sat up in her sleeping bag and looked at the camp below them. "I don't know how the competitors manage to sleep with such noise going on all night and then they have to go and race each day!"

"They don't get much sleep really, I think it is more resting. Still, they seem to get used to it." She was tired and it was only the start of day three.

"Can we camp further away tonight so I can get some sleep?" "Tonight is a good camp; we can camp further away behind rocks, so we'll be out of sight. It won't be so noisy I'm sure of that." He kissed her cheek and brushed a piece of hair back behind her ear. He turned back to his kit, rolling up his sleeping bag before packing it away. "Race briefing in an hour. Do you want some help with the horses?"

"No, I'm good thanks I'll just eat this then get myself sorted out." Dakota hurriedly ate the porridge and dressed before attending to the horses and packed her sleeping bag away into her saddlebag. She really mustn't make a habit of sleeping late again. Her broken night's sleep had put her back with her jobs, Javier had his own tasks to do without having to spend time helping her out. Fifty minutes later Dakota was ready and mounted on Diego in time for the race briefing.

Day three of the race consisted of twenty-three miles over scrubby vegetation and sandy tracks. The morning was very difficult Dakota kept losing sight of the last runner due to the density of the vegetation she had to work her way through leading Cherry. Reaching check point two had taken and hour longer than the previous days and she was grateful when the afternoon gave way to easy riding along tracks with good visibility across the vast but beautiful desert. Now she could see the competitors for miles ahead, like little ants marching up towards the rocky pass ahead where they vanished between the rocks. The plain they crossed was dotted with rocks and sandy tracks. Once she arrived at the entrance to the pass Dakota could see it was more like a track between the mountains, it climbed steadily uphill for around four miles before reaching the check point nestled into the rocks. The last competitor Dakota was trailing behind stopped at the check point for around an hour before deciding they were not going to continue and finish the day; they were too exhausted to carry on. Dakota had to quickly mount up and catch up with the now last competitor who'd left the check point as they had arrived over an hour ago. She estimated they'd now be about three miles ahead of her and halfway to the evening camp. She nudged Diego into trot to cover the distance along the sandy road. The only sound coming from the soft padding the horses' hooves made as they kicked up the sand along the track. Cherry seemed happy jogging alongside and soon they could see the last racer ahead. She slowed to walk and let Diego have a long rein so he could stretch his head and neck. She leaned down and patted him, they had the final competitor well within their sights now, she could relax a little.

Just under an hour later they rode into the camp. Javier wasn't around but she managed to locate his bike behind the rocks just as he had described to her. She removed the saddles and bridles from the horses and sponged them off before feeding and watering. She was just finishing washing the horses' bits and brushing the saddle pads clean when Javier appeared. "Hola my lady, sorry I didn't know you were back in. Last check point radioed in and said you were with the last competitor. I thought you would be at least another hour out."

"I would have been, but they decided to pull out of the race, so I had to get a move on to catch up with the competitor ahead of them, we got back to camp faster than we'd expected."

"It's good to see you, how was it out there today for you?" He took her in his arms, holding her tight against him, she closed her eyes and took a deep breath.

"This morning was hard with all that vegetation to work through I didn't think I was ever going to get out of it but then this afternoon it was so much easier thank goodness or I don't think I would have made it back here until the morning. It was certainly tough going trying to lead Cherry round the scrub and keep the last racer in my sights at the same time."

"Yeah, I had to take a shorter route, there was no way I would make it through all that and the really soft ground, my tyres would've sunk in too far for me to make it out again."

"Poor old Diego went up to his knees at one point but thankfully it was only the one time!" Dakota muttered. "What's for dinner tonight then in our nice, secluded desert restaurant?" She rubbed her hands together in eager anticipation. Javier rummaged around in his pack and pulled out a sausage casserole and vegetarian version for Dakota. "And dessert?" she asked, taking the packets from him to fill from the pot already boiling on the fire. "Rice pudding or sticky toffee?" Javier held up the packets for her to choose. "Sticky toffee please not that I've ever had the freeze-dried version, it might be absolutely hideous." Dakota poked the fire and added more wood before placing the small pan on the top to heat more water. "I think it's going to take a while for the hot water to boil again but at least we can rest up a bit whilst we are waiting, I'm knackered today for some reason" she sat back against the rock and drank her coffee.

"It'll be all the concentrating you've had to do to negotiate the terrain and looking out for the person in front too," Javier replied, "it gives you brain ache!"

"I think that's it; I don't feel physically tired, but I'll be glad to get a decent night's sleep tonight and in privacy too."

An hour later they had finished their dinner and were resting with their backs cushioned from the rocks by their sleeping bags. Dakota had completed her final check on the horses and could hardly keep her eyes open, she was aware if she fell asleep this early, she would probably be awake at some ridiculous hour in the morning so was trying to stay awake for at least another hour or so. Closing her eyes she raised her face to the warm setting sun. She felt so safe here with her man. She had thoroughly enjoyed their time together supporting the race so far even if it had proved difficult and testing at times. Tomorrow would be another day.

That night sleep came quickly and easily to both. The night was a lot quieter than it had been, there were no trucks coming into the camp in the middle of the night and they couldn't hear the generator from their camp behind the rocks. They both slept heavily waking the next morning as the first light appeared on the horizon. Dakota felt refreshed from her good night's sleep. She rose and dressed and tended to the horses. She busied herself filling water buckets and giving the horses more alfalfa to munch on whilst she collected the saddle cloths, she had left on the rocks to dry the night before. Javier looked weary but he was in good spirits as he packed his kit up. "After today we will be over halfway through the race. Let's keep our heads up and plough through the next four days then we can take a few days off at home to recover!" She nodded, a few days off in their flat making love every night sounded like heaven. Right now, though, she was to finish the job out here and make Al proud of her.

Chapter Eighteen

Day four of the race was the long non-stop stage. Dakota was going to be riding from seven that morning until the last competitor finished the fifty miles of desert they would be racing across. She had been told anything up until one o'clock the following afternoon. That was the cut off time, anyone finishing after that would be disqualified from the race. She planned to ride Diego until midnight and then change over to Cherry. She would walk a good way to rest the horse's backs. She knew there would be a plain of around ten miles she could walk and lead them which would give them around three hours or so rest and if she found another suitable spot she would do the same again for Cherry the following day.

Javier was on his bike on one side of the race briefing; Dakota was on Diego at the other. She lifted her hand briefly and smiled over at him, he did the same back to her. He would be off as fast as he could ride once the briefing was over to ensure he would be ahead of the number one racer, the leader. She would be much further back, at the very end with the last person to finish the following day. Javier would have to sweep the course once the first person had finished the race providing water and support to anyone who looked as though they were struggling. He would collect his supplies from the closest check point and go out to the people in need of his help. He had told Dakota he anticipated seeing her quite often on this stage. She was glad he would be around; she felt nervous putting so much pressure on the horses. They would need to eat and drink along the way and Dakota had tried to plan when they would eat with the organisers. The end result had been that she would be able to graze them for an hour or so in a couple of places at check points to allow the last competitors to rest a little. She had also been told that they wanted to get people through the check points as quickly as possible that day due to the miles they had to cover. They didn't want people hanging around and losing track of the time and missing the one o'clock cut off the following afternoon. It

137

seemed crazy to Dakota that at seven in the morning they were moving people on to finish by one in the afternoon the next day!

At seven o'clock prompt the race started. Javier was off in a cloud of dust; she felt her heart go with him. He had been such a support to her over the last few days, had helped her so much she didn't know how she would've coped without him. At night he had been there to help her with the horses, to boil water and prepare their food giving her time to get washed and cleaned up. He had gone through the daybook and their map with her every night showing her what to expect the following day and where she could rest, water or feed the horses. He had stood with the horses, knee deep in water when they had camped close to the river so their tendons could cool, and he had spoken to her on the radio whenever he could just to check there were no problems with her or the horses. He was brilliant; now she felt quietly confident they would finish the race and make Al proud. She understood he'd had reservations about her supporting the event, but Al had told her he trusted her, she knew he did but she wanted to prove to him that she could do it.

At nine o'clock she reached the first check point. The person who was last had made good time over very rough ground and now they were flying out of the check point and onto number two which was eight miles away. Dakota dismounted and walked for an hour before getting back on. The horses plodded along not at all phased by what was going on around them, quietly walking by her side. At check point three, at three that afternoon she managed to graze the horses for an hour and let them rest a little. She walked with them to the next check point which was another six miles further along then remounted and rode as it was starting to get dark. She turned on her head torch and the torches she had to wear on her legs, she had to have a good view of the terrain ahead of them. The course directors had told her that the night stage would be all road based so the horses and competitors wouldn't be in any danger in the dark. At nine-thirty the last person arrived at check point five.

Dakota had to stop the horses a couple of times to let the competitors get ahead, they were so exhausted. She wondered what kept them going, what drove them on to finish the race when they were so weary. At the camp the evening before a couple of

138

people had come over to stroke the horses, she'd asked them what their incentive was for racing. One woman had told her she was raising money for a leukemia charity. Dakota had felt sadness as she thought of her sister Nina but also huge admiration for the woman taking on such a challenge. Dakota asked if she knew anyone with the disease and the woman had told her she had lost her own child to leukemia only the year before. Dakota hadn't mentioned Nina, but she'd thought the woman very brave to take up something like this after losing her child only one year previous. The other competitor had explained he was reaching a milestone in his life and had wanted to do something to mark the occasion. When they had gone, she thought about the other competitors, she wondered what was driving each of them to the finish line. Each one would have their own story, their own goal to achieve and their own reason for taking on such a life changing event. Nobody would finish that race the same person they were when they had stood on the start line. It was punishing, gruelling and painful; Dakota admired every one of them.

It was five o'clock in the morning when they left the final check point. The last competitor had wanted to take a couple of hours to sleep so Dakota had taken that chance to give the horses a feed and let them graze. The organisers had handed her a cup of coffee and snacks as she stood holding the horse's reins in the darkness letting them pull at the thin grass. She stood gazing up at the sky and the stars wondering where Javier was in all this confusion and excitement. She didn't feel at all tired despite being on the go for twenty-two hours nonstop she was wired and wide awake helped by the coffee. She wanted to finish this stage knowing there was only tomorrow, and Saturday left to go and then it would be over.

The dawn had started to break, the sun making its appearance over the horizon far in the distance. Dakota turned off her torches and continued walking behind the last competitor. He had felt rejuvenated after rest and food and wanted to chat, so they walked along side by side. The man was from England, and this was his first ultra-marathon. He found it extremely tough, much harder than anything he had ever done in his life, but he had found himself changing inside as the event unfolded. The first day he had been worried about finishing. Now he knew he was going to finish the race and told Dakota he'd made the decision to leave his wife who he'd discovered was having an affair with her boss. She didn't know, he explained, he was aware of the affair, and he'd come out here to try and find answers. He'd hoped that she'd end the affair but now he had thought it all through and had decided he would leave her once he got back home. Dakota listened to him talk, thinking about the problems with her own family and wondered again what she could do to make things right. "You and the motorcyclist man are you friends?" the man asked.

"We are actually together."

"I saw he helped you with the horses and thought you must be friendly. Do you do this sort of thing all the time together?" The man gently probed as they strolled through the early sun light.

"This is the first time. I come from England too, I came here on holiday in April and decided to stay after I met Javier, and we got together."

"Wow you're brave wanting to live here, it's so different to England."

"We live in San Pedro." She glanced over at the man. He looked exhausted and filthy, but he was still managing to stride out with the aid of his walking poles.

"Do you like living here in the middle of nowhere?"

"I love it." Dakota replied.

"You do?"

"When I came here it was for a holiday, I had broken up with my long term boyfriend and I wanted to get away from it all. I'd no intention of living here but when I arrived, I instantly loved it so much then Javier came into my life."

"D'you have family back home then? I bet they love you being out here, it is a ticket for a free holiday?"

"Actually, it is quite the opposite, they have disowned me since I came out here to live with Javier."

"No!"

"They wanted me to marry the long-term boyfriend and have a family. They are very old fashioned. I'm one huge disappointment to them."

"That's terrible, I'm so sorry for you," he sounded genuine. "Where are you from in England?"

140

"London. My family own a small jewellery business making mainly bespoke pieces for people. I don't think you'll have heard of them, it's called Jumano jewellery?"

"No, I've not heard of them but that's terrible for you, I'm so sorry!"

"It's fine I have had to deal with it. It was hard at first because I'd just lost my sister, and I was over in England for the funeral. They just presumed I'd stay, that I was back from a holiday, it was then I broke the news I was coming back here to live, and they flipped. They've disowned me since." Cherry nuzzled Dakota as if she understood the pain she was feeling. Dakota patted her roan neck.

"Did you tell your parents about Javier?"

"I tried but they thought he was some sort of poor local man with nothing to offer me and had another go at me about leaving Miles."

"Was he your long-term chap?"

"Yes, but it's long over now. I must learn to compartmentalise my parents, keep them at the back of my mind. I have Javier, and he is my life and Al who owns these horses and gave me a job when I had nothing. I owe him an awful lot."

"You have certainly shaken up your life. I'm Paul by the way." He held out his hand and she and shook it, "Dakota."

"That is an unusual name?"

"It is a Native American. My parents are of American Indian descent somewhere down the line."

"Oh I see is that why they are so strict?"

"No. That is just how they are, they have strange ideas and are very old fashioned."

They walked side by side sometimes chatting and sometimes quiet until they could see the finish line ahead. They passed over the line at just after eight that morning which was a race record for everyone to have finished day five. Dakota was glad, she didn't want to be out until one o'clock or longer following the last person in at ten past one for them to be told they were disqualified after trudging fifty miles across the Atacama Desert, that would have made her angry. Now they were finished and in good time too. It was time to sort the horses out and relax for a while.

141

Chapter Nineteen

Dakota walked through the camp leading both the horses. Javier met her halfway and took Diego from her. "How are you feeling?" he asked. "Are you tired?"

"Actually, no I'm not tired, all the coffee I've been supplied with I guess, but the horses are. Let's get them sorted quickly so they can have a sleep and recover then I'll sort us some food." She removed the saddles and bridles and brushed the sweat from the horses' bodies. Javier had prepared their feeds and bundled large amounts of alfalfa on the ground in front of them next to their water buckets. Both horses looked in need of a good rest, so they left them alone to eat and rest. Javier had already started a pot of water on the fire and had meals ready to pour the water into. "I kept asking where you were on the course, so I knew roughly what time to expect you in today. I didn't think everyone would finish as early as they have though, think it is a course record for day four/five finishing so early?"

"Yes, that's what they told us when we finished." Dakota sat down with her back against Javier's backpack and devoured the porridge he handed her. "This taste so good," she said, "so much better than on the go stuff and electrolytes!"

"They can make your water taste like dish water if it gets warm then you struggle to drink it down." Javier explained to her as he busied himself with spooning coffee into the mugs. "That's the scenario I had yesterday afternoon, it really did taste like dish water, but I forced it down eventually." Her stomach full of porridge Dakota felt her eyes start to close, she fought the desire to sleep until she had washed herself down and checked the horses one last time. Suddenly exhausted, she crawled into her sleeping bag and didn't wake until after three that afternoon.

Rubbing her eyes, for a second Dakota wondered where she was then she remembered. Javier wasn't around and the horses had finished their alfalfa and were lying down dozing on the soft ground. Dakota scrambled out of the sleeping bag and pulled on her jeans, t-shirt and boots before fetching more alfalfa from Al's store, heaping it in front of the horses. They didn't seem interested they had eaten enough previously. They would eat what she had just given them later when they were ready for more. She refilled their buckets with fresh water and stoked the fire. Although it was hot with the afternoon sun, she wanted to have a fresh coffee and more food. Dakota had been pottering around for about half an hour when Javier returned to their camp. "You're awake, how did you sleep?"

"Really well thanks. I woke around three and have topped up the horses feed and water and was about to have some more food and a coffee. D'you want some too?"

Javier made the coffee whilst she picked out the food she wanted. Selecting a vegetarian casserole he carefully poured the water into the pouch as she held it.

Early evening arrived. Paul walked over to their camp and stood a little distance back from where they were sitting feeling awkward about approaching their private space. "Hello Dakota, I hope you don't mind, I just wanted to say thanks for walking with me earlier today?" He called over to her.

"Hey Paul, come over and meet Javier!" She stood and beckoned him over to their camp. "This is Javier!" She introduced him and Javier stood and wiped his hands on his jeans. "Hi, I'm Paul," he shook his hand, "I've heard a lot about you during our long walk across the desert this morning." He grinned at Javier.

"I hope it was all good?"

"Of course, Dakota was telling me how you met, and I discovered that she too is from London as am I"

"Sit down and join us," Javier beckoned him into the space. "Are you enjoying the race?" Paul said he was and then explained to Javier why he has here, everything he and Dakota had discussed out on the course about his wife. Javier was shocked to hear his story but knew everyone who took part in the race had their own reasons for taking on such a challenge. Paul was no exception.

It was late when Paul returned to the main camp, Dakota had finished her final check on Cherry and Diego. She'd eaten again and decided she would turn in for the night as tomorrow was the twenty-mile stage then on the final day they would have nine miles to tackle. Javier was next to her, he put his arm around her and pulled her to him. She could feel his warmth through the bag and savoured it. Night in the desert had been very cold especially so if you were tired and she was very tired.

The following morning, they were both awake early. The camp had been quiet overnight, all the competitors exhausted from the long stage had been sleeping. Dakota and Javier had enjoyed a good night's rest. Dakota fed and watered the horses before packing her kit up, everything went into the saddle bags on the horses' backs. Javier had made breakfast. She tucked into the food with the plastic fork, but it wasn't pleasant. Still, it would suffice until lunchtime when she had an array of bars to use up. Javier had already filled her water bottles and popped in some electrolytes; they were fizzing away in the bottom.

At seven, when it was still quite cold, the race briefing started, Dakota was mounted up ready to give her full attention to what the day held in store for her. She wasn't surprised to learn they would be travelling over very rough ground with another two river crossings. She felt for the poor competitors who had already travelled so many miles and had very sore and blistered feet. They now had to face twenty miles of rough stony ground with two river crossings that would undoubtedly soak carefully applied dressings from their feet. She'd realised very early on the severity of this race, why so many people came to do it, to test themselves and their resolve. She admired these people who'd travelled from far and wide to compete in this event as she watched them from the back of her horse. She could see their on-going suffering and pain as they hobbled back to their tents to collect their backpacks and make their way to the start line. She watched them hoping that they would all finish the race after coming this far.

At eight after the briefing had finished, the race started. This was the penultimate day she thought as Cherry took her place next to Diego at the back of the race. Javier was already a speck in the distance in front of the leader of the race spewing up dust in his wake. Dakota rode on through the cool of the morning. As she rode, the heat intensified along with her thoughts. Six months ago, she would never have thought she would be doing something like this with her life let alone in a strange country she had never even visited before and with a man she had only known a few weeks before she had moved in with him. She had never been so happy and prayed that things with her family would sort themselves out very soon. She didn't want to be estranged from them for loving the man she did and for choosing her own path in life.

At the second check point they stopped for a quick lunch. She briefly waved to Paul who was leaving the check point as she was entering. Today he was not the last competitor by at least four and she was pleased to see he was feeling so strong.

Not long after check point two there was a river crossing. The horses waded through, and Dakota stopped on the bank at the other side to wait for competitors to reapply dressings and put on dry socks. She watched quietly as some of them could hardly stand on their battered feet, holding onto rocks to help them gain their balance before reaching for the aid of their walking poles. She saw a few of them dose up on pain killers before carefully climbing to their feet and tottering off ahead of her. Dakota had such admiration for their sheer determination. She thought back to the long stage, how a lot of the racers had struggled hard to finish that stage, but they were still here for the second to last day. To think they would have gone through all that and then not finish today would be just terrible.

As she rode on into the afternoon and over the second river crossing, she came across Paul sitting on a rock resting. "Hey Paul, are you okay?"

"Just having a rest. My blister has rubbed raw on the ball of my foot, the skin has come off and I'm finding it difficult to time my painkillers properly. Before I know it, the four hours have passed, and I've forgotten to take another one then it's just too painful to walk!" Dakota watched him from her saddle, she stared down at the man who looked broken and in pain. "Would it help if I walked with you for a bit, you only have about five miles to go until we reach camp?" She dismounted and took the reins over Cherry and Diego's heads. He looked up to her shielding his eyes from the sun, a smile broke across his weathered face. "Oh wow, that would be just amazing if you really don't mind?" he muttered clambering to his feet. Dakota's heart went out to him as he stood, winced with the pain, almost fell over then with the aid of his walking poles he tottered gingerly along the track leading to the last camp of the race. He was incredibly slow and had to keep sitting down to rest his feet. "They just feel like they are throbbing and throbbing in my shoes. My feet have swollen up so much I dare not take my trainers off because I don't think I'd get them back on again!" Paul explained. She stood and waited patiently for him then he was ready to get back up and walk a little further. Eventually they made it into the camp where Paul collapsed at the water collection point exhausted and in agonising pain. Dakota ran to his aid and tried to heave him up whilst still holding onto the horses. "He really needs to see a doctor," Dakota told the woman who was checking him in. "He's been struggling badly all afternoon; the poor guy needs to finish this race" she explained trying to hold him up. Javier appeared and rushed to her aid pulling Paul's arm around his shoulders to keep him upright. "Wow man, you need help and right now," he told him. "Dakota, can you manage the horses if I get him over to the medical tent?"

"Of course, please do get him over there and stay with him, he's not in a good way." Javier almost carried Paul to the medical tent to get his feet attended to.

Dakota sat drinking her coffee and looking over at the hustle and bustle going on in the camp. It was the last night and everyone still in the race was on a high. The camp was very loud and filled with excitement; this time tomorrow the race will be over and most of the competitors would have a medal around their necks. There will be a lot of medals and some life changing decisions to be made by a few people in the camp once they arrived back home. She watched them hobbling around with their drinks and packets of freeze-dried food feeling pride for every one of them.

It was several hours later when Javier returned to the camp looking very worried. "Hey, I just put more water on for coffee?" Dakota reached for his cup and spooned the brown powder into it, "How's Paul doing?"

"He's not good. The doctor wants him to pull out of the race. The whole bottom of his foot is a really bad mess. The skin has dropped off and the soaking his dressings got today going through those rivers hasn't done them any good whatsoever. The doctor thinks his feet are infected."

"Oh my God," she replied. "What's he going to do? Finishing this race means *everything* to him, you know his story!"

"I know. I told him you'd be with him walking by his side for the remaining nine miles if he chooses to carry on, but the decision really is his. I don't know how he got this far looking at the state of his feet. He had the devils own job trying to get his trainers off."

"Of course, I will walk with him but finishing this race means way more to him than the medal around his neck. He needs to finish it to give him the courage to face what he has got going on back home with his wife. If he fails to finish, it will affect his confidence, and he will go home feeling like a failure. It is such a difficult race this don't you think? After the river crossing, I had to wait for the competitors to re-dress their feet and put on fresh dry socks. Javier you should have seen some of their injuries I can't believe people get up and carry on with such bad blisters and things. I saw one woman's foot was almost unrecognisable it was so bad. She had lost at least three toenails and all her toes had dressings on because of the blisters." Javier knew things like this happened on all the races it wasn't anything he hadn't seen before but it was all new and terrible to Dakota.

"I know, I had to get someone off the course because they passed out with the pain from their injuries. God knows how long they had been out there in the sun, they were not wearing a hat, I found them flat out on the floor unconscious. They're okay now after being on a drip all afternoon in the medical tent but the doctor has said they can't finish the race, they're devastated as you can imagine." He stood staring out over the horizon with his hands shoved deep into his pockets.

The last day of the race had arrived. Ahead of them stood nine miles of baron sandy desert to navigate before the competitors could finally get awarded their medals. The race would finish far out in the desert then the competitors would get taken back to San Pedro on a bus the race organisers had arranged for them. It was common practice after the race for the competitors to go into the church to say thanks for their time out in the desert; the experiences they'd experienced over the week and the friends they had made so it was arranged for the bus to drop them off outside the church in the square.

147

Dakota was at the start line on Diego and Javier was for the final time at the other end of the pack on his bike. There was no sign of Paul and Dakota feared the worse. The race started and the competitors flew off across the sand at an incredible pace. The fact they had only nine miles to cover seemed like they would only just stretch their legs before they arrived at the finish next to the river where it was customary for everyone to jump in and swim around for as long as they could bear the icy waters before the bus took them back to San Pedro soaking wet but very happy. Dakota couldn't believe they were going so fast when most of the competitors were nursing injuries. That must be the power of good painkillers and lots of adrenalin. She looked around the sea of faces still searching for Paul. She felt a hand on her leg and looked down to see him smiling weakly up at her. She smiled and reached for his hand relieved he had decided to try and finish the race. "Nine miles to go, do you think you can keep up with me?' he joked hobbling across the start line and into the unknown. "I'll give it a damn good go," she replied, nudging Diego into a steady walk to keep pace with Paul. "How are you feeling today?" She could see he was already sweating from the pain. "I'm going to finish this race if I have to crawl on my hands and knees then I'm going to get in that river and soak my feet until they damn well stop throbbing." He hobbled along his eyes fixed on the horizon; his chin stuck out with sheer determination. Dakota glanced down at his trainers and could see they had been crudely cut away to relieve his swollen feet. "Couldn't get the damn things on after I visited the doctor's tent last night, so my tent mates helped me design these new and very trendy desert trainers, what d'you think?" He swiftly shot her a glance before returning his stare to the horizon.

"Not sure if they'll set a trend in desert wear" she commented stopping Diego so she wouldn't get ahead of Paul.

"Am I going too slowly?" he asked.

"No, I'm just getting off Diego to walk with you to the finish." She dismounted and led the two horses. "These horses have carried me enough the last few days through day and night, river and desert so they deserve a rest, and I want to give you morale support; I can't do that sitting on a horse watching you struggle!" He grasped her wrist in his grimy sun burnt hand. "Thank you,

Dakota, thank you for all the support you've given me over the past few days I'll never forget you." He forced a smile, but she could see he was very close to tears. His eyes had welled up and he was struggling to control his trembling lips.

"Come on then, enough of the gush let's get this race finished!"

Despite his injuries Paul kept up a good pace and they crossed the finish line in under four hours. He turned to Dakota and hugged her. A week of desert sweat, grime, antiseptic and tears reached her long before the man wearing the odour, despite that she hugged him hard, thrilled he had managed to complete the race. Javier was waiting at the finish line; he walked over to shake Paul's hand. "Well done friend, absolutely well done you should be very proud of yourself!" He slapped him on the back.

"Thanks Javier, I am but I desperately need to get in that river and stop the throbbing in my feet!" He dropped Javier's hand and started to make his way to the river, his medal bobbing on his chest. Dakota and Javier stood together watching him. "I'm so proud of that man I can't tell you," she whispered, "he has dug so deep inside himself to finish the race today; he is just amazing!" She felt a lump in her throat and swallowed hard. Javier reached for her hand and gave it a gentle squeeze. He kissed her gently on the cheek. Her face was grimy, her fingernails harboured a week of saddle soap and horse grease, and her hair needed washing, but she was still the most beautiful woman he had ever set eyes upon. "I badly need a shower," she whispered suddenly aware of how she must look. "Me too, let's get the horses sorted out and then we can go back to the flat and get cleaned up and sorted out."

"Good idea."

Chapter Twenty

Al's barn was just a few miles from where the race had concluded. Al had been busy getting the stables ready for their return. Juan and Nico whinnied their greeting as Javier and Dakota arrived with Cherry and Diego. "Hola, how did it go then?" Al came hurrying over to take Diego from them leaving Dakota to tend to Cherry. "Great, it was absolutely amazing we've had the best time ever and met some brilliant people out there they are just another breed though those endurance race people don't you think Al?" She hugged the old man tightly, "Thanks so much for trusting me to cover the race for you."

"All okay, didn't mind not having a proper wash for a week and it wasn't too cold for you out under the stars at this time of year?" Al was quite surprised Dakota had enjoyed the event as much as she seemed to have done. He shot Javier a glance, "She did brilliantly Al, she literally thrived on it." Javier gave her a weary smile, she smiled back as she cast her eyes over him, covered in a week's worth of filth, sweat, blood and dust she loved him more than she ever thought possible.

They finished putting the horses to bed for the night and were just about to leave. Al hobbled over to her, he seemed a lot older than he had when she had left a few days ago, perhaps the additional work had worn him out. "Hey Dakota, you've worked hard, done well. Take a couple of days off, have a good shower. Come back to work when you smell a bit better." Al was on top form with his humour. She laughed and playfully slapped his arm. "I did my best, but you know how hard it is to stay clean when you're getting hugged by sweaty competitors and looking after two horses sometimes you start to smell like your surroundings!" Al laughed loudly; he'd covered enough races to know.

The old man had been greatly impressed with how she had coped on the race with the two horses out in the hot desert for most of the day. Even with Javier's help in the evenings he hadn't been there to help her with the technical descents and difficult terrain she'd crossed with the horses, terrain totally unfamiliar to her. He was pleased she'd done well and had enjoyed it; he was quietly confident she would be more than capable of covering future races.

The bike came to a dusty halt at the steps to the flat. Dakota and Javier had spotted competitors on their way back to their hotels after giving thanks at the church. They had scanned the dirty, sunburned faces they passed searching for Paul. They had failed to locate him. Dakota thought he'd probably spend the rest of the day seeing to his feet, treating and dressing them properly and packing his bag for the flight home the following day. She thought about how he'd feel when he arrived home; what he would say to his wife? A terrible thing to have to do but he had his reasons. She knew she would never see him again; now she understood what Javier had told her. She would be part of these people's lives for a week, she would watch their suffering, rescue them from their plight, listen to their stories then never see or hear from them again. She would go on with her life here in Chile not knowing what was happening in Paul's, wondering if he was okay or if his life was falling apart. She hoped he'd be strong enough to face his wife and the life changing decisions he had to make.

They dumped their bags in the kitchen. Dakota insisted Javier have first shower, she was too busy trying to sort filthy clothes, clothes she doubted would ever be clean again, and shoving them into the washing machine. The smell of the desert, the horses and their sweat brought back not so distant memories of the struggles she'd overcome with the horses.

Javier emerged from the bathroom, a towel wrapped carelessly around his middle, dripping water onto the floor. She glanced up from her position on the floor at the washing machine door about to scald him for wetting everywhere; he looked beautiful. Would she ever spend a day in the rest of her life not admiring this gorgeous man she shared her life with. Not only was he beautiful inside but completely irresistible on the outside. Her heart melted, her stomach did an insane somersault, instead of scalding him she wrapped her arms around him and kissed him.

Dakota lathered on the shower gel and several applications of shampoo. She watched as the water turned sand coloured and then foamy and finally clear. She stood for a while under the jet of hot water savouring its feel. She emerged feeling and looking like a new woman. She noted Javier had hung the washing outside on the small line above the stairs. "Tell me Javier, you've not hung the washing out dressed like that?" she laughed, he still wore the carelessly wrapped towel around his middle and it wasn't hiding much. "Yeah, thought I'd give Ruben the shock of his life," he shot her that cheeky smile she could never resist, and she felt her heart melt for the second time that day as he reached out and slowly pulled her towel from her damp body. "Come on, we've got a week to make up for!" He took her arm, led her into the bedroom where she could resist him no longer and gave in to his powers of seduction.

When they woke it was getting dark. "Hey, come on, it's getting dark out, we promised ourselves dinner out tonight!" Dakota pushed him gently and he groaned. "Would you prefer to stop in?" she asked, a little disappointed, "I thought we might meet up with some of the competitors on their last night?" She hoped to see Paul. Javier pulled himself up onto his elbows and rubbed sleep from his dark lashes. "Okay just give me a minute and I'll be with you." He yawned and got out of their bed. Dakota dressed in clean clothes. It felt good to be wearing clean, fresh clothes instead of ones she'd worn for two days and sometime slept in if it had been exceptionally cold. She brushed her hair and tied it back in a band. He dressed and was ready. "Where d'you fancy going then?" he asked straightening his clothes. "How about the bar we met in?" She applied the finishing touches to her ponytail. That bar would always hold a special place in her heart. It wasn't anything special, but it was where, on that April evening he had walked into her life. It was only months ago but it seemed like they had been together for years. They always sat at the same table.

The cold beer was a huge improvement on the electrolytes dissolved in water which, along with coffee, had been their staple hydration during the race. "It tastes so good, doesn't it?" she smiled indulging herself another mouthful of the amber liquid. "Yeah, almost as good as you look," he spoke quietly. "Did you really enjoy the race as much as you told Al you did?"

"I loved it. Bring on the next one is all I can say!" She moved her bottle to one side to make room for the pizza the waitress had just brought out. "Do you really want to do another one? Don't you feel tired, were you not scared at points?"

"Of course, I'm knackered, there were places that were challenging but it was brilliant." She started to cut the pizza then paused, "I was thinking the other day when I was out in the field, how much my life has changed since I met you. If someone had told me six months ago, I would be here doing this with you I would never in a million years have believed it but now it feels like I've been here forever. The race is something I knew I would enjoy; it was so real, so raw. Talking to those people and hearing their stories, seeing their suffering but also their faces when that medal was placed around their necks, it was life changing for a lot of them!"

An endless stream of competitors passed by as they sat at the small table outside the bar, on their way to the church. They smiled and waved as they sat watching the procession. "We're almost famous now," Javier joked, "All these fans waving to us, but they'll have forgotten us by this time next week when they are all back to their normal lives!" Dakota doubted it, how could anyone go through something like that and then forget the people who shared the event with them? She didn't say anything for a while and then, "I wish we could've seen Paul one last time to say goodbye, to wish him all the best." Dakota felt saddened, she'd spent a lot of time with Paul and now he was gone. "Yes, he was a nice man," Javier agreed. "Maybe he'll be back next year to do it again."

"Do you think he might be?"

"I don't know. Some of them finish so badly you think they will never do another race then they are back to do it again. Some don't finish the first time but then they are back the following year to finish the race, and some don't come back at all. You can never tell."

They finished their beers and pizza and sat in the cool night air watching the last of the competitors walking back to their hotels preparing for their last night in Chile in the comfort of their hotel room before taking flights back to normality wherever that may be for them. Javier reached for her hand and stroked it with his thumb, "Do you think you'll be here next year?"

"What do you mean by that Javier, of course I'll be here next year with you and the year after that. Why did you ask me that?" She was shocked why he'd asked her such a thing; she thought he was over his insecurities, she felt sure he knew how much she loved him. Had this set him back? "Javier what's going on, why did you just ask me if I would be here next year, you're worrying me?"

"I'm sorry, when I saw you with Paul, I realised how different you are with people from your own background, I wondered if you miss them, if this race has made you see how much you miss the people back home and you want to go back but feel you can't tell me?"

"Oh God, I don't believe this, different? What do you mean, how am I different?" she stammered.

"You speak freely with them. You got on so well with all the competitors you came into contact with, but you were different with the English ones."

"It's good to speak freely to people, Javier you know I struggle with the Spanish language, I don't miss England or the people. We've been through all this; my life is here with you." Her face was flushed, she felt she might cry. This wasn't what she'd been expecting. "It might take me a while to learn Spanish, but I *will* learn. Our life here is different to what I've been used to, please try to understand that." She paused for a while before continuing, "The majority of the time we spend together it's just me and you or me and Al, not many other people unless I have a ride to take out. I enjoyed the race because it was new and exciting and there were lots of people to talk to." She glanced over to him seeking his approval.

He felt cross with himself for upsetting her. "I wasn't criticising you; I was just amazed at the person you became when you were out in the field. I never in a million years thought I'd meet someone who wanted to be out there in the thick of it, helping, supporting and encouraging people but I have, I met you. I don't want to lose you Dakota, but I had to ask in case you'd changed your mind." She stared at him frowning slightly "But you won't lose me I love you, when are you going to

154

understand that, Javier!" He looked drained and tired, and she wondered if that was where all this doubt he was having was coming from. "Come on, let's go back and have a good night's sleep. Things will seem different in the morning." Dakota stood and pushed the heavy metal chair away scraping it on the floor. She took cash out of her wallet and left the money beneath her plate. "Come on my man lets go back to bed." She held out her hand and he wearily took it.

Javier stared up at the ceiling. He wasn't seeing the cracks in the plaster or the cobweb in the corner. He was reliving the previous week's events; he had come to realise how much he loved this woman sleeping next to him, how much she meant to him, and it scared him beyond his wildest dreams. He knew she would finish supporting the race, but what he hadn't known was how much she would flourish. The terrain had been tough at times, she had walked a lot of it leading the horses. She had met competitors who'd struggled hard, she had given them support, walking alongside for miles, chatting to them, asking about their lives back home and they had finished. He too had hoped that they would see Paul again, wish him the best but he knew more than anyone things didn't always work out like that. Sleep wouldn't come easily as it never did when he'd been out supporting events for more than a couple of days. His body seemed to think he should be sleeping on the desert floor, not their bed. He glanced at Dakota who was sleeping soundly. Her glossy dark hair fell over her face shielding it from him. He reached over and brushed it away so he could drink in her beauty. She looked so peaceful lying there next to him. What did she see in him?

Over breakfast the following morning Dakota was upbeat, events of the night before put to one side, "So what do you fancy doing today then handsome?" she handed Javier the butter. "What do you want to do my beautiful lady?" He scraped his knife along the butter and spread it thickly on his toast. "And please don't say you want to go out into the desert for a sleep over!"

"We need to get food then I thought we could have a walk around town, have a few drinks out or something?"

155

"Yeah, sounds good to me!" He finished his toast and wiped his fingers on his jeans. It was a habit that would've infuriated her had it been anyone else other than Javier doing it. Together they cleared away the pots, Dakota hung out the last bits of washing from the race. All their clothes had eventually come clean taking two washes for some items now they were all drying and ready to be packed away for the next race that would probably be next spring.

Ruben handed over the shopping bag stuffed with their food order. "So, you're going to support the next race then?" he asked Dakota as she took the overflowing bag from him. "If Javier can put up with me for another race, then yes I am up for another one!"

"Good for you, I have to say when I first met you, I didn't think you would be the sort of girl to take up motorbikes let alone horses but its good you enjoyed it." He shot her his best black toothed smile. "Thanks Ruben, that means a lot to me!" She hauled the overflowing bag up to the flat busying herself packing it away in the cupboards whilst Javier continued chatting with Ruben in the shop. "She did great Ruben. Al is so pleased with her as am I, it's like she was born to it."

"Al's been in here, said he hoped that she'd manage okay with the horses and everything she had to do out there. He said if she could cover the races, he'd make enough money to keep the horses over the winter. I don't recon he's thinking about selling up these days now he has Dakota I think she'll have a job with him for as long as she wants it."

"That's great news. She loves working with Al and the horses and it seems to be suiting everyone!" He turned to see Dakota had returned, "Come on let's go and see what has been happening in San Pedro in the last week since we decamped to the desert."

Dakota wanted to visit the church. They pulled open the heavy wooden doors and stepped inside. They took seats on opposite sides of the aisle. Dakota offered a silent prayer to thank God for keeping them safe during the race, for looking after Cherry and Diego, she thanked God for Javier, for bringing him into her life. She prayed that they would be together forever. Lastly, she asked God to let her parents forgive her and mend the rift that had grown between them recently. She didn't think it likely that wish

156

would be granted, she hadn't heard anything from them and didn't expect to now. It looked as though she'd lost them forever.

Walking back into the late morning sunshine they visited the small mini market outside the church where Dakota wanted to pick up a few extra provisions. Inside were a few of the competitors walking around making last minute holiday purchases. Their flights were not until later that day, so they had time on their hands. Dakota knew some of them had very long flights home. People came from all over the world to compete.

After a quick lunch back at the flat they visited a different bar and sat drinking for the rest of the afternoon in the sunshine. They were both tired and needed to spend the afternoon relaxing. Al spotted them and came over to join them. He asked how they were feeling, Dakota said they were tired but in a good way. "Well, the horses are all fine I'm pleased to report."

"They were so good on the race I couldn't have asked for better. They really looked after me." Dakota said.

"I've had time to think about things, about the business whilst you were away with the horses. I feel confident we can manage between us if you are still happy for things to continue as they were Dakota?"

"More than happy Al!" She was starting to feel a little bit drunk and hoped that Al would leave before she started to slur her words. She had consumed too many beers in too hot sunshine! It was time to go back to the flat and have another sleep. Al drained his drink and departed. "Right, I'm off, I'll see you on Tuesday Dakota, I have a ride booked in for two for you to take out."

"Thanks Al, see you Tuesday!" She said waving him off from her chair, thinking she might fall over if she were to stand.

"Dakota are you okay?" Javier asked looking concerned.

"I'm starting to feel very drunk Javier, that beer has gone straight to my head" she tried to stand up without wobbling, "I think I need to go back home for a sleep." He took her arm, and they walked back to the flat.

Chapter Twenty-one

Tuesday was colder than it had been lately, there was a chill in the air. Javier planned to spend the day doing maintenance to his bike, to try and clear some of the sand out of the mechanics. Dakota was already on her bike making her way to Al's barn to take the ride out. When she arrived, Al was in the stable grooming Nico. "Will you take Juan today; I think Cherry is a bit under the weather?" he asked. Dakota opened the stable door and went to Cherry where she was standing looking a little subdued. "Hey, Cherry, what's the matter, are you not feeling too good today then?" Cherry nudged her pocket looking for a treat. "No treats today lady if you are not feeling good!" She stroked her soft nose, the little mare perked up as Dakota lavished attention on her. "She seems okay now Al, but we'll leave her here today if you are not sure."

Dakota groomed a very grumpy Juan, he was stamping his foot and shaking his head up and down as she brushed his coat. She saddled him and Diego up whilst Al prepared Nico for the ride. At ten o'clock their customers arrived at the yard all ready and excited for their ride into the desert. Dakota got them mounted on Diego and Nico and she swung her leg over the back of Juan and landed softly in the saddle. Taking up her reins she led the way.

The couple didn't speak much English, so the ride was mainly just the pair talking between themselves. Dakota listened to them talking in Spanish, she could pick out a few of the words Javier had taught her. She smiled to herself thinking of the game she would play; they'd lie in bed at night, he would try to teach her, she would get him to repeat himself, pretending she couldn't pronounce the words and then she'd tell him it was turning her on. It would always have the same ending; she would tease him into a sexual frenzy. Maybe she needed to try harder with her Spanish lessons.

The wind was gentle on their faces carrying the smell of wood smoke from somewhere off in the distance. They arrived back at the barn on schedule. Al dealt with the clients, he did after all speak fluent Spanish and Dakota saw to the horses. After they had been groomed, she fed them and then went to look on Cherry. She was prancing around in her stable wanting to go out for exercise. Dakota put on her headcollar and took her out for half an hour so she could stretch her legs.

Dakota returned Cherry to her stable and left her to eat her alfalfa. She tucked into her small lunch and Al made a pot of coffee for them to share. They chatted for a while about Al's other barn where he moved the horses to and from during peak season. They were going to have to make a trip over there and make a few repairs, clear down the old feed and alfalfa that was stored there and take away any saddlery that needed repairing. Dakota wondered if Al wanted to be rid of the place, just keep the barn they currently worked from, it was just a short distance from San Pedro and her and Javier's flat. It was a lot of upkeep, if they could try and work their bookings from San Pedro it would make better sense all round

Later that afternoon Al and Dakota had made the trip to Calama in Al's battered truck to collect more feed for the horses. Al was busy putting it away in the feed room, all neatly rowed up in date order. Dakota was holding the horses for the farrier whilst he trimmed their feet. He spoke very poor English so she asked Al to swap duties, he could chat to the farrier, and she could heave the feed bags around. She arrived home later that evening dirty and hungry.

Javier had been busy working on his bike all day and was covered in oil and grease. He undressed in the kitchen and put his clothes into the washing machine before heading into the bathroom for a shower. Dakota prepared their evening meal and poured wine from the fridge. Once showered and dressed Javier sat at the table and she served up their meal. "This looks great!" He tucked into the food on his plate. "Sorry I'm back later tonight, we had the farrier stop by to get the horses feet trimmed and I forgot he was coming. They should've been done last week but because we were out on the race, they had to be put back a week."

"Did it go okay?" he asked.

"Fine, but honestly Javier I've been giving some thought to my Spanish lessons" Javier's eyes brightened instantly

"Oh yes" his cheeky grin appeared

"I'm being serious Javier, I had to take a ride out today for two hours and I couldn't talk to them, I've got to take this more seriously"

"Dakota, I do try to teach you." He looked up from his dinner and winked at her "Okay, the way forward is I'll teach you sentences rather than words then you'll learn quicker, be able to talk to people."

"Whatever you think but I need to know what I'm talking about by next season, and I'll need to learn to write it too?"

"I can teach you how to write in Spanish later, once you know what you are saying," he grinned at her, he really was the loveliest person she had ever known.

She refilled his glass and put the bottle back into the fridge. "Man, I do love you!" She said ruffling his thick black hair.

"And I love you too" he grabbed her wrist and pulled her down to where he was sitting and kissed her quickly on her cheek. She flicked him playfully with the tea towel she had in her hand then started to clear the plates from the table. After the pots had been cleared, washed and put away she felt weary. "Let's go into the other room and relax for a bit. I'm still tired and I have no idea why, I've had plenty of sleep."

"It'll be the adrenalin from the race. It takes me ages before I can properly sleep at night and not wake up and think I'm on the long stage and I've fallen asleep at a check point or something equally as bad."

"Really? Is that what happens to you? I've not had any of that, I just feel tired. Goodness knows how the horses must feel." Javier sat on the sofa with Dakota spread across his lap. He stroked her long hair running it slowly though his fingers. It was so soothing she started to drift off to sleep and dreamed of the desert. This time she was halfway up a very rocky outcrop with Cherry who was stuck and starting to panic. Diego joined in the panic and pulled away from Cherry dragging her off Cherry's back and onto the rocks below. She woke with a start and realised she'd been dreaming. Javier was also asleep, his head tipped back on the back of the sofa, his hand was rested on her shoulder. She carefully extracted herself from him, stood up and stretched her back and hips, she was stiff and slightly sweaty from the dream.

160

She'd take a shower before turning in for the night. She woke Javier and he staggered off straight to bed.

Dakota stood under the shower rinsing the shampoo from her hair. The dream had disturbed her, it had brought to the forefront of her mind how easily an accident could happen when she was out in the desert, what if it happened and one of the horses got seriously harmed or she got harmed and the horses ran off and she was unable to catch them? She started to turn things over in her head worrying about the welfare of the horses, should she really be looking after them, was she as capable as she thought she was?

Al looked at her with shock on his face, "What? Of course, you are capable I wouldn't let you out with the horses if I thought you weren't up to the job now would I? Yes, you probably will fall off at some stage, it's happened to me lots of times in fact more times than I can remember but the only one you need to worry about running off is Juan. The other three would stop if you fell and wait for you to get back up." Al handed her their first morning coffee, "Now don't you start getting bad dreams and things just because that man of yours does!" he instructed. She placed her mug down on the floor and looked into the old man's greying and weatherbeaten face. "You and the horses mean so much to me Al I just couldn't live with myself if I let you down. You gave me a chance when I had no job and couldn't speak Spanish, I owe you a lot."

"In that case you'd better keep working for me then," he joked. "Come on don't get all down about it everything will be fine. The race you have just done was challenging and to be honest it was probably the worse terrain you will encounter on a race and you managed that just fine so you have nothing to worry about at all." The old man put an arm around her bony shoulders and hugged her against him.

Dakota felt at ease after discussing her concerns with Al and she was all ready to take the horses out for their daily exercise whilst Al got on with the stables. She quickly finished her coffee and saddled up Cherry, she could lead the other three from her. A couple of hours later she was back at the barn with all four horses unharmed. Al had finished the stables and helped her groom the horses off from the ride. He did still relish grooming and handling them despite telling her he wanted less of the hard work. The horses had been a part of his life for so long she wondered if he could ever really let go and sell them. Hopefully not she thought running the body brush over Cherry's roan body.

Chapter Twenty-two

Javier hurried outside and shoved the phone at Dakota, he had a concerned look upon his face. Dakota scowled wondering who it must be on the phone to make him look so worried. "It's your mum Dakota, you were outside, so I answered I hope you don't mind?" She frowned at him and took the phone covering the mouthpiece with her hand. "Of course I don't mind we live together for goodness sakes!" She removed her hand and took a deep breath. "Hi Mum" she said, wondering what sort of reception she was about to get this time. "Hello, Dakota, how are you?" her mother spoke softly.

"We're fine thanks Mum how about you and Dad are you both alright?"

"We're fine too, thank you. I had to call you because we had a visitor come into the shop the other day and he claimed to know you. Well not actually know you but he had a story to tell your father and I."

"Oh?"

"His name was Paul; he told us you were supporting a race he was competing in Chile last week. You supported the event on horseback, he said if it wasn't for you, he wouldn't have finished the race." Dakota smiled thinking about her new friend Paul back in London calling in on her parents to tell them all about their daughter, helping her despite having problems himself. He was a true friend.

"Not just me Mum, it was Javier too."

"Yes, he did mention him but said it was mainly you who supported and encouraged him, you often walked alongside him instead of riding your horse. He said you walked the full nine miles of the last day to encourage him to finish. Is that true Dakota?" She sounded incredulous.

"Yes, that's right I did just that. The night before Javier took him to the doctor's tent and got him patched up so he could finish the race." She didn't know where this conversation was going but her mother sounded quite impressed. "Your friend Paul has been into the shop, he spoke to your father and I about our relationship

163

with you, how you felt about things." Dakota felt her mouth go dry wondering just what exactly Paul had said. "He was a very gentle man and explained to us that you miss us and want to try to mend our relationship. He also told me that you will not be returning to England, you have your home and a very nice man in Javier. He said you are very happy; he could see that for himself when you welcomed him into your camp one night?" She continued.

"Yes, that's pretty much what happened." Dakota stood holding the phone running her hands through her hair wondering what bomb shell her mother was about to drop next.

"Please understand this is the first step in a very long path Dakota, we all must work at it, but your friend made us understand why you enjoy your lifestyle in Chile so much. I think it's time we started to call each other more often and try to mend broken bridges. What do you think?" A wave of relief swept over her and a worried Javier let out a deep breath. He'd been terrified Dakota was set for more heartbreak, but it didn't look like this call was bad news.

"I think that would be a very good idea, Mum." She replied remaining cool and calm but giving Javier the thumbs up sign. "Shall we start by you telling us about this race and how you were involved in it?"

Dakota took a deep breath and relived the events of the race from start to finish. She started from when she first went to work with the horses and Al, how their relationship had strengthened and he'd said she could cover the race; how Javier had supported her helping with the horses, going over the map and road book every night to show her what to expect the following day. She told her how she'd met Paul, and he'd left Chile without having a chance to say goodbye. She had wanted to wish him well, but it was too late he had already left. Her mother listened to everything she said and cried. "Dakota, we miss you so much please come home at least to visit us sometime soon?"

"Mum I will come to visit sometime, and I will bring Javier with me." Her mother fell silent on the other end of the phone for a few seconds and then said, "If he is your life now, you'd better bring him so we can meet him. Does he speak good English?" she asked. "Oh, and by the way we found out Miles has another woman in his life, she's moved into his house to live with him." Dakota smiled to herself, it'd been her house, her mother was only telling her to try and provoke a reaction. "That's great news, please pass on my regards to him I'm so pleased he is happy," she told her, "And Mum he does speak good English much better than my Spanish. It has been really good to talk thank you so much for calling me." They said their goodbyes and hung up.

Javier had been sitting on the seat on their tiny patio, he'd been studying Dakota's face, watching every expression during the conversation with her mother. "That didn't sound too bad from this end anyway?" he patted the seat next to him.

"Seems she's changed her mind about things with you and I" Dakota sat on the bench next to Javier and told him what had happened. "It was Paul who changed their minds," Dakota sighed loudly, and fidgeted about on the bench. "He called into their shop, told them how we'd supported him on the race, it seems it's made her realise I am worth having as a daughter after all." He put an arm around her shoulder and pulled her close to him. She closed her eyes feeling the comfort his arms always offered her, "I wish I'd taken his details because I'll never be able to thank him for what he's done." She felt a tear trickle down her cheek, and she quickly brushed it away, but Javier had already seen it and hugged her hard. "It's good news though isn't it that they want to be in touch with you again. Paul was a good man and he's done a good deed for you by speaking to your parents" he said kissing her temple.

"I know, I just wish I could thank him properly. I want to know how things have gone for him in the last week since he got back to England. I want him to be okay after he broke the news to his wife that he was leaving." She put her phone down on the table and stared up at the deep blue sky above them, the clouds looked like cotton wool drifting slowly by. "I really didn't think this day would ever happen you know?" she turned to face Javier; he was looking concerned.

"Why did you think it wouldn't happen?" he frowned.

"My parents are so stubborn it's untrue. I can't think what Paul must've said to them, but it has obviously done the trick. They want us to go and visit sometime."

"Us? am I invited too?"

165

"Of course you are. They know we're together now and Miles has got himself another woman thank goodness I think that must be why they are cutting me some slack."

"What does that mean?"

"Not being so mean!"

"That's cool. I'm so pleased for you; things are improving with your parents. It must've been hard for them, for you all losing Nina then being estranged from you by their own choice of course. I think that's probably why it's taken them so long."

"We'll have to see what happens. Mum did say it's the first step in a very long road so anything could happen." She gently she took his face in her hands, "Javier, you will come with me to England to meet them, won't you?" she whispered stroking his cheeks with her thumbs pleading in her eyes for him to go with her and meet her family.

"Yes of course I'll come. I told you before, I won't leave you ever Dakota, I never want to spend another day without you by my side." She smiled and kissed him softly on the lips.

"Come on let's go and get some dinner I'm starving!"

It was Al's day off and Javier had gone to the barn with Dakota to help her with the horses as he usually did when Al was not around. They'd finished the jobs in good time and were riding out across the desert towards the river. The decision had been made that they would ride out for longer, they'd planned lunch out on a high point giving them a great view across the huge plains of the Atacama. Dakota loved to watch how the desert changed over the weeks and months since she had come to live in San Pedro.

It had been several weeks since the race had concluded, Javier and Dakota hadn't really been out any distance into the Atacama together since then. It was a cold morning; they could see their breath out in front of them and flaring out from their horse's nostrils. Taking one of Al's lesser used maps they decided to follow a different route so Dakota could familiarise herself with it for next seasons rides. They rode down a steep bank and into a canyon with a small river flowing through. Dakota hadn't really got her bearings, she let Javier take the lead.

They followed the river for about an hour before having to go single file along the bank and through some dense vegetation.

Javier brushed the Pampas grass back from his face with his arm. The grass shed fluff as they brushed against them. Dakota rode ahead and tried to duck out of the way of the grasses. After a few minutes they came to a much wider expanse where the grasses grew further away from the riverside, and they were able to ride together again. "Wow it must have been a while since Al did this route, he's not been down to cut back the grasses. Maybe he was hoping we wouldn't find the map and that'd save him having to do the job," Dakota joked, "We'll have to come down and sort this lot out before next season rides start, it's virtually impassable."

"It might be an idea," Javier replied brushing the last of the Pampas grass from his jacket, "I don't think your clients are going to appreciate being whipped around the face by Pampas grass!"

"Maybe some of them would like it," Dakota laughed, "you never know!"

"No, you don't but I don't want to think you'd take people like that out on your own!" Sometimes Javier struggled with Dakota's sense of humour and didn't understand what she meant. She never corrected him or tried to explain unless he asked her.

For lunch Dakota located a high spot where they sat and gazed out over the ever-changing desert. Al had always marked lunch points to be at a good viewpoint allowing his clients to admire the raw beauty of this incredible place. They sat eating their lunch in silence. Dakota cupped her coffee mug trying to warm her hands. It was cold now, too cold to drink water so she took a hot drink along for their lunch stop. Tiny cars moved around on the dusty roads in and out of San Pedro throwing up huge dust clouds in their wake. Dakota tried to locate their flat in the sprawling town but without binoculars she couldn't even try to find it. They sat for a while longer, watching the tiny cars and bikes finding it slightly hypnotic as they flowed back and forth. Below them they could see the breeze whipping up tiny cyclones of sand that soon faded, not having the strength to become anything more than just a few seconds. Dakota watched as tumbleweed bobbed around like wiry green balls. It was so calm, so peaceful. She loved to ride out into the desert and enjoy the silence.

Javier packed away the flask and they mounted up ready for the ride back to the yard. Dakota hoped they wouldn't have to tackle any more overgrown areas or sharp Pampas grass on the route back. Javier had studied the map during lunch, he said the going looked good. She didn't want to be too late back to sort out the horses and give them their evening feeds before darkness fell. Nudging Cherry and Diego into trot then canter they covered a good few miles of flat desert trails before negotiating another steep descent. Dakota felt they must be coming back down to river level so almost back to the barn. She checked the map again to get their bearings and spotted the small buildings ahead that marked they would be roughly an hour away from Al's yard. She was pleased they'd managed to follow Al's map without him going through it with her. She felt confident now she'd ridden the route with Javier next to her to help out if she had been in any difficulty. Each time she came out into the Atacama she felt more at ease, she was getting to know the place and Al's maps very well. Every time she discovered new routes and different territory she embraced it; remembered as if it was imprinted on her mind.

Nico and Juan whinnied a welcome to Cherry and Diego who called back in response. "Hey, you guys you can speak to each other in a minute when you're back in your stables," Javier told them reaching down to pat Diego on the neck. "You've been a good old boy today, Diego." He swung his leg over the saddle and landed beside the horse's shoulder. He loosened off the girth and led him into the stable. Removing the saddle and bridle Javier started to brush the remains of the Pampas grass out of Diego's coat. Dakota had done the same with Cherry who had tumbleweed, and all sorts matted in her tail. She ran the body brush through and untangled the weed removing large clumps of it and brushing the cots out. "Cherry old girl, you have half the floor of the Atacama in your tail here," she murmured as she picked the weed out, "and the other half on your legs by the look of it!" She leaned down and brushed the mud and debris from the horse's legs. Cherry reached down and nuzzled the top of Dakota's head with her nose. "Hey girl, you want some treats?" she reached into her pocket and pulled out a handful of treats and fed them to the impatient mare. She took them very politely from her hand, crunching loudly whilst Dakota finished her grooming.

Dakota handed Javier feed buckets for Diego and Nico and took Cherry and Juan's herself. Slipping them inside the stable doors they locked up the barn and left for the night. Dakota was on the back of Javier's bike, her arms tight around his waist, clinging on as they sped towards San Pedro. Her face was against his back, and she breathed in his smell. Today it was mingled with the smell of horses, she thought that made him smell even better. She closed her eyes and clung to him as the wind whipped her hair back. She was so happy; she knew life could never get any better than this.

Chapter Twenty-three

It was late November; it was mid spring in Chile. It was cold but not like it was in London in the dark month of November. Dakota had only worn a light jacket in the daytime up to now, even in the coldest of the winter months in June, July and August she had never had to put more than a fleece on. She found the Chilean climate suited her well. She was looking forward to the arrival of summer in January, but Javier had warned her it could be as late as February some years. She did think it very strange that the Chilean summer was the British winter and the Chilean winter the British summer.

Dakota had her parents on her mind. They'd called and spoken with her a couple of times since their initial call in October. She felt they were gradually starting to recover from the loss of Nina if only a fraction. They had joined a local church group to help them. Paul had not been again to visit them, not since the day he had recalled the events of the race to her mother and father. Dakota hoped she would be able to thank him for being instrumental in mending the relationship between her and her family, but he had never been in touch again. She wondered about him often and had asked if her mum would pass on their details should he ever visit the shop again.

Dakota wearily carried the shopping up the stairs to the flat. Javier was still out working but she had finished for the day. Al had not been well the last couple of weeks, and she'd been worried about him. Dakota felt he'd been over doing things at the barn with the horses. She'd taken up the job of making the drive to Calama to collect the horse feed and alfalfa. She usually accompanied Al when he made the hour or so drive but today she had made the trip alone. Al had made the call to the store to order and pay for the collection in advance. Dakota had driven the sixty-two miles from San Pedro to the horse feed store. Pulling up outside she could see the men watching her from the warehouse; wondering where Al was. Thankfully Javier's evening Spanish lessons were proving useful, and she'd managed to explain that Al was not well, and she had come in his place so please could they load her truck with goods Al had ordered. The men had understood her basic Spanish and proceeded to load the pickup truck with the feed. It'd taken well over and hour to drive back with the loaded truck, but Dakota had managed to unload the alfalfa and bags of feed into the store just as Al had shown her all those months ago. She wished the horses could eat hay, but the grass didn't grow much, there wasn't enough of it to feed. Hay was a very expensive commodity in Chile Al had explained one morning over their customary coffee so the horses ate alfalfa instead. She often thought how different the horse's smelt out here compared to grass and hay fed horses back in England.

Dakota heaved the shopping bags onto the worktop in the kitchen and unpacked the goods. Once finished she ran herself a shower. She stood underneath savouring the warm water on her body as she soaped away the smell of horses and feed. She let the pounding water wash over her aching muscles for a minute longer then turned the shower off and stepped out to dry herself. She heard Javier come into the flat and called out to let him know where she was. He walked into the bathroom to find her wrapped in a huge fluffy towel with another on her head absorbing the moisture from her wet hair. "Hey, just how I like you best, naked and wet!" He snatched the bath towel away from her leaving her with only the towel on her hair. Holding out her hand, "Javier come on I'm soaking wet; can I have the towel please?" she asked.

"No, I think I'm keeping this" he moved his hand with the towel in behind his back. She stepped forward and tried to grab it, but he moved away too quickly. She stood in front of him and reached behind his back but still he was too quick for her. She stepped onto his boots and put her arms around him to try and get the towel back. She could feel he was very aroused, so she pressed her breasts hard against his grubby t-shirt making him take a breath. She ran her hands inside his t-shirt and swiftly tore it from him leaving it in a heap. The towel wrapped around her hair fell to the floor on top of his t-shirt. He was getting more aroused by the second, he scrambled out of his jeans almost falling in his haste, he grasped beneath her thighs and lifted her pushing her hard up against the tiled wall in the steamy little bathroom. She wrapped her arms around his neck and gasped as

171

he entered her, her legs around him she pulled him further into her; Javier drove himself inside her wetness and erupted making her cling to him even tighter, gleaning every bit of pleasure from him. Slowly he kissed her neck and lowered her to the floor. He held her, small, wet and naked against his warm, strong body feeling love neither of them had ever known.

Later they sat at their small dining table in the kitchen Dakota had made vegetarian lasagne after persuading Ruben to stock pasta in his little shop. Despite Javier being an avid meat eater, he was consuming the lasagne as though it were to be his last meal. "Slow down Javier you'll scrape the pattern off the plate if you're not careful." She watched him scraping away the morsels left on the plate. "There's loads more left if you want it?"

"Yeah, can I have some more please if there's enough left?" She pushed her chair back from the table and went to the worktop where the lasagne was cooling. "Here you go." She loaded two more heaps of the lasagne onto his plate and handed it back to him. "Have you had a busy day today judging by your appetite? Did you get anything to eat at all?"

"It wasn't too bad then I got home and found a naked nymph in the bathroom and things got a million times better" he smiled at her; his eyes had a mischievous glint to them. "Umm I see!" she took her seat opposite to him and continued with her dinner.

"How was your day? Is Al any better, did you hear anything from him?"

"I went to Calama to fetch the feed and alfalfa for the horses. I spoke to Al briefly he said he'd call the supplier to pay in advance and make sure they had the order ready for when I got there."

"And did they have it ready for you?"

"Yes, I had to use my poor Spanish to speak to the guys and tell them what I was doing there. I think they just wanted to watch me more for the comedy value than anything, they're the same men that are there when I go with Al, so they know who I am!"

"Did they understand you?"

"I got everything I went for, so I presume so." She finished her plate of lasagne and sat waiting for Javier to finish his second helpings. "I unloaded it all and hopefully it is as Al would like in the storeroom."

"D'you know when he'll be back at work?"

"Next week I think but we're not busy so I can manage with the horses on my own." She wondered if the horses missed Al. She thought they must do as he'd been looking after them for years now. She wished she could tell them he would be back soon.

The following morning Dakota was busying herself mucking out the horses when her phone rang. She hurriedly fumbled in her jeans pocket to answer but didn't recognise the number. Frowning, wondering who it could be calling her out here she answered "Hello?"

"Hello Dakota, it's Paul, from the race…"

"*Paul*," she shrieked down the phone, "How lovely to hear from you, how are you doing?"

"I've been thinking about you and thought I'd better call and explain myself somewhat. Better late than never I suppose! I hope you didn't mind I went to visit your parents after I returned from the race. I felt you'd helped me so much and I didn't even get a chance to properly thank you. I thought it was the least I could do under the circumstances."

"Yes, I'm so grateful you've called because I wanted to thank you for going to see them and explaining everything about the race."

"Is everything okay with your parents?" he asked tentatively.

"My mum called me after your visit and told me what you'd said to them. It certainly struck a chord, now she calls me every few weeks and we're back in touch again. She even asked me to visit and said I could bring Javier!"

Paul laughed, "I did tell her how good you both were to me, if it hadn't been for both of you, I wouldn't have finished that race." He sounded distant; she wondered what he was doing as he spoke to her. "How are things with you now, did you make your decision about your wife?" She didn't know if she should ask or not but decided she would anyway. "Yes, I did, I told you I'd decided to leave her but when I got back, she told me all about it, that it was over, and she'd been stupid and wanted to try again. The easy thing would've been to walk away and leave her, but I love her and after she admitted everything and said it was over I told her I knew about it. She was devastated I'd not said anything,

173

but we've decided to make another go of it so here we are several weeks post-race and still together!" He sounded happy.

"I'm pleased for you Paul, you deserve happiness!"

"Thanks, and I'm delighted for you now things are better with your family. How is Javier by the way?"

"He's fine. I'm at work with the horses now and he's at work too but not with me today unfortunately. I'll tell him you called and send your regards?"

"Yes, that'd be great. Can I call you both again sometime?" "That would be cool, I'm so pleased you rang I've spent so long wondering how you are and sorry we didn't get a chance to say goodbye to each other please do keep in touch I'd like that very much."

"It was your mum who passed on your number, she said every time you call you tell her you wish you could see how I was getting along, she said you were upset that you didn't say goodbye properly. She had my number from an order I placed at the time I went in to see them. She called me yesterday, asked if it was okay if she passed my number on."

"Wow she really is changing. Please keep in touch and take care Paul."

The call ended. Dakota felt delighted, now she knew Paul was okay and had decided to patch things up with his wife despite their differences. He'd said he would keep in touch and hopefully when they went back to England to visit her parents, they could even meet up and talk over old times. Dakota threw the muck into the wheelbarrow with great enthusiasm. She felt incredibly happy with how things were going in her life.

Dakota rode out alone that afternoon feeling life was good, she had Javier, a job she loved, the relationship with her parents had improved and she'd heard from Paul and top it all off Christmas was on the horizon! The sun was shining as she swung her leg over Cherry's back and into the saddle. She took the other three horses by their lead reins and ventured off into the desert. On these rides alone she used the time to think about things, process what life had sometimes thrown and sometimes gifted her. The call from Paul was filling her thoughts as they trudged across the sand on a circular route that afternoon. Later, back at the barn as she was putting Cherry's saddle and bridle away, Al appeared round the corner of the stables making her jump. "Al! God, you made me jump, how are you? I didn't expect to see you until next week?" she asked concerned as to why he'd made an early appearance. "Feeling much better now thanks Dakota. I'm just going to have to start slowing down, taking more of a back seat with things out here you know? I've been told I'm doing too much."

"Are you okay, come and sit down here?" She moved buckets that were taking up the space on their bench. "I'll put the coffee on, you can tell me all about it?" She smiled at him reaching for the pot they brewed coffee in. "Just let me finish here a moment." She hurriedly put the horses bucket feeds into the stables. She would finish the alfalfa when she had spoken with Al. He sat down on the bench whilst she busied herself with coffee. "Here," she handed him his mug. "I have really missed you Al and I know the horses have too!" He chuckled but she could tell he wasn't filled with his usual joviality; he seemed to have grown old very quickly. "Have they been telling you so?"

"Not actually, but they look out for you. When I turn up in the morning, I get the feeling they think only half the troops are here." She sat next to him with her coffee mug in her hand ready to listen. "Tell me what's been happening with you Al?"

"The doctor has told me to take things easier Dakota it's my heart and I have high blood pressure; it isn't good this getting old business." She stared down at the ground for a long time before answering him. "Why don't you let me take over here completely Al you know I can manage, and you fetch the feed and do the deliveries at the stable blocks for the rides next season, I'm sure the guys will load the feed into your truck for you and I can unload it this end?"

"I don't know, part of me thinks I should sell up and retire completely. I thought I could manage with you helping me out as much as you do but now, I just don't know, I have the other stables to think about too not just these." She could see the conversation was upsetting the old man, his eyes had started to glaze over, and he was staring away into the distance. He loved his horses and parting with them would be very painful. "Al, what do you want to do, tell me honestly?"

175

"I want to be twenty-three again and able to cope with four horses, taking out rides and all the running around and planning that it involves. I hate being old, having my body dictate to me what I can and can't do and how much it tires me out." Dakota felt so very sorry for him this dear old man sitting on the old wooden bench next to her. She had loved working with Al, he had taught her so much about horses, the desert and life in San Pedro. He'd been like a father figure to both her and Javier and she felt incredibly sad to see him so upset.

Dakota persuaded Al to return to work but on light duties. She would muck out and heave the feed around and Al would groom and tidy around. He would collect the feed, but she was to unload it. Al had asked if there was any chance, they could get Javier to come and help out on the odd day and Dakota said she felt sure he would be able to. She rode home that night with a heavy heart. Javier was already home when she got in and sensed her mood. "Are you okay today beautiful lady, you seem a little down?"

"Not really," she put her arm around his neck and kissed him tenderly. "Old age is a cruel thing Javier," she said lifting her eyes to meet his. "Poor old Al is in a state, he doesn't want to retire but the doctor has told him he needs to. His blood pressure is through the roof, and he has a heart condition."

"Um, yes, I know, he's been like it for a while, but he does seem to have got worse very quickly, doesn't he?"

"I managed to get him to agree to groom if he feels up to it and tidy around. He'll drive to Calama to collect the feed as we need it, and I'll take on the bulk of the horse care and unload the feed once he gets back. He just can't manage it anymore." Javier took her hand and led her into the lounge they sat on the sofa, the window was open, and they could hear the noise of the town outside. Dakota continued, "I'll be okay managing without him, but he's asked me to see if you'll come and help out the odd day here and there as we need it?"

"Of course I will, that goes without saying I would help Al with whatever he wants me to do." She sat silently staring at the wall chewing the inside of her cheek for a few minutes and then took Javier's hand. "You know I sold my house in London; I have enough money to buy Al out of the business if he wants to sell it so we could take over the horses and the treks. He's worried about having to sell the horses, but this way he wouldn't have to," she paused for a while, the plans running through her head. "He could come and visit us every day if he wanted and just sit and drink coffee and chat. He knows I love the horses and would look after them well, he wouldn't have to worry about anything. What do you think?" Javier looked at her for a long time before replying. He could see how enthusiastic she was, and he knew how much Al and the horses meant to her. "I think if that's what you want to do then let's do it, let's go to the barn tomorrow and speak to Al. The worse he can say is no!"

"Seriously, do you think we should do it?" Her mood had changed to excitement.

"Absolutely, but it will be tough you know?"

"I know, but we have enough money to buy the business and build a small house on the land at the side of the barn, that would allow us to live on site and we wouldn't have to travel every day."

"I take it this isn't a spur of the moment decision then?" he smiled wryly realising she had given this a great deal of thought. "Do you *really* want to do this with your money Dakota, it will mean getting a lot more bookings than Al has coming in, we will have to advertise if it is to justify both of us running it and a house too?" he warned.

"I know but we have friends in England who could put something online for us and we could take bookings in advance, we could advertise so much better and make this really work." She was so excited then suddenly felt guilty for feeling that way, it was only going to be made possible because of Al being ill. "I hope Al is okay about it. I don't want him to think I feel he isn't running his business properly?" she added feeling acutely aware she could hurt the old man's feelings with her proposition. "He wouldn't think that at all. He knows you're a driven person, a determined person who will only have his and his horses' best interests at heart. Shall I come down with you tomorrow and we can speak to him then?"

"Yes, let's talk to him tomorrow, let him know it is an option if nothing else and we can put his mind to rest."

Chapter Twenty-four

Early the next day Al was already at the barn huffing and puffing putting morning feeds in for the horses. Javier and Dakota rode up on his bike. "Hola, morning Al," Dakota shouted as she dismounted and removed her helmet. "How are you feeling today?" She asked running her fingers through her hair before hugging him. She collected the coffee pot to fill and heat up. "Yeah not too bad but I haven't started the mucking out yet." Al replied. He looked tired and jaded.

"Good, I've brought Javier along with me today to help with that whilst you are not even supposed to be thinking about it!" She wiggled her finger at him disapprovingly. "Now you be in charge of the coffee and when it's ready we need to sit down and talk to you!"

"Gracious! Well, it sounds like a brilliant idea to me!" Al slapped his hands on his thighs then shook Javier's hand and then Dakota's. "It would make me so happy if you took over the business it really would!" He was smiling so broadly Dakota couldn't believe his mouth would stretch so far. "And you don't mind if I come down and see you all every now and again?"

"I'd be cross if you didn't," Dakota replied. "Honestly Al I'm so pleased you have agreed, it will be great for all of us don't you think?"

"Yes, it will, and you'll keep my maps for your rides?"

"I wouldn't dream of changing them in any way at all." Javier had all the maps out on the floor and was pouring over them with Al. "You need to go over a few of these with me though Al I'm not one hundred percent familiar with this one and this one," he pointed to two of the maps. "And that one we went on a while back I will need to sort out the vegetation down there before we start taking rides out that way again it's like a wilderness!" Al laughed. "Yes, it is. I wasn't going to take any rides out that way again, but you are welcome to now if you want to it was just such a lot of maintenance, I couldn't really be bothered with all the work it entailed, clearing such a large stretch of land just for a few rides each season so I left it."

178

"I will go down and sort it all out so once the season starts again, we can use it."

"How are you planning on running things with clients? You know by now we don't really get a lot of customers, have you any ideas or thoughts on how you will improve things?" Al asked. "I'm hoping that friends and family back in England will put something on the internet for us, maybe develop a web page or something along those lines so people visiting San Pedro know we are here and what we offer. Hopefully that will bring some business our way and we'll have an idea of what we can expect to make for the season. I want us to make enough money to be able to keep Javier and myself busy here," Dakota explained to him. "Will you be able to help us out the odd time if we are busy with things, just keep an eye on this place if all four horses are out?"

"It would be my absolute pleasure!" Al was still smiling and poured them all another cup of coffee to celebrate their business deal.

Javier and Dakota rode out together that morning with their life together in a new light. "If you're serious about building a house out here we'll need to start making enquiries about it" Javier said nudging Diego into a trot to catch up with Juan. "I think we need to start sorting that out sooner rather than later though, don't you?" Dakota turned to face him, "We don't want to be living in a mess and trying to run a business in the middle of the tourist season, do we?"

"I'll speak to a friend of mine who's in the building trade and see how quickly he can sort us out once we get the plans done and approval for it, that could take an age." He was thinking of all the things he would need to do, "I'll let Ruben know we will be moving out at some stage just so he knows ahead of someone telling him we are planning on having a house built." Javier was in a state of mild panic about it all. He'd been expecting to spend the rest of his life in the small flat over Ruben's shop and covering races to make his money. Now they were on the brink of buying their own business and having plans drawn up to have a house built too! He knew Dakota had money, but he'd never asked her about it or what she had intended to do with it. He thought she was going to use it when times got tough over the

179

winter months, now he realised it was the best thing they could have done, buy the business and the horses and make it really work. Dakota was so clued up on running things and she had friends and contacts in England who could help them.

At lunchtime Javier went off on his bike to locate his builder friend and discuss houses. Dakota sat with Al and explained to him that they wanted to build a house on site so they could always be with the horses. "You know Dakota you're a good woman, you have a very kind and big heart" Al said, "You make that man of yours very happy. In all the years I've known him I've never seen him like this." Al continued, "Javier was ten years old when I first knew him, I've known him a long time." Dakota remained silent. "You two will be very happy here with the horses and I hope very much to be part of your lives for a long time to come. I was worried what would happen to them if I had to sell up but now you've put my mind at rest, I know the horses will be in good hands and well provided for. Thank you, Dakota, for being such a good friend." Dakota smiled at him and put her hand on his thin leg. "It is *you* Al that has been the good friend. How would I have managed all this time if you hadn't given me a chance and let me come and work with you?"

"It has been a pleasure my girl, a real pleasure and I can't wait to get back and tell my good lady wife the news she'll be so pleased. She will be glad to hear that the plans I got approved for a house on site will be put to good use now too if you want to use them that is."

"*Really*? You already have plans? that's brilliant news I'm sure it will save us time somewhere along the line if we can use them? Are you sure you want us to take over the running of everything from today, do you not want to wait until the funds have been transferred?" Things were just getting better, Al had planning permission for a house on site so now things could get moving even quicker! "You may as well start running it all now, the money will be transferred by the end of the week and then all this will be yours. I have planning permission for a house next to the barn I just never got the money or the inkling to build it. The plans are for a four bedroomed house, you are welcome to look at them, to have them if it's the sort of place you want to build. I'll put you in touch with my lawyer." Al was also running though the list of things he was going to have to do, "I'll make sure I call the feed supplier to let them know you'll be taking over and they give you as good deal as they have me all these years. I'll settle the account then it'll all be ready to be transferred into your name." Al was well on the way to the final stages of handing over his business. He seemed to have everything in hand and ready for Dakota and Javier to take over. She'd never dreamed it would be so easy.

Dakota was swept away with how fast everything was moving, and Al had been open to the changes she wanted to put into place. He'd explained to her if he had the money and the opportunity he would have built a house at the barn. He was pleased to hear their plans and ideas for making the business work. "I'm always here for you if you need me to come and make coffee or just want me to come down and groom a bit."

"Al, please don't offer to do that because I want you to be here all the time. It won't be the same without you." She rather hoped he'd pop down and visit them daily. She wanted him to be part of the changes they were planning to make; she didn't like the idea of him turning up one day to see they'd altered everything. "One thing though Al, can I keep the coffee pot and use it when you come to visit?"

"Yes," he laughed, stood up rather shakily and handed her the pot. "Here, now this is officially yours!" She took the pot and hugged the old man.

"Thank you, Al, thank you for everything!"

To celebrate that evening Javier had been out and bought a bottle of champagne. He'd never drunk champagne before, but he knew Dakota liked it and he wanted to celebrate their good news. "How was the afternoon with Al, he hasn't changed his mind has he?" Javier asked getting the champagne out of the fridge. "Where did you get that from?" Dakota spotted the bottle in Javier's hand. "I didn't know such things existed in San Pedro let alone you going off and getting your hands on a bottle!"

"I went to the hotel and asked them to sell me a bottle so we can celebrate the news, our news."

"Oh yes, how did you get on with the builder?" Dakota returned to the kitchen.

"Good news, he doesn't have a lot on now in terms of building work so we can be first on his list."

"Wow, I have to tell you that Al has plans for a house to be built at the barn, I've brought them back with me to see what you think"

"Oh yeah, Al told me ages ago he had planning permission for a house next to the barn and I had completely forgotten about it. We can look at the plans after dinner and see if anything needs changing but if it doesn't, work can start in as little as two weeks' time." Dakota's mouth dropped open, she stood holding the champagne glasses in the middle of the kitchen floor staring at him "That is just amazing, you certainly wouldn't get a house started in two weeks in England unless you dug the foundations yourself!"

"If you don't want any changes to the plans and things go as predicted we can move in the start of February all being well."

"Best fill these up then!" She put the glasses down on the work surface and opened the plans on the kitchen table. She knew how to read plans it was something Miles had taught her so she could understand the layout of the house. She explained it all to Javier, it was perfect. "Brilliant I couldn't have planned it any better myself," she said as she chinked her glass against his, "this is just perfect!" She folded the plans ready to hand over to Javier's builder friend.

"I called the bank today and have arranged transfer of the money into Al's account, but he's more than happy we start running the business from now and he'll take a back seat."

"I can't believe he's taken it so well! I thought he'd be really upset to be giving it up. It's been his life for so many years, but he's glad to have us taking it over. I suppose if it were anyone else, he might have his reservations."

"I think he's a lot sicker than he lets us know and the business has been a worry to him for a while. He didn't want to sell the horses and that was stressing him out too now he's sold them to us, he knows we'll look after them and he knows our plans so he can be as much a part of all this as he wants to be. All this has put his mind to rest and given him enough money to look after Catalina and himself for the rest of their lives." Dakota said hoping that Al and Catalina were also raising a toast to their part of the deal. She hoped Catalina would be happy now that Al was retiring and would be taking life a little easier.

They sat on the sofa drinking the champagne and discussing plans for their future. It had changed on a dime, one day in the flat where Javier thought he would live forever and the next they are discussing plans for running the business they've just bought and getting a huge house built. "Javier, can I ask you something?"

"Pretty lady you can just about ask me anything" he winked at her; he was such a smoothie she thought.

"You've never asked about my financial situation, why is that?"

"Umm, that's your business, I thought you'd tell me if you wanted me to know how many pesos you have?"

"You know I had a lot of money from my house sale that I kept to one side for our lives out here."

"No Dakota that is money from your house sale it is money you earned, I know you wanted to use it to live out here but what would you've done if you'd had to move back to England, you'd have no money if you'd spent it here living with me."

"But Javier, you looked after me when I moved in here, you paid all the rent and everything until my house sold."

"That's different, I need to look after you."

"No you don't Javier, that is old fashioned!" He was alarmed by her harsh words, "No that is how it is I'm the man in this relationship and I look after you!" He told her gently taking her hand in his. She lifted her eyes to meet his, his kind eyes, his handsome features framed by his mop of hair. He melted her heart every time he gave her that look. Afraid she had been a little harsh with her words she spoke softly,

"Javier, I have a lot of money by Chilean standards. I have enough to build and furnish the house and to buy Al out of the business and still have money left over. I want us to run the business together, by that I mean you support races on your bike, and I will continue with the horses but when you are not working, I would like us to look after the horses together and take rides out. What do you think?"

"Yes, absolutely I agree, I want this to work but I don't have a business brain like you do. I don't understand websites and internet pages, so I must leave that side of things to you." That didn't matter one bit to Dakota, she didn't care if he had a business brain, he was everything to her and she wanted him to be as happy about this as she was. "Dakota, you know I want you to be happy here with me and I'll do everything in my power to make that happen."

"I don't completely understand websites and internet pages either that's why I need someone in England to do it for me. I have the foresight but not the ability to do it. We will do this together Javier, and it'll be our home and our business."

He leaned over and kissed her cheek. "You're the boss and I'm the muscle," he flashed her his cheeky smile.

Unable to sleep with the excitement they tossed and turned in bed that night. Earlier in the evening Javier had broken the news to Ruben his landlord. "I saw Al a few weeks back, he didn't look well at all. I'm glad to hear that you've taken the horses over from him he'll be pleased to have good people looking after them," Ruben had shaken Javier's hand. "And that woman of yours, when are you going to make it decent?" Javier felt himself blush at the very thought of asking Dakota to marry him. "Don't know yet. We haven't been together that long you know; it isn't even a year yet, it's way too soon to know if she wants to marry me or not."

"Not even a year and you're having a house built and buying a business, but you don't want to put a ring on her finger? Can't you see the woman loves the very bones of you Javier, I can bet you she'd jump at the chance to be your wife. Now get on and ask the question!" Although the last thing Ruben had wanted to do was open old wounds his comment had done just that. Javier lay in bed thinking of Petra, the woman who he'd been so sure would be his wife all those years ago. She had left him in San Pedro alone with his heart in a thousand pieces. He was sure Dakota knew how he felt about her but what if he was wrong? What if she felt the same way as Ruben had suggested? What if she thought buying a business together and having a house built would equate to a diamond ring sometime soon? Dakota was nothing like his ex in any way at all, but it plagued him, and he lay awake turning it over and over in his mind. Was she getting her house in order ready to become Mrs Gonzales?

He tossed and turned, at three-thirty Dakota sat up and looked over to him, the bedroom was in pitch darkness. "Javier what is it? What's bothering you my darling?" She reached over and stroked his hair gently, "Are you worried about what we are about to take on?"

"No, it isn't that" he replied quietly lying with his back to her.

"Well, what is it then?" She touched his shoulder and gently rolled him over so she could look at him in the darkness. "Tell me please Javier?"

"I don't know how to tell you Dakota," he stared up at the ceiling terrified of the impact his words could have on their relationship. "I don't know how you're going to react to what I have to say." Her heart started to thud hard and fast in her chest and her mouth went dry. Was he about to tell her he didn't want to buy the business or get the house built? Was he about to announce that he didn't love her enough to want to spend the rest of their lives living and working together or had he had enough of her and wanted her to return to England without him? She swallowed hard, "I think you need to tell me whatever it is." She spoke quietly, the bed sheets gripped in her hand preparing herself for the worse. He shuffled up the headboard and faced her across the bed. He took her free hand in his and looked into her face, the features he could only just make out in the darkness. "Dakota, I can't marry you!" He said letting go of her hand, waiting for her reaction.

"What? Is that it?" she was so relieved it hadn't been anything worse. "You don't mind?" Javier choked.

"Why would I mind? We've never spoken about marriage; we haven't even been together a year yet Javier. I was with Miles five years and thought he was the one until I had my eyes opened and realised, he wasn't. Why would I want to rush into marriage?" Javier was so relieved he fell back onto the bed with a thump. "I thought with the business and house you would want some sort of commitment from me!" he breathed.

"I have commitment from you Javier, I have you turning up to be with me every night and still here in our bed with me in the morning why would I want a ring on my finger to change that? I know how you feel about me, you tell me every single day."

"It was something Ruben said that made me think about it then I started to panic thinking you wanted me to propose so we could live the dream."

"Well, you didn't need to panic and if Ruben really knew me he would realise what I think is important in life and diamond rings are not part of that equation," she leaned over and kissed him, "I love you Javier Gonzales don't ever forget that." He held her against him until the light of morning shone through the curtains waking them.

Chapter Twenty-five

It was mid-morning on Christmas day. Dakota and Javier were at the barn with the horses cleaning them out and hurriedly handing out feeds so they could rush back to their flat and spend the rest of the day with Al and his wife Catalina. Dakota was cooking a traditional English Christmas lunch for them all. She had even managed to get her mother to send her a Christmas pudding and after dinner mints. Dakota was so excited about spending their first Christmas together. She hurried around cleaning out and emptying the wheelbarrow as Javier heaped alfalfa into the horse's buckets. "Just think this time next year we won't have to ride to the barn, we can just step outside our door and walk over a few steps to the horses it will be so cool!" She gasped as she hurried from one stable to the next. "Okay I think we are finished here. We'll be back later my lovelies." Dakota locked up the barn behind them and swung her leg over Javier's bike. Gripping his jacket, she hung on as the rode back to the flat.

Back home the turkey was cooking away filling the flat with the aroma. Javier had never had an English Christmas dinner, and Dakota was looking forward to getting it all out on the table with a vegetarian version for herself. Al and Catalina where at the door shortly after they arrived home, Javier sat them down on the small sofa with himself and Dakota on the floor where they exchanged gifts. Al and his wife had brought Dakota a small silver horse necklace. It was beautiful she put it on fastening it around her neck. "Thank you both so much it's beautiful!" She was thrilled with such a thoughtful gift. Javier handed Al his present Dakota had spied whilst perusing in the mini market by the church. It was a new and shiny coffee pot. "I figured you gave me yours, so you'll need another one now!" Javier had a bottle of wine and Catalina had a small bracelet with a horse on. Al's wife didn't speak very good English, but they managed to spend the most wonderful day together laughing and enjoying Dakota's best efforts at lunch. After the huge feast they sat in the lounge and played cards. Dakota went into the bedroom to call her parents back in London. Sitting on their bed she made the call back to England. "Hi Mum, its Dakota," she said hearing her mother's voice on the other end of the phone. "How's Christmas in London this year?"

"There is only your father and I so it's very quiet," she replied, "how about you, what's your Christmas like in San Pedro?"

"I have Al and his wife here and Javier. They're playing cards in the lounge at the moment. I have just made their first English Christmas dinner, and they thoroughly enjoyed it especially the Christmas pudding and after dinner mints you very kindly sent. We don't have things like that out here," she explained.

"Really? That's terrible, no Christmas pudding?"

"Nope none at all but we had one at this house and I really appreciate you sending it for us Mum." Christmas pudding had always been a firm favourite of Dakotas, her mother knew this and had thought to send one to Chile for her.

"Thank you for your gifts, Dakota, it was very thoughtful of you. Please tell me more about your business and your new house plans if you have the time!"

Dakota proceeded to tell her mother about their business which was well underway, Paul had taken it upon himself to help them with the website and internet page. They had already received a lot of bookings for the end of January through to May and they were still coming in. Dakota told her about their house, the building work was well underway, and they hoped it would be finished by the beginning of February if everything went to plan. Dakota had been to Calama to choose fixtures and fittings, and she'd ordered furniture as their flat was a lot smaller than the house would be and she had four bedrooms to furnish. As Dakotas mother listened to her daughter's plans and ideas for her future in Chile realisation dawned on her she wasn't ever going to come back to England to live. "And how is Javier? What will he do with himself once you start your season with the horses?"

"We are going to be running everything together. He rides too and helps me with the horses all the time. The only exception is when he is away covering a race but if the organisers want horse cover too, I'll be with him on the race just at the other end of the field and on horseback instead of the bike."

"I see, are you truly happy with this man Dakota I mean truly?"

"I am. I'm happier than I have ever been in my entire life. He is my life, and I never want to be without him."

"I understand. Well, I hope you have a good Christmas ours is almost over now being four hours ahead of you in the UK and a happy new year to you all in San Pedro." She rang off. Dakota wasn't sure if her mother was starting to come around to her way of thinking and realise, she wasn't just sitting around in the desert watching the stars but making a go of her life, setting up their business, building their own home and having Javier by her side through it all.

Back in the lounge the excitement had reached fever pitch as Catalina was beating the men at cards. Dakota was off to finish the horses for the day and would see them when she got back later. She needed the time away to think about her parents back home alone without either daughter enjoying lunch with them this Christmas day. Dakota's thoughts turned to Paul and wondered what he was up to on this day, how would he be spending it and were things still on the mend with his wife she wondered? Last time they had spoken was when she had asked him to help her with the website and they had been getting along really well with their reconciliation. Paul told her they'd been away together and were planning to renew their vows the following year. She'd asked him if he would ever take part in another race and his reply was probably not. She hoped they would meet again but their rare and long phone calls seemed to suffice. Her thoughts drifted to her ex-Miles; she hoped he was having a good Christmas too with the new woman in his life. He hadn't been a bad man in the grand scheme of things, and she didn't want him to be miserable.

The horses heard her coming and whinnied their welcome. She took them out for an hour walking and thinking how glad she would be when they lived at the barn, and she could make a corral for them then they could have turn out all the time and not have to stay in the stable most of the day. When she returned home Al and Catalina were getting ready to leave. Al hugged her. "Did you give those horses my regards?" he asked.

"Always Al and they did ask when you were coming to see them again?" She smiled and kissed Catalina on the cheek. "Soon I will come soon once Christmas and New Year is over, I will come and see them. I miss them too you know," he patted her shoulder and shook Javier's hand. "Good night both of you and thank you so much for a truly wonderful day, we've enjoyed it so much." Dakota hugged Catalina; she was such a frail woman Dakota wondered how she had ever managed to help Al with the horses at all. She looked as though a puff of wind would blow her over, but she had a strong grip as she hugged Dakota. "Thank you for English Christmas dinner," she said, "thank you Dakota!" She kissed her cheek for a second time then left hand in hand with her husband.

"Right then big man, are you washing or drying?" Dakota asked running hot water into the sink, piled high with the dishes from lunch. "Drying!" He grabbed the tea towel and started to dry and put the pots away. The draining board was tiny, she had to wait for him to catch up due to the volume of pots the Christmas day dinner had created. "Good job we have Ruben down below to lend us these dishes," she commented, rinsing the huge roasting dish off and handing to him to dry. "We won't have him quite so close when we're living with the horses though, just remember that."

"I know but at least we will have more space to store more groceries and more pots and pans to cook with."

"Very true," he replied, "but I will miss the flat and living in the middle of town. It will be very quiet living in the desert." Dakota stopped washing up and looked over at him. "Are you having second thoughts Javier?"

"No, I will just miss living here that's all. I'd much rather live with you in our big house with four horses as our neighbours." He flicked her with the tea towel, and she splashed washing up water at him. "Don't!" she warned, "Or you'll get very wet!" Javier continued drying up the pots and pans putting Ruben's pots to one side so he could take them down to him in the morning when the shop would be open again.

After everything was cleared away, they sat quietly on the sofa reflecting on the day. Dakota's mother had sent her a parcel containing everything she loved and knew Dakota wouldn't be able to obtain in Chile. Inside the parcel as well as the Christmas pudding and after dinner mints, was a bottle of orange liqueur. She poured herself a large glass and added ice, offering one to

Javier. "Can I taste yours first in case I don't like it?" she handed him her glass and he took a mouthful. "Okay lady, I like it I'll have some if you don't mind sharing?" Dakota poured him a glass and added ice cubes. "This is one thing I miss from England which is weird because now my drink of choice would be Pisco if we were out drinking cocktails."

"I don't know how you can drink that dreadful stuff," he was referring to Pisco, "It's disgusting!"

She laughed, "Each to his own Javier, each to his own!" They chinked their glasses together in a toast and sat savouring the liqueur. Javier casually reached into his pocket and brought out a small box. "Hey, looks like Father Christmas forgot this one!" he handed her the tiny box. Inside, a beautiful pair of earrings to match the necklace Al and Catalina had brought her. "Javier they are beautiful absolutely beautiful," she gushed fastening them into her ears, she stood to admire them in the mirror, "Thank you so much!" She kissed him then padded over to the drawer to retrieve his gift. "And he didn't forget you either!" She handed him a larger box, inside was a mobile phone.

"Wow my first ever mobile phone!" He marvelled at it turning it over in his hand and wondering how he would ever figure out using it. "Thanks Dakota that is brilliant!" A while ago he had told her he'd never owned a mobile phone and, to be quite honest, Dakota found it tiresome waiting for him to arrive home before she could start dinner or if she was running late, she had to call Ruben to go upstairs and let him know. Sometimes he borrowed one, when he was out on races or multi day events so she could at least try to get hold of him if there was an emergency. Now they were running a business together they needed to contact each other at all times. "I've programmed everyone's number in - mine, Al's and a few others I could think of but all in all about six numbers!"

"Thanks," he smiled staring at the machine in his hand. "You need to teach me to use it now!" He handed the phone over to her and his first lesson began.

Dakota was snoozing in bed the next morning when her phone rang startling her. It was early she thought, looking at her watch, only six-fifteen. Who could be ringing her now? She saw Al's number flash up. "Hey Al, this is early, are you okay?"

"It is me Dakota, it's Catalina." The old lady started to cry on the phone. Dakota sat upright in bed. "Catalina what's the matter? What's happened?" Her heart started to pound hard in her chest. Javier rolled over and sat up taking the bedcovers with him, his eyes wide. "Catalina, can you tell me what has happened, why are you so upset, has something happened to Al?"

"Wait I hand you to my son." Dakota was now even more puzzled; she didn't even know Al had a son let alone one that lived close by. "Dakota this is Al's son Sergio I'm so sorry my mother wanted to call you this early, but I have bad news" Dakota looked over at Javier, her face was as white as a sheet. He was staring at her, waiting for news. "What's happened, why is Catalina, er, your mum so upset?" she asked Sergio.

"My father passed away early this morning. He died in his sleep. My mother said you two were to be told before anyone else, that is you and Javier?" Dakota felt grief hit her like a train, the tears welled up in her dark eyes and tumbled down her cheeks, she looked at Javier and he knew, he cast his eyes down to the bed clothes and bit hard onto his bottom lip. "I'm so sorry, so very sorry. Is there anything we can do to help?" her voice was trembling despite her best efforts.

"No. Thank you. Thank you for your kind words and for making his last day so pleasurable. My mother told me what a lovely day they spent with you yesterday, she wanted me to tell you they had talked about it well into the night when he fell asleep. It was most probably the last thing he thought about before he passed away. I will let you know about funeral arrangements if you would like to attend?"

"Of course we want to come, please keep me updated and if there's anything at all we can do please let us know." She ended the call and looked at Javier. He was still staring at the bed cover. "Javier, I didn't even *know* Al and Catalina had a son," she wept into her hands. "How come he didn't tell me I thought I was his friend?" she sobbed. Javier moved over the bed and took her in his arms. She sobbed against his shoulder; he held her tighter and closer.

"They weren't close Dakota. He hardly ever spoke about him to anyone so don't take it personally." He hugged her feeling her tears fall down his bare chest, struggling to control his own grief.

192

"He's going to let us know about funeral arrangements but it's so sad, so very sad he won't be down to see the horses again, he won't be dropping by to have coffee and a chat with us, he won't be there to tell us any more of his stories or see how the house is progressing, Javier, what will we do without him?" She wept uncontrollably. Javier felt horribly miserable. Al had looked after him, looked out for him for most of his life and now, in the blink of an eye he was gone. "Dakota, you know he will always be with us." She dried her tears dabbing her face on a tissue Javier handed to her. Her fingers felt for the necklace Al and Catalina had given to her only the day before. "All the plans we had included him in, I thought he'd live forever!" She started to cry again Javier handed her a bundle of fresh tissues. "Come on, we need to go and tell the horses" He climbed out of bed and dressed feeling a huge weight in his chest, the weight of grief sitting like a rock. He didn't know life without Al but now he would.

At the barn Dakota cried almost all the time she was with the horses. Javier spoke to the horses in Spanish. He told them Al had passed away that perhaps they'd feel his presence around them for a few days. Dakota didn't ask him what he had said to the horses, she thought it might be something to do with the Chilean belief in afterlife. They rode out in silence, somehow the grand plans for their house and corral now seemed a necessity and not something wonderful to look forward to. Dakota wanted to be with the horses more than ever and to take care and love them. If Al was up there watching, she wanted to make him very proud.

After a couple of hours out in the fresh air they turned the loop and rode back to the barn. Even Juan was subdued today. Dakota sensed they knew something was amiss in their lives. It wasn't like a normal Boxing Day; she wondered what would be happening at her parent's house. Usually on Boxing Day her mother would cook a huge ham, and everyone would gather there for the day and eat the ham or in Dakota's case a vegetarian version and then cheese and biscuits and pickles for tea followed by Christmas cake and home-made trifle. This was another tradition they didn't have in Chile, but she was going to make it one of theirs once they moved into their new home.

The heavy atmosphere stayed with them after they returned home. Sergio called to let them know the funeral would be in two day's time at the church in town. The church where both she and Javier often prayed; the next time they would be entering the church would be to say goodbye to their dear friend Al.

Dakota was going through the motions. She made Javier turkey curry for dinner that evening. He had never eaten curry before or indeed half of the things she had got him to try in recent months. He enjoyed the meal she had prepared. She didn't feel hungry so settled for a glass of wine instead. "You not eating Dakota?" he asked noting the speed in which she was consuming the wine in her glass.

"Not hungry" she said, downing the wine and pouring another one.

"You need to eat though?" He said softly.

"Drop it Javier!" She snapped snatching her glass and taking it into the lounge. He stood, pushing back his chair and followed her, confused by her sudden and unexpected outburst.

"Have I done something?" he stood there in front of her with his hands on his hips. "Dakota, what have I done?" She looked at him, how he stood with his legs slightly apart, socks with holes in on his feet, his expression of surprise and sadness at how she'd spoken to him and his striking good looks. Her love for the man standing in front of her was unfathomable; yet she was trying to push him away because she was hurting in a different way. He was hurting immensely; she could see that. Al had been his friend since he had been ten years old. Twenty years of friendship and she had known Al only eight months. What right did she have to stand there and subject Javier to her grief when his must be so much worse? But he was there, standing in front of her ready to support her, to see her through this as if she'd been the one to have known Al all those years. Dakota felt herself crumble and she fell into a heap on the sofa crying as though it was her last day on the earth. "I'm so sorry Javier please forgive me I'm so, so sorry" she sobbed.

"What for? What have you done?"

"I'm sorry, your grief must be ten times worse than mine, here I am not able to help you, being an emotional jelly fish," she sobbed into his t-shirt soaking it with her tears. "Dakota don't be silly, I knew Al for twenty years yes, that is true, and of course I'm very sad to hear that he has passed but you knew him better than I did recently, and you worked closely. He loved you like a daughter he told everyone that."

"Did he?"

"Well, he told Ruben anyway, and he told me. He trusted you with his horses from the very start. You hadn't been working with him that long when he let you cover the race. Why d'you think he sold us the business and was so happy about it because it was *you* that he was selling his beloved horses to!"

Her sobbing lessened, she lifted her tear laden eyes to meet his, "Really, is that what you think?"

"That is what I know because I've been told by various mutual friends. You were the one who he doted on, so you have every right to be as upset as you are. I'm here for you and I always will be," he hugged her, stroking her hair, "Now come on, I need to finish that curry before it gets cold. Come and talk to me, tell me how you learned to make curry!" He led her back into the kitchen and sat her on the chair opposite to him with her wine and, whilst he finished the last of the curry, she told him how she had learned to make it.

Chapter Twenty-six

It was seven months to the day since Dakota had stood in the church in London attending Nina's funeral. Now it was another funeral. This time it was inside the majestic old church in San Pedro that had the smell of age, weddings, christenings and many funerals. She glanced around at the beautiful figurines in the alcoves and the well-maintained paintwork, she remembered the first time she had set foot inside this wonderful old building, the sense of comfort and calm it had enveloped her in. It was the most beautiful church she had ever been inside and not because of the stained-glass windows or any of the magnificence of the church Nina's funeral had taken place in, for this church didn't have any of that, not a single stained-glass window or fancy brass candle stick was to be seen. This church felt full of love.

Al's coffin was at the front by the alter. The service was long. A lot of people had known Al in his life and a lot of people wanted to pay tribute to him. At the end of the service everyone filed out behind the coffin and on to the small graveyard. The congregation stood and watched Al's coffin disappear into the ground. Dakota's heart was heavy as she looked on, but she also felt this was the ideal place for him to be laid to rest, here in the sunshine with all his friends around him.

Later at the wake everyone gathered at one of the bars in town. There was a lot of laughter as people recalled their own stories of Al who, it seemed, in his youth had been a bit of a character. Some of Al's friends came over to speak to Dakota. They said Al had said such a lot of wonderful things about this remarkable girl who had appeared from nowhere, but no one knew who she was. Everyone knew Javier and once they put two and two together, she was to be known as 'Javier's horse woman." She was sure she had been known as worse things in her life but wasn't sure if she wanted to continue being known as 'Javier's horse woman'.

Catalina shuffled over; the small frail woman hugged Dakota tightly. She looked up into her eyes, the old lady had aged in what seemed overnight. The man she had loved since she'd been not much more than a girl had been taken from her, her whole world had imploded, and she was left alone. Her English was worse than Dakota had ever heard her speak because she had more important things on her mind than trying to master a foreign language. Dakota tried her hardest to understand her but then she called Javier over to join them as Catalina had things to say. Indeed, she did, Sergio has asked her to go and live in Santiago with him, his wife and children who would soon be off to university in America. There would be lots of room for her and she would be well looked after. She didn't want to go, she wanted to stay here in San Pedro, to be able to come and sit at Al's grave every day if she wanted to. Sergio had said she would be all alone here but if she wanted then she could stay but he wouldn't be able to visit more than twice a year as his holiday permitted. Dakota felt incredibly sorry for the old woman, she had lived here in San Pedro her entire life. She'd met and married Al here and bore his child, now they were asking her to leave and live in a big city something that was totally alien to the dear old lady.

Once the wake was over Dakota and Javier walked slowly home hand in hand. Dakota felt drained and exhausted. They discussed Catalina's plight and Javier too felt sad for her. "What will she do if she stays here?" Dakota asked, "she will be alone but at least she has her friends and Al is buried here. If she goes to Santiago, she will have Sergio and his wife who couldn't even be bothered to come to her father in laws funeral. What sort of life will that be for her?"

"She'll chose what she thinks will be the best for her but if she decides to stay here there'll be a lot of people around who'll support and look out for her including us." Dakota squeezed his hand.

"You're a good man Javier, a really good man and every day I thank God for you and for bringing you to me all those months ago."

"I think it should be me thanking him for bringing you to me. It was you that made the six and a half thousand-mile trip to San Pedro" he reminded her. For both of them it felt as though Dakota had lived in Chile all her life, not just the eight months it had been.

They strolled slowly through the streets until they arrived at their favourite bar. They sat outside as they always did and ordered pizza. At their table they sat silently each of them lost in the memories they had of their time with Al. Dakota would always remember him sitting on his bench after he had handed her a mug of coffee and chatting. He always had time for her, he always gave her sound advice and helped her with anything she had found challenging. Javier remembered him in many more ways from all the years he had known the old man. He remembered Al helping Javier fix his first bike, then his first motorbike when his father was away working. He remembered the time latterly when he'd been out in the Atacama and had supported him with the horses, more recently he'd let them take Cherry and Diego out into the desert, the vast desert where Javier had realised, he was deeply in love with Dakota. His thoughts drifted back to that day when they'd argued, and he'd made her cry. He gave her a sideways glance, she was sipping her wine, the late afternoon sun shining on her black hair and her olive skin glowing from the kiss of the Atacama sun. It was at that moment everything slotted into place, he completely understood this was the life for her, she thrived on it, and they really were good for each other. Their life was moving on now and he must move with it if they were to stay together. Their life together, their home and work were all about to change.

Javier poured them each a large glass of wine. He sat on the sofa, Dakota sat on the rug on the floor, and they talked. Tomorrow they would be riding a new route Javier had discovered in the large pile of maps. Their intention had been to speak to Al about it, but time had run out. They were going to discover the route themselves without Al's help. Dakota was pouring over the map on the floor. Javier was pointing out the markers they were to look out for. It would be another four-hour trek but most of the bookings they had taken were for half a day rides and some for full days. They'd not taken any bookings for multi day rides and Dakota was pleased, it would mean less ferrying around of food and supplies if the horses were only out for a day or half day, she could leave everything at the barn.

The following morning, they were at the barn early. The day was cloudy and overcast. Dakota had decided to take Juan and Nico on their ride and to leave Cherry and Diego at the barn. The builders were already on site and working, Dakota asked them if they would be able to put up some fencing enabling them to let the horses out each day. She had never liked the idea of them being stabled all the time. When they moved into the house, she was planning on having them outside with access to the stables if they needed it. She could put alfalfa into buckets and have it around the corral so they would always have food available for them to pick at if they wanted. The builder had agreed to put up the fence the following day when he had his two apprentices to help him.

The sun finally made an appearance, and the clouds moved from the sky. It was warm and it looked as though summer was arriving in San Pedro earlier than Javier had anticipated. It was still December, but they wore t-shirts and light weight jeans. The first hour of their trek was in silence. This happened a lot, Javier liked to concentrate on the route and Dakota had her thoughts. Javier rode behind as this time it was Dakota reading the map and she needed her full concentration for the route they were riding. Later they stopped for water. Javier reached over and took her hand in his and gently squeezed it. "Are you okay?" he asked raising his eyebrows.

"Yes, I think I know where we're heading now." She replied studying the map. "No, I mean are you okay?" She looked up from the map to see him frowning slightly, a concerned look on his face. "Yes, I'm okay. This is going to sound weird I know but I feel like Al is with us today? Silly, I know, but I feel he is almost walking in front of us, guiding me somehow."

"That would be Al alright. Remember, when you are next on the long stage of a race, he'll be watching you from the heavens!" Javier chuckled and let go of her hand. "I will miss him so much!" She felt the lump in her throat start to rise and she swallowed hard, determined not to cry again.

"We all will but we'll never forget him, that's the main thing and we'll keep his traditions and ways of doing things."

"We will!" She replied, nudging Juan on in the direction on the map.

The terrain was getting a little rough underfoot, so Dakota dismounted and lead Juan over the rocks. "I don't want them twisting something because they are having to concentrate on us," she told Javier instructing him also to dismount. "What would Al say?"

"It was Al that designed this route, so he must've ridden it!" he protested.

"But how long ago? Look at the route we did with the Pampas grass that attacked us then he told us he wasn't going to bother doing that ride again because of the maintenance involved, this might be just as bad." She carefully led Juan down the shingly slope and onto the flat track below. "You can get back on now." Dakota swung her leg over the saddle and waited for Javier. "In your own time," she giggled. "Come on Javier you can't be this slow when we have rides to take out!" she teased as he struggled to mount.

"Getting your leg over isn't as easy for me as it is for you these days!" He complained finally getting into the saddle and straightening himself up.

They rode on without encountering any further obstacles, Dakota wondered why Al had not sent her on this ride before. Maybe it was just one he was saving up for her when he thought she might need a map reading challenge. The ride had proved challenging but enjoyable and she marked it as one to do again.

Back at the barn Javier's builder friend had worked wonders. He'd pulled out all the stops, called his apprentices, got them onto site and they were halfway through the corral construction. Dakota was thrilled with the sight that greeted them. "That's great, now the horses will have somewhere to stretch their legs, and they'll not have to stay in their stables all day, it will be brilliant for them, thank you so much" her face was alight, thrilled and excited at how quickly things were progressing. "How are things going with the house do you anticipate it being finished on schedule?" she called up to where the builder was working. "By February first without fail" he assured her from the precarious position he was in. "I'll get more people in if I think we're going over schedule on it." Dakota turned to Javier, "They are good chaps getting it done so quickly for us" she said.

"It isn't like bricks and blocks though, it's glorified mud really but you can see, all the houses round here are made of it, and they last. It doesn't take as long as it would in England to build a house here." Javier turned away and led Nico into his stable where he started to unsaddle him. Dakota led Juan into his stable and followed suit, handing him some treats as she took his saddle off. Juan seemed to be shaping up into a nice horse now, he realised who was the boss and seemed to be accepting it. Dakota had tried hard with him, and, at times, he had tested her to the limit but now she believed they had come to an understanding.

Before leaving the barn, they had a brief look around the beginnings of their new home. Dakota was really impressed with how quickly the house build was progressing, it was to be the home of their dreams, and she was excited. It would be great to live on site with the horses close by and to be on hand for any customers that should drop by without a booking. She'd never been comfortable leaving the horses so far from home, not being able to hear them should they be in distress. It was something Al had felt strongly about too, that was why he'd had the plans drawn up in the first place.

That evening they started making lists of what they needed for their new home. Javier realised all their current furniture would probably fill one room. Dakota had bought some antique pieces from Calama when she had visited to collect feed for the horses. The furniture was to be delivered once the house was ready. They would need another three beds plus all the bedding, drawers and wardrobes and that was just the bedrooms! Dakota wasn't worried, she'd done this before when she'd bought her house in London. She had started from scratch, had nothing when she'd moved in and then she moved out and had left it all to Miles. That wasn't going to happen here, this was going to be her and Javier's home for life. They would live here, grow old here and retire here. She was busy with lists and calculators working out budgets, this was totally alien to Javier and he was getting stressed out about it all, how much it was going to cost and the scale of the project in hand. "It's okay we'll get it sorted eventually there's no immediate rush you know?" She had tried to soothe him, patted his knee as she looked into those beautiful brown eyes of his, "If it takes us two years then it doesn't matter, why d'you think that it's such a mission?"

"Dakota, we have four bedrooms to fill just with bedroom stuff not including the lounge, kitchen and dining room, study and utility room as you call it!"

She smiled, "Dear Javier don't panic. We have the money and next time we go to Calama for feed we can go and have another look around at the shops and get a few more pieces. Don't forget I've done this before; I know how much it entails. I can get all my soft furnishings sent over from England, so we won't have to buy any bedding or curtains, don't stress about it," she reassured him, "it'll all be fine!"

They sat on the rug together, backs against the old sofa, exhausted from all the planning and list making. Their happiness was tinged with a little sadness at having to do all this without Al to consult, run things past and give approval. She'd hoped so much that he would be a big part of their new life, but that wasn't to be. Now he was gone, and she had to do it all herself. Javier seemed to be so distracted, she wondered if his heart was in it, was it too soon to be forging ahead with the house when they had only buried Al a few days ago?

It was New Years Eve. It was early evening, everyone was out in the small town of San Pedro drinking, eating and making merry, ready to welcome in the new year. Dakota and Javier were preparing to go out, a night eating and drinking on the town. Dakota wore a pair of leather trousers and a very tight top which hugged her curves. Javier's eyes were out on stalks, he couldn't stop staring at her. "Are you really going out like that?" he asked.

"Why what's wrong with it?" She said looking down at what she was wearing.

"Nothing is wrong, you just look incredible and every man in San Pedro will want a piece of you lady, I can almost guarantee it" he smiled, he felt proud this beautiful lady was his, she'd changed her life and his, moved six and a half thousand miles to be with him, to share his life, his work and his bed.

"They can want then, in case you'd forgotten Mr Gonzales, it is you who has me in your bed at night to do with as you wish!"

He laughed, "Yeah I sure do, you look a million dollars!" He buttoned up his shirt and held his arm out for her to take. "Let's go and hit the town!"

Outside in the street the noise was getting louder, the town was filled with an electric atmosphere. There was a lot of laughing and excitement as people made their way to restaurants and bars to see in the New Year. Dakota and Javier were planning to visit their bar, the one they had met in all those months ago, their favourite bar. The walked slowly along the street hand in hand greeting friends and people they knew along the way. Just as Javier had predicted, Dakota did attract a lot of male attention, but she only had eyes for him, and he was proud to have her out with him. She was so different to other women Javier had known in every way; she didn't take any notice of the men staring at her because as far as she was concerned, she would wear what she wanted. She wasn't out to catch a man she already had the only man she would ever want in her life, and she was very happy with him. Next year would be the start of everything – their new life, home and business together. It would be the start of something brilliant.

At midnight they all cheered in the New Year with drinks and merriment. Javier took Dakota's face in his hands and kissed her passionately inside the bar, making everyone cheer again. It was after two o'clock in the morning when they finally left and walked to the church in the square to say a prayer. They walked home though the empty streets. Everyone had gone to bed and there was not a sound. How different to New Year in England she thought, where it seemed the trend these days to set fireworks off, people would be returning home throughout the early morning hours drunk and shouting. There was none of that here it was silent, the only noise was Dakota's heels on the rough road.

Inside the flat Javier made them a mug of coffee and they sat in bed sipping the hot liquid. Dakota thought about her parents. She wondered what they were doing. She didn't want to call them as they were four hours ahead of Chile time, they would've gone to bed hours ago and were probably almost at the time where they would be getting up. She hoped they would call her in the morning to wish them a happy new year. Coffee finished and the mugs on the bedside table she turned off the light and turned over snuggling down into the covers. Javier held out his arms and she moved over to him in the darkness. He smelled so good she thought, unable to resist him she started to run her fingertips over

203

his chest and collar bone and up over his shoulder to stroke the back of his neck. He moved to her and kissed her gently, moving to her neck where he worked his way down. She moaned softly unable to resist him, she let him seduce her. She could feel his hardness and moved her hand to take him. She worked him a little, she knew it wouldn't take much, he was more than ready for her, "Come on big boy, show me what you're made of!" She whispered softly to him as she flung the covers back and mounted him. The night was still young, for them at least.

Chapter Twenty-seven

It was New Years Day, and they didn't wake until eight o'clock. Dakota was in a panic; it was so late. "But the horses will be wanting feeding come on Javier get your act in gear, will you?" She threw his jeans on the bed followed by his t-shirt and socks. "They haven't had any food since last night!"

"Nor have I but you don't stress about me having breakfast" he complained pulling his clothes on in a hurry.

"You can feed yourself, but they can't. I can't expect them to stand there in the stables feeling hungry just because we were at it half the night" she said angry with herself for oversleeping and not setting her alarm.

"Yeah, but it was worth it don't you think?" he reached for her wrist and pulled her back onto the bed and started kissing her. She really didn't want to resist him, but she had to. "No Javier, come on we need to sort the horses out!" She sat up and pushed him off. "I'll sort us some breakfast to eat quickly if you promise to hurry up?" Javier resigned himself to having to get out of bed quickly if he wanted his breakfast. Dakota busied herself in the kitchen making toast and cereal for them all the time worrying about the horses. They were creatures of habit and routine and leaving them later than was expected was bothering her.

Eventually they were at the barn. Javier hurried around heaping alfalfa into the buckets in their stables and Dakota sped around with bucket feeds ensuring they were fed and watered despite arriving an hour later than usual. In recent times if she'd been late, it wouldn't have mattered because Al would've been there or if she had a day off Al would've covered. Now it was down to them, and she felt responsible. How much easier things would be when they were living on site, she couldn't help but think as she filled and distributed the water buckets making the morning routine complete.

That afternoon the fencing was finished, and the horses had a turn out corral. Dakota led them out one at a time into the corral and turned them loose. Last to go out was Juan because she didn't want him stirring up the others by running around. They all walked around curiously sniffing the ground and the new fence posts. The corral was around two acres in size, so it was big enough for them to have a trot around. Dakota was planning to make another corral at some point so they could have more room but for now this was more than ample. The horses had a little trot and then they started to feel more confident and had a little buck and canter around once they had their bearings and knew where the boundaries were. Cherry was the most excited about it all and trotted around with her tail held high and nostrils flared. Dakota and Javier stood watching them. "This'll save us so much time and they'll be able to have a day off being ridden, relax a little bit" she said leaning on the fence and watching them play. "I don't know why Al didn't do this ages ago it would've saved him so much time!" She had piled alfalfa into large buckets around the corral so the horses could eat and stretch their legs this was much more natural for them than having to stand in a stable all day and wait for someone to take them out. She thanked the builder's apprentices who had turned up early on New Years Day to get the job finished and for getting the job done so quickly. Now her horses were happy at least.

After they had spent the morning mucking the horses out and the afternoon watching to see that they didn't decide to try and jump out of the corral Dakota felt confident enough to leave them for a few hours whilst they went back home to sort things out for their New Years Day dinner. They didn't seem to celebrate things as much out here as she had done back in London, so she had decided to cook them a nice dinner that evening and wanted to go back to start preparing things. Javier was glad they were going home he wanted to catch up on his sleep.

At the flat Dakota started taking out vegetables and preparing them for the evening feast she had planned. She had wine in the fridge already chilling and was using the last Christmas pudding for dessert. She took the pudding out of the plastic wrapper and looked at it still in its plastic bowl ready to be microwaved. Back home she used to buy them in bulk and store them up until summer when she would use the last on around August time. Out here they were not heard of, and she made a mental note to get her mother to send her a bulk package next year so she could use them throughout the year. Perhaps once they had their own house, she would try making one herself. She did remember thinking about it before when she worked full time and thought it seemed very time consuming. Maybe she would make Christmas cake next year instead that wasn't quite a huge task. She unwrapped the pudding and removed the lid piercing the plastic on the top so she could cook it for the three required minutes in the microwave. Thank goodness Javier had one of those, it had saved them from a big wait on many an occasion when he had arrived home late and had been hungry. Things would be better now he had his phone though; she could call him.

Later that afternoon Dakota was back at the barn. The horses had remained in the corral and were now standing around nose to tail swishing their tails to keep the flies off each other. They whinnied when they saw Dakota arrive on her bike. The stables where all ready so the horses just needed to be put inside and checked over before she left for the night. Things would be much easier now; all she would need to do is ensure that the droppings were removed from the corral on a regular basis to discourage the flies. She led the horses into their stables and checked them over to ensure they had not suffered any injuries whilst they had been in the corral. They were all fine and ready for their dinners. Everyone fed and checked she swung her leg over her bike and rode back to the flat.

Javier was up when she got back home and had showered and poured her a glass of wine. "How were they, still in the corral I take it as I had no phone call to tell me otherwise?" He smiled and handed her the glass. She took a sip.

"They were fine. Standing nose to tail when I got down there and happy to go back into their stables. It must be so good for them to be out in the fresh air without someone on their backs or leading them." She was happy the horses now had some freedom.

Dakota had cooked Javier beef wellington. As much beef wellington as she could with the ingredients she'd managed to find. There was beef, mushrooms and pastry so that would suffice she had thought putting it all together. She was having vegetarian lasagne. She was glad she'd managed to persuade Ruben to stock pasta. He too had been pleased she'd made the suggestion because he'd sold out of every kind of pasta he'd been able to source during the first week! Now he stocked pasta sauces as well as pasta and had been doing a very good trade out of it. He had mentioned to Javier he was to let him know if Dakota wanted any other type of ingredients that he didn't usually stock so he could hopefully boost his sales on that line too. She had managed to introduce him to a few things, but he was not ready to take on vegetarian frozen meals no matter how hard she tried to persuade him. As she sat in the kitchen waiting for the dinner to cook, she remembered conversations she'd had with the shopkeeper. She'd tried to get him to stock vegetarian sausages at one stage she remembered fondly. "What? They make such things as sausage without meat in it?" He was disgusted as she'd tried to persuade him it would be a good idea. "But it would be great, I could have a sausage sandwich on a Sunday morning when Javier likes his fry up!"

"What is a fry up for goodness sakes?" She'd then gone into full detail to explain what a full English fry up consisted of. "That sounds much better than sausages with no meat in. Don't think I am going to start stocking things like that in my shop I would lose half of my customers" he had firmly dictated.

"You would gain more custom from me though!" She tried again to persuade him.

"And I would probably lose Javier if you tried to turn him into a vegetarian that I can guarantee. I hope you've not tried that yet. Good luck to you if you have?"

"No of course not. What he eats is up to him I wouldn't try and get him to give up meat unless he decided he wanted to."

"If that day ever arrives come and see me again and we can talk about vegetarian sausages again." He had smiled showing his blackening teeth and handed her the bag of shopping she'd gone down to his shop to purchase.

After the New Year dinner had been consumed and the pots cleared away, they sat at the small dining table in the kitchen and talked. Dakota's mother had called her that morning when she'd arrived back from the barn. She'd been courteous but Dakota had the feeling that all was not okay back in England. Her mother had been a bit short, and she wondered if she was having another bad episode because Dakota lived in Chile and not London. She'd hoped she was getting used to the fact, after all, it wasn't about to change. Her father seemed to be taking it in his stride now and she couldn't help but wonder how much of her father's anger had been fuelled by her mother. She'd only remained on the phone a few minutes then said she was having guests that were due to arrive any time and had to go. Dakota told Javier, "She just seemed odd again. I hope we're not going to have another falling out because I don't live close by," she said gazing into her empty wine glass, "I'll get the bottle out of the fridge!" She walked over to the fridge to retrieve the wine. "Your parents need to get used to the idea. D'you think it would help if we went to visit them soon?" Javier suggested.

"No, I don't think we can now we have the house build going on and who do we have to help with the horses now Al isn't here? There is only you and me and we need to stay here until after the next tourist season. If we go it'll need to be in six month's time when we've found someone who we trust to look after the horses." Javier understood she didn't want to go back, not just because of the house and horses she didn't want confrontation. Perhaps her parents would reconsider and come out to Chile to visit them once the house was ready. That was to be a conversation for another day but not today.

They lay in bed, she in his arms and they talked well into the night about their plans. Javier had seen a change in Dakota he hadn't expected but nevertheless was grateful for. She seemed to have developed a large lust for life, to get things up and running and sorted out. Once she'd seemed almost laid back and had gone where life had taken her. That had been the Dakota he'd first met and fallen in love with. Now she was different. She was taking each challenge as it presented itself and got on with conquering it. She was incredibly strong and self-assured. She had been the one to arrange the house and get the business set up. She had been the one with the capital and incentive to do it. Javier had only dreamed of having his own flat one day far in the future let alone a big house with land and horses. He had been impressed with how easily she had got on with things, never made a fuss or dwelled on issues she just took everything in her stride. Now they were only weeks away from the start of their new life together and he couldn't wait.

Chapter Twenty-eight

The day of the move had arrived. Javier and Dakota were standing outside their newly completed, immaculate four bedroomed home hand in hand gazing up at the size and beauty of the place. The furniture was being moved inside the freshly painted rooms. The kitchen had been completed only the day previous due to a delay on the cooker Dakota had ordered but it had all been worth it, their new home was amazing. Javier squeezed Dakota's hand before hurrying indoors to help the men move the last pieces of furniture inside their home. It was things from the flat that indeed did just about fill one room. Dakota remained outside waiting for the antique furniture from Calama she'd ordered weeks ago to arrive. She worried the delivery men wouldn't find the house but as Javier had already told her, the men lived in Chile and would know directions to San Pedro and just about anyone in San Pedro had known where Al kept his horses and their house was being built, they would find the house he had assured her.

The horses milled about in their corral watching all the movements over at the house with interest. Dakota knew Javier was right and started to help move things inside, tired of waiting for the furniture men to turn up. It didn't take long for everything from the flat to be moved into the house. Javier had felt a tiny bit sad to leave the flat after it had been his home and his place of sanctuary for many years. He would miss his friend Ruben too and the convenience of the shop downstairs. The idea of living with Dakota the woman he wanted to share the rest of his life with in this grand, beautiful new home made him realise just how lucky he was. Ruben was only a couple of miles away and he'd be popping into San Pedro all the time.

They stood on the steps of the new home arms around each other waving off the men who'd helped them move in just as the furniture van appeared. Two large Chilean men jumped out and rolled up the back of the lorry ready to move in their new furniture. Dakota directed them as to which room everything needed to go into. Two antique beds were taken upstairs along with three sets of drawers and three wardrobes. There were two new sofas to fill the large lounge space and a desk and chair for the office. Dakota was pleased with how everything looked and started to unpack the plastic wrapping from the sofas. They were leather, Dakota hoped they would be hard wearing for when Javier flopped around on them in his work clothes. She didn't even want to entertain the idea of fabric sofas, how on earth she would get them cleaned out here!

At last, everything was inside the house and unpacked. The furniture men had taken away the plastic wrappings after Dakota had given them coffee and homemade cake she'd made at the flat. They collapsed onto the sofas in their large lounge and looked around at everything in wonder. "I didn't think it would still look so big once all the furniture was inside," Dakota commented gazing around the lounge, "Al certainly wanted a large-scale house, didn't he?"

"It is amazing, absolutely amazing!" Javier marvelled at it all. All the new furniture, fixtures and fittings and soft furnishings that she had hung before the furniture had arrived, he had never in his entire life visited anywhere as grand as this house let alone lived there. "You've done a fantastic job with everything, I can't believe this is our home now," he grabbed her around the waist and kissed her. "Shall we christen the sofa?" he asked flashing her his best cheeky smile and knowing he was pushing his luck.

"No, we won't christen the sofa thank you very much," she pinched his cheek playfully, he let go of her. "Come on, we've bedding to unpack and clothes to hang in the wardrobes." She trotted off upstairs, Javier following along behind her knowing his work was far from finished. "As you sleep on that side of the bed you can have that wardrobe, and I'll have this one. I figured we'll only need one set of drawers between us now that we have a wardrobe each?" Dakota busied herself hanging clothes on the rail inside the wardrobe. Javier slowly started unpacking things into the drawers folding them as he went but his mind was not on the job. "Isn't this just the best thing ever? I never thought I'd live anywhere like this it's great" he wandered aimlessly round the bedroom with a pair of socks in each hand flapping them about as he continued, "I can't believe we're finally in and have all this new stuff, its completely unreal!" She smiled at him. It was possessions she'd been used to having back in London and living in a new house but here it was different. This was no new build on a housing estate that came with fixtures and fittings, carpets and curtains this was a house they had instructed people to build from scratch with local materials and right out in the Atacama Desert. It might not be as far out as Dakota would have liked but it was far enough. This was her dream. The dream she had not realised until she'd arrived here on her Harley Davidson. Now she could never imagine living anywhere else but San Pedro with her beloved Javier. She glanced over at him; he was staring out of the window at the horses down below in the corral. "You happy?" she asked joining him. She slipped her arm around his waist, "D'you think we'll be happy here Javier?" He turned to face her putting his arms around her neck. "I'm very happy and yes, I do think we'll be happy, very happy this is going to be our home for life Dakota, we will run our business from here, raise our family here, we will grow old here, we will never move." He kissed her on the nose making her laugh, "You've done all this you did everything. You've made me the happiest man in the world you know, in the months we have been together, you really have. Don't ever leave me, d'you promise?"

"Javier, you know I won't leave you," she gazed into the depths of his deep brown eyes knowing she could never leave him or San Pedro, this was indeed going to be their home for life. She kissed him softly on the lips. He tasted of coffee, "This is the start of our new life together, lets finish unpacking then we can open some wine and celebrate!"

The horses had been fed, had alfalfa added to their stables and had been put away for the night. The corral had been cleared of muck and the dinner was almost on the table. The day seemed to have gone by so quickly, but they had achieved so much. It was easy having the horses on site; being able to pop out to them. Next week their first customers since they had moved in would start arriving for the Atacama rides. Dakota was excited as the first arrivals were English and had booked using the website Paul had made for them. Her first customers for a four-hour ride and then she had more the following week. In fact, she realised, she had a full week, so it was good that the horses were fitter than they had been. She turned the cooker off and served up steak, potato wedges and vegetables to Javier; she had stuffed aubergine with potato wedges and vegetables. They opened the wine and raised a toast to their new life together.

That night they slept in their old bed they had moved from the flat. It was a very comfortable bed, and Dakota hadn't seen the point of getting another one. The bed linen was freshly laundered and smelt of the desert winds. Dakota lay awake staring at the night sky through the open window. It seemed that all the stars in the universe had gathered outside their bedroom. The gentle breeze flicked at the edge of the curtain, there was not a single sound to be heard. It was so different to the flat in the middle of the town where every night there had been laughter and noise from the people passing below or visiting Ruben's shop. Javier slept soundly beside her she could hear him breathing. She gently pulled the covers back and stepped out onto the floorboards. Padding over to the window she pushed it open further. The sky was the deepest black with the stars that looked as though someone had thrown thousands of diamonds across the black velvet of the night. The moon was big and silver above the Atacama shining like a large coin. Dakota had never seen anything like it before and stood leaning on the window staring into the night filled with wonder. "It's beautiful, isn't it?" he whispered as he joined her at the window. "The night sky in the Atacama Desert. You wait until we have a thunderstorm out here then we'll know about it!" he said gazing up at the stars. Dakota turned to face him.

"Why would it be different to any other storm?" she asked puzzled by his comment. "Here, we have in the middle of summer, around now actually what people call the Altiplanic winter when moist air comes in from the east and brings the unsettled weather arriving in the middle of our summer. The storms can be magnificent, but you have to damn well be careful of the lightening." He told her of people he'd known struck down by the lightening out in the desert. "It isn't like it is where you are from where most of the time you don't get struck, its more trees and houses."

"Wow thanks for warning me," she muttered climbing back into bed. "I hope I'm not camping out one night when we have a blaster of a storm then!" Javier hoped that she wouldn't be either it could be deadly.

The morning dawned clear and bright. Dakota woke, stretched and smiled to herself realising where they were. This was the first day of their new life together in their new home. She scrambled out of bed, ran her fingers through her dishevelled hair and went to the window. The sun was shining, and it promised to be another glorious day. She could see the river in the distance and the desert beyond. For miles and miles, the raw, untouched beauty of the desert sprawled out before them. She quickly dressed and went to see to the horses. She hurried around handing them buckets of feed and topping up the water before returning to make breakfast. Today she would take the horses out on a half-day ride getting them used to longer rides again. They had been out on a few longer rides lately because Dakota knew she had bookings to take out and the horses hadn't really done a great amount of work since the end of the season. Now they were back to fitness and would certainly be fit enough for next week's schedule.

Dakota spooned porridge into the bowls on the table as Javier appeared in the doorway. He hadn't combed his hair, and his shirt was only half fastened. He had rips in his jeans and looked extremely dishevelled she glanced up at him and her stomach did a somersault. How on earth could someone look so damn hot after just getting out of bed? Putting the porridge pan onto the drainer she stood with her back against the sink staring at him. "What?" he asked looking down at himself, wondering what she was looking at, "Why are you staring at me like that lady?" he stood with his arms open trying to figure out what the expression on her face meant. "You want me or something?" that cheeky smile appeared, and her stomach did another flip. "Something" she replied.

"You DO want me!" he laughed bounding over to her he grasped her arm and pulling her to him. She could feel his heart beating through his shirt. In the warmth and comfort of his arms she closed her eyes and breathed in his smell. "Come on we've got all the time in the world lets go back to bed!" He led her upstairs and seduced her on the bed, the same bed where his seductions had taken place so many times in the past months. She lay in his arms afterwards breathing hard. A fine film of sweat covered her body. He was such a fabulous lover, he knew exactly how to satisfy her and never failed in the quest. She wondered if they would ever get much work done now that they lived so far away from town and with the horses on site it was a recipe for passionate nights and lust filled mornings. She didn't care, she had everything she'd ever wanted right here.

Later they were out riding the horses across the desert. The sun beat down, but the gentle breeze had remained with them from the previous evening, and it threw up tiny tornados which danced beneath their horses before blowing themselves out. They had crossed the river a couple of times, ahead was the long-anticipated lunch stop. Javier was riding Diego and leading Cherry. Dakota was riding Juan and leading Nico. They fastened the horses securely to a tree that would afford them some shade and unpacked their lunch. Sitting on the rocks Dakota asked, "Are you happy we've done all this Javier, you don't think we've jumped into things a bit too quickly do you?"

"Yeah of course I'm happy, it's just so hard to take it all in. I never in my lifetime thought I'd be living in a fantastic home with the woman of my dreams. If you had asked me a year ago, I would've said I was going to spend the rest of my life living alone in the flat. I woke this morning disorientated because I thought we were in the flat just for a second."

She laughed, "I woke up and realised straight away. I'm so glad that we did this you know?" She said taking a long drink from the water bottle. "I know we didn't really have a choice when it came to how quickly we did things, it was Al who had decided that, but I always knew it would come to this at some stage."

Javier knew it would be hard for them at the start, but they already had bookings coming in and when Dakota was out with clients, he was in charge of the horses left behind and the stable duties. He knew it would be fine, that things would work out. The only thing he was worried about were the impending races, how they would manage to cover them if nobody was at home looking after the two horses left behind. They'd hoped that Al would've taken up that duty but now there was no Al and nobody they trusted to care for the horses. Still, they hadn't been asked to

215

cover the next race yet, so they had plenty of time to find someone trustworthy.

The breeze dropped and the afternoon was hot and clammy. Dakota felt uncomfortable riding in the close heat. "I wouldn't be surprised if we have a storm tonight it's so close" Javier commented. "You'll be able to see the lightening first hand if we do but we'll have to make sure the horses are away in their stables." Dakota had been planning on leaving them outside a few nights a week but on his warning, she made a mental note that tonight would not be one of them. In fact, they didn't have to wait until the evening for the storm as the sky turned very dark when they arrived back at their home. Quickly they put the horses into the safety of their stables. Dakota ran outside to the saddle room and hung the saddles up before quickly distributing the feeds. Javier was outside collecting buckets from the corral as it started to rain soaking him before he had finished the task. His shirt was stuck to him, she could see the outline of his muscular body beneath the linen. The sight of him in his wet shirt brought back memories of that very morning when they'd gone back to bed and how she had dug her nails into his firm toned buttocks as he had brought her ultimate pleasure making her scream for him. She thought how much she would like to do it again later when that wet shirt of his was in a heap on the bedroom floor on top of hers. Putting her thoughts aside she closed the stables and ran into the house. Standing in the hallway they gasped and laughed before comparing how soaked they both were considering it hardly ever rained in the Atacama, and it was after all, the driest desert in the world!

The first huge crack of thunder boomed overhead making Dakota jump. "Wow that was loud!" she exclaimed, "very loud!" A flash of lightening appeared and lit up the whole house. "Oh my God look at it!" She hurried to the window and looked outside at the lightening flashing over and over again in front of them. "You see now why it is so dangerous?" Javier asked standing at her side. "You see if you are out, you must take cover or crouch down on the ground so you are the lowest point and won't get struck you must do that Dakota do you understand?" She glanced over at him and could see how serious he was about it but wondered why they had never had this conversation before now.

"Yes, I understand, I won't be going out purposely to get myself struck you know?" she added.

"It is so dangerous please promise me you will do as I ask of you Dakota?"

She could hear the fear in his voice and turned to face him taking his hand in hers, "Javier I promise I will do as you ask," she smiled and kissed his cheek. "Now come and let's get these wet clothes off and shower or bath?" she smiled, "We now have the choice of both!"

"Bath. We can both fit in there!" he grinned.

"Come on then!" She ran up the stairs two at a time and he followed pulling his wet shirt off as he went. She poured the water into the huge bath, they hurriedly undressed and got in. Javier was already hard; he grabbed the soap rolled it around in his hands giving them a good covering, he then proceeded to run his soapy hands all over Dakotas body. He covered her in the foam feeling his hands slip over her breasts he could hardly contain himself. She laughed and grabbed the soap from him and followed suit, covering his shoulders, arms and chest, she reached under the water to his hardness; he took a deep intake of breath then he pulled her legs towards him until she was straddling him in the bath. She felt him inside her and grasped the edges of the bath as he rubbed his soap ladened hands over her body making her ache for his touch. He worked her thrusting himself harder and harder until an almighty crash of thunder was heard above them as they reached their climax. They lay in their very large bath staring up at the light fittings, their hearts pounding, breathless. "We seem to be making a habit of bathroom sex!" she commented.

"I think we need to do it in every room in the house before the end of the week lady" he lifted his head so he could see her at the opposite end of the bath. "What do you think?"

"I don't think I'll be able to walk if you want to do that let alone take out rides next week, I'll be a mess," she scrambled to her feet and reached for the towels.

The final evening check on the horses happened later that night. They'd not seemed at all bothered by the storm and were happily munching their alfalfa when she looked over the door checking on each of them. The storm had cleared the air. It had hardly rained at all after the first burst that had wet them both to the skin and she could see all the stars above their new home. Javier appeared on the front steps as she made her way back to the house. "Here, thought we could sit out here for a bit and watch the night sky with a glass of wine?" He was such a thoughtful man. She took the wine from him and kissed his cheek. "You are lovely you know that?" She whispered in his ear, "I love you Javier please don't ever change."

"Not likely to now I don't imagine. I've been stuck in my ways for too long." He took a sip of the wine. It was cold and very dry against his tongue. She sat down on the steps next to him and looked out across the dark and now very calm and still desert. "This is just so amazing." Dakota felt extremely grateful to have such a lovely house in the best spot in the whole world with such a fabulous man to share it with. Sitting only inches away from her Javier was having the same thoughts. They sat in silence for a while just watching the night sky and listening to the horses moving around in their stables. Javier fetched the wine bottle from the fridge, and they sat and drank the second glass out on the step.

It was early afternoon the following day and they had just turned the horses out into the corral after another half-day ride. Dakota's phone rang "Javier it's my mum I'm going inside to take this." She called over to him taking the phone inside so he could finish the horses. She answered, "Hi Mum how are you?"

"Dakota we are fine how are you both and how is the new house coming along?"

"Oh, Mum it is incredible. It's huge but not like the houses in England. It's built mostly of a sort of mud brick thing, but it has four bedrooms and at night I can see all the stars from the bedroom window."

"That sounds lovely did you get all your linen and curtains I sent over for you?"

"Yes, I did, thanks for sending those they're all on the beds or hanging at the windows now. We had all the furniture delivered but the house still looks partly empty, we need to get used to it not being overcrowded that's all." Her eyes tracked around the lounge she was standing in before continuing. "Last night we had a terrible storm apparently they do happen at this time of the year

218

even with it being summer over here it is called Altiplanic winter, Javier has been telling me all about it," she mumbled remembering the deafening thunder and their passionate sex that had happened during the storm. Her mother's tone changed slightly as she continued. "Dakota I'm calling to tell you something, I have some news for you. It's Miles, he's decided to get married to the woman he met after you two broke up."

"Well, that's good isn't it, Mum?" Dakota asked wondering why it would be a problem. "No, it isn't good news for goodness sakes, I wanted you two to get back together. All this time you have been playing around with your horses and Javier we've been sitting here waiting for you to come to your senses and return to London. All this time Dakota, I have been playing your game and now it is too late he's marrying someone else!" Her mother screamed down the phone at an alarmed Dakota.

"Mum when will you realise it's not a game I'm playing? I'm here with Javier for keeps. Would I have gotten you to send over the curtains and bed linen if I was coming back? Would I have sold my house in England and had this one built and bought the business if I'd intended to return?" Dakota was getting angry with her mother she could feel her temper rising. She stopped talking and took a deep breath. "That was when I realised it was going a bit too far," her mother replied, "And when that Paul chap turned up, I *tried* Dakota I really tried to accept this new life style of yours but we miss you and we want you home married to Miles not floating around some far flung desert wasting your life like you are doing."

"Please try and understand I don't want to keep going over and over this all the time. I'm living here now, and Miles has his own life why can't you be happy for him with his new woman and for me here with Javier?" Dakota was exasperated. She could hear her mother sigh on the other end of the phone, and she knew it was far from over. "I've been speaking to your father; he told me I must accept you are doing this but it's hard. It's especially hard without Nina here now."

"I know Mum, I know it must be hard for you both without either of us. Why don't you come and see us, we have the house you can stay here?"

"No, I don't want to go to Chile I told you that before!"

There would be no talking to her mother and Dakota realised she was wasting her time. They finished the call with a few pleasantries and then she hung up. Sitting on the sofa Dakota felt like she was beating her head against a brick wall with her parents. Would they never understand and accept this was her life now? Would they never want to see their daughter happy with the only man she had ever wanted?

The door opened and in walked the reason for all the strife. He smiled at her and her heart melted. God, she loved him so much. She wouldn't go back to England without him. She didn't want to face life without him by her side. *He* was the very reason she'd been put on this earth. Her heart beat for him and she loved him more than she had ever loved anything in her entire life. He was her entire world. Feeling weary from the verbal battle with her mother Dakota smiled weakly back at him. "Hey, how did it go?" He asked flopping down on the sofa next to her.

"Oh, don't ask. Miles is getting married, and it seems that my mother still thinks I should find it within myself to marry him and hurry home before he marries this other woman!"

"What? She knows you're here with me and thinks you'll go back and marry another man?"

"She was hoping I'd go back but yet again I have told her I'm not going back. It seems now that my dad has at least accepted I'm staying here. It has made me really annoyed if I'm honest with you, I thought she'd accepted it and now it seems that isn't the case at all." Dakota was frowning down at her phone. "Damn it, she's spoilt my day," she put the phone down on the table. "I'll come out and finish the horses now I think."

"No need, they're all sorted so we can have lunch and then we can get on that computer and sort out what other bookings we have," he nodded his head towards the computer in the study. "Yeah, I do need to do some book work and other boring stuff it is starting to run away with me." She complained moving into the kitchen to start their lunch.

Chapter Twenty-nine

The two English clients where riding Cherry and Diego, Dakota was on board Juan. The clients were friendly and had chatted away to Dakota about her life in the desert, how she had met Javier and where she came from in England throughout the whole of the four-hour ride they'd signed up for. The horses had been very steady and looked after their riders. Dear sweet Cherry had picked her way carefully across the river despite Juan trying to take a bite out of her rump as she stepped into the icy waters. Dakota had hoped he'd gotten over his naughty streak, he hadn't shown any signs of being a worry for months but now they had clients he seemed to have regressed somewhat. Dakota told him off for trying to bite Cherry. The two clients she was riding with were from Devon and had come to Chile on a sightseeing holiday. For a whole month they were travelling around seeing everything they could fit in. This week they were in San Pedro for four days before flying back home. They were accomplished riders, and Dakota had enjoyed their company very much. Arriving back at their house Javier had met them and taken the horses from the couple to sort them out. They had paid Dakota and put in a hefty tip too telling her they would remember their ride in the desert forever. She felt happy it had gone well, and they'd enjoyed the experience.

Dakota often thought of her first ride in the desert although it was longer than four hours, five days in fact! She'd loved every minute of it and had known she would remember it for the rest of her life. She had vowed to ensure everyone who she took out on a ride would see the best of the desert depending on the route that she took. Sometimes it would be the steep rugged beauty of the slot canyons, the dense vegetation along the riverbanks, the view from the highest point on their rides or the flat rolling expanse of the desert plains where they could canter for miles and miles without meeting a single person.

Once their clients had left, Dakota helped Javier with the horses. They were turned out in the corral for the afternoon. Dakota had made a mental note to spend more time with Juan to try and sort his issues out. Perhaps he thought he would test her resolve and patience when she had clients to look out for or perhaps he just liked being naughty from time to time. Either way she couldn't have him misbehaving when she had to be responsible for people's safety.

That afternoon Dakota spent in the saddle room cleaning saddles and bridles. The blankets that went under the saddles were brushed off and left outside to air. The whole room was swept out and left with the door open to get rid of the dust that had accumulated. After the saddle room was finished, she started on the feed room. Peering inside she wondered what Al would have said if he could see it now. Javier certainly wasn't the tidiest person to have helping her, she was always telling him to put things away with the bags of horse feed in date order, but he often didn't listen. She rearranged all the feed, so it was in date order with the oldest at the front and the newest at the back. She scrubbed all the buckets out to get rid of the bits of feed that remained stuck to the sides and then she cleared the corral of droppings.

Finally finished she went inside to lie down for an hour whilst Javier was collecting shopping from San Pedro and catching up with his friends at the bar. She loved having him around all the time, but it was important he didn't lose touch with his friends, so she had sent him off for the afternoon. He said he would be back in time for dinner. Whilst she lay on their old bed with her eyes closed her thoughts were plagued by her mother's phone call the day before. Dakota couldn't help but wonder where all this was going. Would they ever accept her life in Chile? Would every phone call be contentious and upsetting? She knew she was fighting a losing battle with her mother, but Javier was her life, and she wasn't going to give him up to make anyone happy.

Waking after slightly longer than two hours sleep Dakota went into the office to do more paperwork. She rang the feed merchant and paid them for the last bill then checked her emails. She had three more bookings for two weeks' time, that was good news, she was pleased people were interested in seeing the desert from horseback. She hoped all her clients would be as nice as the people she'd taken out that morning. Dakota had chatted to them for longer than she'd spoken to anyone since arriving here except for Javier, Al and dear lovely Paul. It was so nice to have people who spoke English, and she didn't have to struggle with Spanish. She knew at some point she would probably get people who only spoke Spanish then she would have to make more of an effort than she did now, but at least Javier's Spanish lessons were paying off and she had improved.

Rising from the chair in the office Dakota stretched and yawned. She would fetch the horses in now and then Javier would be back for dinner. Outside it had turned cooler and the wind had got up whipping sand around in the corral. She hurried around fetching the horses in just as Javier appeared with the shopping in his backpack. "Do you need a hand?" he asked her as he removed his helmet, "or shall I start dinner now I'm back?"

"You start dinner please?" She was just putting in the bucket feeds and checking that everyone had enough water then she was going inside.

"I need to spend more time sorting Juan out." Dakota commented over pasta in Arabiata sauce. "He's being naughty again. He tried to take a chunk out of Cherry's backside this morning when I was out with the clients just as she was stepping into the river too!"

Javier glanced up at her from his fork of pasta, sauce dripping into the bowl. "What are you going to do with him?" He asked forking the pasta into his mouth.

"Just need to work him a bit harder, I think. He does have a bad streak that one Al used to warn me about him and, to be honest, I thought he'd got over it, but it seems not!" Dakota spooned in more pasta. Javier had turned his hand to doing more cooking since they'd moved into the house. He had managed previously in his flat but had told her he felt more inspired with a big kitchen and a huge cooker at his disposal. "This sauce is fabulous," she said, "you might get the job of cooking now you've proved yourself in the kitchen!"

"It's a job I think we should continue to share" Javier replied.

"Good idea, you can cook six nights a week and I'll do one night," she joked, "no, seriously it is a good idea if we share the job I agree."

The next day Juan and Diego were saddled up ready to go out for a ride. Dakota had decided to take the route they had

223

discovered shortly after Al had passed away. It would take half a day so they would be back by mid-afternoon after their later start that morning. They mounted their horses and set off along the route. Dakota still had the map. After only riding the route once she didn't feel confident that she knew the way to go without checking the map at intervals. Javier had convinced her he could remember but she didn't want to get lost so she tucked it away in her pocket where it would remain unopened unless Javier got them lost. Along the vast sandy floor of the Atacama they rode. Their horses were restless shaking their heads and stamping their feet when their riders stopped but Juan didn't misbehave himself. They reached the incline that seemed worse since the rain a few days ago. Dakota dismounted and led Juan down mounting at the bottom. Javier followed and managed to mount easier this time perhaps because he knew she was secretly watching him pretending to be fiddling about with her reins. They cantered gently for a while until their home and stables came into view then they slowed to a walk so the horses would return cool. Dakota was pleased they hadn't had to look at the map once. She'd remembered the route better than she had thought she would, and Javier had followed her lead knowing she was going in the right direction. He always had confidence in her despite how often she failed to have confidence in herself.

They were almost back at the barn feeling happy and tired they were chatting and letting the horses walk on a long rein to wind down. Suddenly and without warning Juan decided to take advantage of the long rein Dakota had been riding him on. He leapt forward and snatched at the bit before bolting in full gallop. Dakota was slightly unseated but managed to catch her reins and eventually pulled him to a stop. As the horse skidded to a halt, he threw a huge buck tipping Dakota off his left shoulder and into a crumpled heap on the floor where she landed with a thud. Juan trotted off to the corral with his stirrups flapping against his sides and reins hanging down in front of him. Javier launched Diego into gallop pulling up hard at the spot where Dakota lay. He hurriedly dismounted almost falling off in his haste to get to her.

She was lying face down and motionless on the dusty desert floor as he fell to his knees beside her. "Dakota, Dakota can you hear me, *can you hear me?*" Javier carefully rolled her over cradling her head with his hand. He was shaking like a leaf, tears running down his face, leaving tracks in the dust. He could see she had hit her head on a rock embedded in the desert floor. There was a lot of blood running down her face from the huge gash on her head, it was matting her hair. He trembled as he leaned down and whispered her name "Dakota…." but he knew the light had gone out in her eyes. He held the woman he loved more than life itself and closed his eyes. His heart broke into a million pieces. Their dream was over.

Epilogue

In a private London hospital Dakota opened her eyes. "Javier," she croaked, "Javier, where have you gone?"
"Who is Javier?" her sister Nina asked.

The End